The Mystery of Lewis Carroll

Also by Jenny Woolf

Lewis Carroll In His Own Account

The Mystery of Lewis Carroll

Discovering the Whimsical, Thoughtful,
and Sometimes Lonely Man Who Created
Alice in Wonderland

JENNY WOOLF

ST. MARTIN'S PRESS ☙ NEW YORK

To Tony, with all my love

www.stmartins.com

ISBN 978-0-312-61298-6

First published in Great Britain by Haus Publishing Ltd
First U.S. Edition: February 2010

10 9 8 7 6 5 4 3 2 1

Contents

Acknowledgements

Many thanks to all the people who have been involved in the making of this book. I appreciate the work of those at the publishers who have worked so hard to get it right, and my agent Andrew Lownie. I would like to give particular thanks to Jaqueline Mitchell for her wise and conscientious text editing and her tireless willingness to explain the finer points of the publishing process to me.

I am grateful to Mark Richards, Chairman of the Lewis Carroll Society, London, who has offered help and advice and allowed me to borrow all sorts of books from his collection over the years, even though it may sometimes have seemed to him that I would never return them! I am also very grateful to Karoline Leach, for so many useful and interesting discussions over the years. And many special thanks to Beth Mead, descendant of Wilfred L. Dodgson, who has been kind and supportive throughout.

I am grateful also to Yoshiyuki Momma, Clare Imholz and many other scholars, collectors and members – too many to mention individually – from the various Lewis Carroll Societies in the UK, the USA, Japan and worldwide.

The combined expertise and energy of all these enthusiasts has brought so much hitherto obscure information about Lewis Carroll into the public domain.

It was important to me that the book was readable as well as accurate, and I am hugely grateful to my family, particularly Tony, Kath and Vanessa, who have spent hours of their time in discussing the book, and reading and commenting upon the manuscript from a reader's point of view.

Last but certainly not least, I am very grateful indeed to Edward Wakeling, who has generously shared his time, expertise and extensive databases with me, and has offered staunch moral support and encouragement over the years.

In addition, I have consulted many biographical works on Lewis Carroll, including those by Carroll's nephew, Stuart Dodgson Collingwood, Michael Bakewell, Anne Clark, Professor Morton Cohen, Derek Hudson, Karoline Leach and Donald Thomas, together with the Diaries edited by Edward Wakeling, and the Collected Letters and many other works, large and small, edited by Professor Morton Cohen.

I am grateful to the owners of the material who have kindly allowed me to quote. They include the Alfred C. Berol Collection; Fales Library, New York University; the Harry Ransom Humanities Research Center, The University of Texas at Austin; the Special Collections Department, University of Colorado at Boulder Libraries; Rosenbach Museum & Library, Philadelphia; Guildford High School, England; The Syndics of the Fitzwilliam Museum, Cambridge; Morris L. Parrish Collection. Manuscripts Division. Department of Rare Books and Special Collections. Princeton University Library. Extract from 'In the Shadow of the Dreamchild' by Karoline Leach, Peter Owen, Ltd., London; Extract from 'Lewis Carroll' by Derek Hudson by kind permission of Constable & Robinson Ltd, London. thanks to A.P. Watt Ltd. on behalf of the Executors of the C.L. Dodgson Estate for permission to quote from copyright material by Lewis Carroll, from the Letters and other books edited by Professor Morton Cohen and others. Every effort has been made to trace copyright holders of text and photographs to clear permission. I regret any inadvertent omissions, which can be rectified in future editions.

Photographic illustrations courtesy of: the National Portrait Gallery p 10; Getty Images pp 66, 180, 237, 264; Corbis p 264; Topham Picturepoint pp 38, 126, 211; National Media Museum Science and Society Picture Library p 238; Private Collection p 94.

Foreword

If you read all the published biographies of Lewis Carroll (real name Charles Lutwidge Dodgson), you would end up with confusion rather than clarity. There have been scores of books written about the author of *Alice's Adventures in Wonderland* over the last hundred years. The earlier biographies give you more fact (albeit limited in scope), and the later ones give you more fiction.

Over the last 20 years I have read some very strange biographies of Lewis Carroll, that to my mind are about a person I do not recognize at all. Having studied him for well over 30 years, researched all the available primary source material, edited his private diaries for publication, reconstructed his photographic register, and written extensively about him and his activities, I thought I knew him fairly well. But I gasp when I discover that some biographers think he was a repressed man, a philanderer, a child sexual-abuser, a shy introvert, a man with a guilty conscience, a murderer, a psychopath, a fraud, or an oddity – suggestions made by a variety of writers. These suggestions probably tell us more about the biographers rather than Lewis Carroll himself.

So it is refreshing and delightful to introduce a new biography that speaks sense about the man. All biographers have to interpret the information they have available to them, but desperation should not lead to pure invention, and the search for a 'new angle' should not lead to myth-laden nonsense.

Jenny Woolf's biography of Lewis Carroll takes notice of the evidence that is now available to help us understand and appreciate this famous Victorian poet, mathematician, writer, photographer and children's author. This book gives a good account of what we know about Dodgson's life, and I like the way it is written. I don't agree with every sentiment expressed, but that doesn't matter. She has painted a picture of the man based on her thorough research, with accurate descriptions, and her evidence is clear and well presented.

Her analysis of Dodgson's financial activities, taken mainly from the bank accounts that she discovered and published, provides a most interesting chapter covering much new ground. Her chapter on 'children' is excellent, strongly emphasizing, rightly in my view, the need to understand Dodgson in his own context – the Victorian standards, attitudes, and mind-set of his time.

This book beautifully demolishes the nonsense written about him from the 1920s onwards. There are aspects of his personality that surprise and confuse us, mainly because there are apparent contradictions. Was he shy and withdrawn from society or gregarious and comfortable with others? Was he always witty in his conversations and correspondence or did he have a serious side? Was he conventional by Victorian standards or did he sometimes act in an unconventional manner? Did he follow the moral and ethical codes of his day or did he rebel against the norms of Victorian society? Was his personality gentle and easy-going, or was he strong-willed and pedantic? This biography answers these questions and reveals many different aspects of Dodgson's character – some for the first time. Lewis Carroll's personality is many-faceted and complex.

Maybe this is what attracts us to him – he is a very interesting person.

Edward Wakeling

Editor of *Lewis Carroll's Diaries: the Private Journals of Charles Lutwidge Dodgson*

A Personal Introduction

"'Things flow about so here!" she said at last in a plaintive
tone, after she had spent a minute or so in vainly pursuing
a large bright thing that looked sometimes like a doll and
sometimes like a work-box, and was always in the shelf
next above the one she was looking at.'

Through the Looking Glass

The more closely Lewis Carroll is studied, the more he
seems to slide quietly away. The elusive author of *Alice's
Adventures in Wonderland* has been portrayed in innumerable
ways over the last hundred years. He has been posthumously
psychoanalyzed, condemned and criticized for his supposed
sexual perversions and drug use. He has been pitied for his
apparent repressions, his hidden tragedies and his emotional
frustrations. He is said to have suffered from various disorders
that range from Asperger syndrome to epilepsy. He has even
been suspected of committing terrible crimes – in the intervals
between his religious devotions, of course.

His personal contemporaries, those who would have recognized the stiff-backed, pale-skinned Oxford don as he strode
down the street, have also left differing, though generally less
dramatic, impressions of him. Many of these people lived and

worked alongside him for decades. Their recollections make perfect sense individually yet, taken together, they do not present a coherent picture. When compared with each other, or with aspects of Carroll's work, the real man that they try to describe starts to twist, dwindle and disappear, like a sheet of paper devoured by fire.

So was Lewis Carroll a quiet and boring scholar whose life was utterly devoid of incident, or was he as sharp and imaginative as his 'Alice' books suggest? Was he mild-mannered or passionate? Prim or bohemian? Reserved or sociable? Creepy or cuddly?

I have had an itch to know more about Carroll since, at the age of seven, I was given a copy of the combined volumes of *Alice in Wonderland* (as the first book is more commonly known) and *Through the Looking Glass*. I found it impossible to figure out what the stories were about, but something about Alice and her adventures greatly appealed to me. I read the books laboriously by myself all the way through, and asked for more. When I discovered there were no more, I requested Lewis Carroll's address, so that I could contact him and ask him to write some. I still remember how disappointed I was when I learned that he was already dead. My dreams of having a friendly correspondence, and perhaps a meeting with him, fell in ruins about my seven-year-old ears. I think I have been trying to track him down ever since.

The bare facts of Lewis Carroll's life are clear enough, and can be summed up in a couple of paragraphs. His real name was Charles Lutwidge Dodgson, and he was the oldest son of an Anglican clergyman. He was a devout Christian, and grew up in a large family in the north of England. He attended boarding school at Rugby, then came to study and live at Christ Church,

Oxford, when he was 19. Christ Church then was a dusty, closed-in old place, which became less dusty, but not much less closed-in as the years went on. Carroll lived quietly there for the rest of his life. He never married. A mathematician by profession, he was a photographer in his spare time. He was fond of children, and told a special story for one little girl – a story which became famous. He shunned fame, and made just one trip abroad, then never left Britain again. He taught, he wrote, he prayed, and then he took early retirement. He died, aged nearly 66, while at the home of his spinster sisters near London.

That, then, was his life: yet there was so much more to it than that.

The Oxford college of Christ Church, *Aedes Christi*, provided the constant physical background to Lewis Carroll's life. Originally a monastery, then a theological college, Christ Church (often abbreviated in Carroll's correspondence to 'Ch.Ch.') is still one of the wealthiest and most important institutions in Oxford. Re-founded by Henry VIII in 1546, it has traditionally educated the offspring of the rich and powerful, and its foundation includes Oxford's cathedral church. The college is certain of its own importance, and it treasures its own history and sense of continuity. Standing on the edge of riverside meadows, its noble buildings are dominated by Tom Tower, designed by Sir Christopher Wren. Superficially, it seems that little has changed in hundreds of years. History seems to permeate the golden-yellow stones. Great Tom, the tower bell, still strikes hourly throughout the day, and chimes 101 times each night at 9.05 pm. The main gate is guarded by bowler-hatted custodians, and the main archway leads into a spacious, grassy quad, overlooked by many windows, with a fountain in its centre. Scholars still climb the fan-vaulted, worn stone staircase to dine daily in the paneled Great Hall.

Yet, despite its sense of inward-looking continuity and apparent changelessness, the college – like Oxford itself – is now entirely different from the place that Lewis Carroll knew. These days, Harry Potter fans flock to see Christ Church's splendid hall, which they know as the original of Hogwarts' school refectory. Visitors are more likely to see groups of tourists than a couple of dons ambling past in academic robes and caps. Buses and coaches and taxis roar past the ancient main gate, and crowds of trippers trudge along the pavements from famous 'sight' to souvenir shop to teashop. The city of Oxford itself has become large, sprawling and, beyond the sublime historical areas, frankly drab.

Wherever Carroll's shade may be glimpsed, it is not here. His Oxford existed in an age that was pre-motor car and pre-mass tourism. It was a city that was quiet, small, old, provincial, apart. Its refined flavour can now only be experienced briefly in the occasional sight of a sunlit empty alleyway, or in the stillness inside the cathedral when the tour groups are elsewhere. For Carroll lived not only in a different time, but truly, in a different world.

His Oxford may have vanished beyond recall, but his books are still alive. What is more, they have remained relevant in a changing world. To me, reading them first as a child, then as a teenager, and finally as an adult, this continuing dynamism has seemed one of the strangest things about them. How could a book keep changing? Of course, I knew that really *I* was the one changing, as I grew up. Yet the feeling of shifting uncertainty, the sense that none of what I read had been quite what it seemed, was the element that kept drawing me back. This unusual, if not unique, quality of the books set me wondering what Lewis Carroll himself had been like. So I opened the best-known biographies and started reading.

I found more than enough detailed information about Christ Church, Victorian religion and mathematics, and also plenty of speculation about Alice and all those engaging little girls. Yet although there were plenty of facts, and more than enough theories, it was hard to get an idea of Carroll the man. He was sometimes portrayed as a drearily unpopular social retard with a creepy interest in pre-pubescent girls, or, alternatively, as a shy saint, too innocent and religious to realize what women were for. Or he was presented as a pathetic loner who was woefully unlucky in love with anyone over the age of seven. Sometimes he sounded mad, sometimes dull, sinister, or just boring. In fact, rather than seeming like a real person, Carroll the human being came across almost as a sort of space into which commentators poured their *own* heartaches, yearnings or fears.

I read all the books that I could find about Carroll, but quickly discovered that there are few truly intimate memories of him. From his birth to long past his death, no members of his close family circle discussed his adult existence with outsiders. Except for a handful of letters to newspapers, mainly correcting errors of fact, they said nothing to the wider world about him. His scout, or servant, at college did not discuss what he knew, and his oldest friend, Thomas Vere Bayne, left only the briefest, dullest recollections of him.

Carroll himself shunned publicity, and had little to do with his colleagues in later life. He was gregarious when he wanted to be, but only on his own terms. Privacy was an important element of his existence.

I bought each volume of the complete edited version of his diary as it came out, but, despite the diary's extensive notes and annotations, Carroll's own words were not revealing either. His jotted comments became increasingly clipped and guarded as the years went by. Essentially, it seemed as though he was writing the diary with one eye on posterity. His letters, though usually charming, lively and interesting, nearly all reflect a public face.

What I read just did not fit together to create a believable picture of the man who had been 'Lewis Carroll'. His inaccessibility was maddening. Of course, it did not help that in the years after his death Carroll's family descendants, for what must have seemed to them good reasons, kept such a tight hold on much of the information that could later have cast light upon his unusual personality. Major documents about his personal life, originally carefully preserved, had apparently been destroyed some years after his death; if not destroyed, they must have been extraordinarily carelessly handled – at any rate, they were now nowhere to be found.

Because of these large gaps in information, various peculiar theories have come to fill the gaps. Some were mad, some were sad, others positively baroque. Carroll and his stodgy clergyman friend, Thomas Vere Bayne, were supposedly jointly Jack the Ripper, taking time off from their clerical duties at Oxford to travel up to London and murder prostitutes. Carroll was said to be autistic or epileptic; and there were fanciful Jungian assessments of his psyche, and detailed analyses of the many secret messages that were all-too-imperceptibly supposed to be hidden in his work.

Karoline Leach's book *In the Shadow of the Dreamchild*, published in 1999, broke new ground. Leach not only pointed out how many of Carroll's personal documents had been tampered with, but also showed how intensely secretive and, indeed, deceptive, Carroll himself had been. Leach's book was clever, elegantly written and well researched, but, unfortunately, many have not found it easy to believe in her major contention that Carroll had an affair with Alice's mother. Yet her book accurately pinpointed what I had suspected: that there was much, much more to Carroll than initially met the eye.

So I decided that the best way to understand Carroll would be to start with an open mind, look carefully at as much original source material as possible, think what might sensibly fill the gaps in the present information, and build a picture of him from that. I would consider everything, but I would focus on those aspects of his life which seemed best to reflect the man himself. I wanted to avoid the risk of creating yet another portrait of

Carroll which said more about its author than it said about him, so I would try hard not to make confident assertions about his thoughts. Biography inevitably floats in the ocean between fact and fiction, but I wanted my feet to be touching the factual shore.

I also fantasized that I might find some new and unsullied information against which to set a clear new picture of Carroll. It would be information which had never been seen before, and which had not been overlaid by constant interpretation and re-interpretation. This significant new document, I conjectured, would provide a fresh background against which to re-evaluate existing material about Carroll and it would also allow me to assess whether I was working along the right lines. Admittedly, it seemed unlikely that anything like this would turn up, for every scrap of paper Carroll ever wrote fetches gigantic prices at auction, and few collectors keep completely quiet about what they have. Still, unlikely things do sometimes happen. And in this case, something did.

One day, sitting at my desk, I took a routine call from a PR lady about a hotel which her company represented in Oxford. The hotel had once been a bank, patronized by many important members of the university in Victorian days, she said. It had been taken over by the multinational bank Barclay's, which had run it for some years before closing it down and selling it for conversion.

After her call, on impulse, I called the archive department of Barclay's Bank, and asked the woman who answered if they had any records of a 19th-century Oxford account in Carroll's real name, C L Dodgson. She did a brief check, then returned to say that yes, indeed, they had the entire account. It ran from 1856 to 1900.

Had they ever shown it to anyone? I enquired.

No, she replied. Because nobody had ever asked.

So, of course, I asked. And, within a week I was on the train to Manchester to investigate forty years' worth of Carroll's personal and private bank account, unseen for over a century.

What I discovered, in a windowless book-lined room over several weeks, was a breakthrough. Here were hard, unaltered and previously unknown facts, the accounts shown exactly as they had been when the clerks closed their big leather-bound ledgers over a century before. No devoted members of Carroll's family had scrutinized this material. Nobody had had the chance to obliterate records of certain payments, and insert others they thought more suitable. The fact that this material was utterly untouched made it unique as an important new source of Lewis Carroll information.

Transcribing the account and putting it together with other research was a monstrous task, but, when transcribed, the bank account record stretched over nearly 45 years. It cast a bright, narrow but utterly truthful beam of light over one little slice of Carroll's adult life. For the first time in a hundred years there were some new facts! The rows of inky figures – red ink in many cases, signifying overdrafts – did not look inviting, but when carefully studied they said interesting things about Carroll. New angles on familiar themes were revealed, and people who were barely mentioned in the letters and diaries were shown to have been important in his life.

The account also raised one significant new question. Carroll paid nearly one-quarter of his annual salary to someone called 'Forster' in 1861, a year for which his diaries have mysteriously disappeared. Who was 'Forster' and what was the payment for? As yet, nobody knows.

The bank account was an amazing find, and a lucky one. It showed me that if one vital document can be found, then perhaps others can too. As indeed, they were. Even as I was researching this book, I came across a cache of papers in the archives of the University of Colorado.[1] The university is not particularly known to be associated with Lewis Carroll studies, but it happens to own a letter that casts new light on Carroll's relationship with the Liddells, the family of the so-called 'real' Alice. Like the bank account, this letter had been lying, catalogued and publicly accessible, for all to consult – except that nobody had ever done so.

So now, perhaps, it is time to take a closer look at Lewis Carroll, and see what we can see.

Author's note

It is always a problem to know how to refer to Carroll. Should he be 'C L Dodgson,, as his friends and family knew him, or 'Lewis Carroll', the famous author? I have, for no particular reason, chosen the latter.

Lewis Carroll with his 10 brothers and sisters at the Rectory, Croft-on-Tees, Yorkshire. Carroll can be seen seated on the ground to the centre left. The photograph may have been posed by Carroll, with another party removing the lens cap in order to make the exposure, or it may have been taken by his uncle, Skeffington Lutwidge.

1

'My Father and Mother were honest though poor ...'

Family

… An island-farm – broad seas of corn
Stirred by the wandering breath of morn –
The happy spot where I was born.
'Faces in the Fire'

It is a curious thing that Lewis Carroll, so closely associated with Victorian childhood, hardly ever spoke about his own childhood. Not only did he refrain from discussing his youth, but almost nobody else left personal memories of it either. His brothers and sisters supplied only a few carefully edited recollections of him as a boy. Those family letters which survive hardly refer to him as an individual.

His arrival in the world, though, received a few lines of public notice. It was the tradition among the middle and upper classes to announce the birth of offspring in *The Times* of London. So it was that on 31 January 1832 the newspaper carried an announcement of the birth of the baby who became Lewis Carroll.

Carroll's real name was Charles Lutwidge Dodgson, and he had been born a few days earlier, on 27 January 1832. He was the oldest son and the third child of the Revd Charles Dodgson and his wife (and first cousin), Frances. His birthplace was a small parsonage in Morphany Lane in the village of Daresbury,

Cheshire, where his father was perpetual curate. There had been two Dodgson sisters before him and there would be eight more children after him, following at a rate of one every year or two. Every one of the eleven survived, and throughout Carroll's whole life he would be a vital and valued member of this huge and self-contained group. Always in his background, always in touch, his siblings remained of great significance to him throughout his life.

Not only the eleven children, but the family's numerous aunts, uncles and cousins were close-knit. They all knew that upon the Revd Dodgson's death, Carroll, as the oldest son, would become the head of the family. If any of the brothers and sisters needed help with their problems, it was to him that they would go, no matter how old they might be. Carroll's whole existence was to be spent in the full knowledge and awareness of this large responsibility.

The England where the Dodgson family grew up is still sometimes portrayed in idealized form on traditional Christmas cards. It seems like a jovial land of Mr. Pickwick, of stagecoaches and poke bonnets and roast beef, of simple country folk and inns and ale. The reality, of course, was less comfortable. Huge technological and social changes were under way, and public attitudes had yet to catch up with them. As the Dodgsons' first son greeted the world, slavery was legal, cholera was rife in cities, Roman Catholics were barred from Parliament, and tiny children were being worked to death in factories. Married women had no legal right to keep their own earnings, and public executions were still a popular form of entertainment.

Such repressive, sometimes savage attitudes towards women, children, religion and crime would take many years to change. Whether or not Carroll accepted them (and mostly he did not), these attitudes shaped him and his contemporaries and provided the intellectual and social background to their early lives.

Daresbury, where Carroll spent the early years of his life, was then a pleasant small village with a population of around 150 souls, at the centre of a scattered parish in flat, lush countryside. The parsonage was some distance both from the village and the church, and it was so countrified that even the passing of a cart on the road was said to be a matter of great interest for the children.[1]

The Revd Dodgson, though well bred and well read, was however not well off. He was a brilliant scholar who had obtained a double first at Christ Church, yet as a mere perpetual curate he was ill-paid and doing a job far below his intellectual capacity. Without influential people to lobby for him, there was little he could do but make the best of it, and his situation was a matter of some pain to him and his friends. His poverty and enforced lack of status would not have been lost on his eldest son.

The family's life in Daresbury was very rural. They kept livestock and grew some of their own food, but of course, living in a Georgian country house and growing one's own vegetables was not quite the charming existence that it might be today. Both parents made the best of their lives with Christian cheerfulness, and if the Dodgson siblings' tight-knit, cooperative and upright adulthood is anything to go by, their youth was orderly, austerely religious, affectionate and generally happy. The Revd Dodgson worked hard at ministering to his widely dispersed flock, and took in extra pupils to help bring in a few extra shillings to feed, clothe and educate the family. His wife searched endlessly for inexpensive ways to manage the household and her brood of growing children, as her stream of dashingly underlined letters to her sister eloquently testifies:

... <u>Loui</u> I have only got the llama Wool High Dress she had last Winter & for <u>Carry</u> & <u>Mary</u> I have got <u>nothing</u> for the <u>morning</u> – the <u>few</u> High Dresses they had last Winter are <u>quite</u> <u>done</u> – their Pelisses must also pass down to the younger ones (the <u>two</u> smallest being wanted to make <u>one</u> for darling Edwin … <u>Can</u> I get wr<u>ong</u> in choosing the above for them in Darlington? they would be less expensive there I should think …[2]

The Dodgsons stayed in Cheshire until 1843, when Carroll was eleven, after which they moved to Croft-on-Tees, north Yorkshire, where Carroll's father had gained a well-deserved promotion to rector. In 1852, he was made residentiary canon of the ancient cathedral at Ripon, Yorkshire, and after that, he and his family spent time in Ripon as well as at Croft.

There is but one recorded remark from Carroll about himself as a child, contained in a letter to a lady friend, and it is brief. He wrote, during a diatribe about how he disliked boys, that he had been a 'simply detestable' little boy.[3] He was probably joking, but, as a boy, detestable or not, he hardly figures individually in preserved family letters and papers. Any family friends who remembered him chose not to come forward with their memories of his youth, and even the neighbours had almost nothing to say.

In fact, since Carroll did not attend school until he was 12 years old, it can fairly be said that he had little significant childhood existence outside his large, extended family. From the very start, he was one of a group, not as much of an individual in his own right as someone from a smaller family would have been. He had to take his place, wait his turn, and join in.

Letters still in the Dodgson family's possession, telling relatives how glad and happy their children made them, show that both parents delighted in their family life. In the very busy but well-organized household, the offspring were distinguished by their initials and referred to mainly as 'treasures' and 'darlings'. There is a surviving letter from 1837, which Carroll, then about five, 'wrote', with his hand guided by an adult. Couched in baby talk, it sends a 'kitt' (kiss) from 'Charlie with the horn of hair', its existence showing that adults in his life doted upon his babyish quirks of speech and his infant curls.[4]

The few reminiscences of him which his nephew Stuart Collingwood coaxed from Carroll's brothers and sisters when writing his biography, present a quaint, charitable and clever child, demanding to know what logarithms were, and making personal pets of snails and toads and worms. Perhaps understandably, the book is not very objective yet, within the limits of presenting a conventional picture of his uncle, Collingwood tried hard to show him as the quirky human being he essentially was. He had been a child, he said, who seemed 'to have actually lived in that charming "Wonderland" which he afterwards described'.[5]

As he grew older, Carroll emerged as the family entertainer, involving his brothers and sisters in vast imaginative games in their huge garden. Railways being the latest thing at the time, he made a train from a wheelbarrow, a barrel and a truck. It would carry its young passengers from one 'station' in the rectory grounds to another, in accordance with a long and deliberately ridiculous list of railway regulations that he concocted for them. He learned sleight-of-hand and dressed up to amuse his siblings with magic shows. He helped make a toy theatre – he was good with his hands – and wrote puppet plays which he and the older ones performed. They also wrote and illustrated several family magazines under his guidance, and when he was away from home he wrote them long, loving, and entertaining letters.

One of these letters, written in his twenties and addressed to his youngest brother and sister, then aged 12 and 9, has survived. He had just become a tutor at Christ Church, and it gives an account almost worthy of the Marx Brothers of how Oxford lectures were supposedly conducted via a sort of Chinese whispers system through doors and all along corridors:

Tutor. 'What is twice three?'
Scout. 'What's a rice tree?'
Sub-Scout. 'When is ice free?'
Sub-sub-Scout. 'What's a nice fee?'
Pupil (timidly). 'Half a guinea!'
Sub-sub-Scout. 'Can't forge any!'
Sub-Scout. 'Ho for Jinny!'
Scout. 'Don't be a ninny!'
Tutor (looks offended) ...'[6]

Family life seems to have been very harmonious, with no sugges-tion that any family members were left out or badly treated by the others, although Skeffington, the second brother, may have had slight learning difficulties and seems to have been a worry at times.

Viewed from a century-and-a-half away, the inter-relation-ships and personalities of the family members have, of course, mostly faded to obscurity. But because they were such a major influence on Carroll, it is worth taking a quick look at what is known about his sisters, his brothers and other close family members.

Just as his family rarely discussed him with outsiders, so Carroll spoke little to outsiders about them. No descriptions remain of any of them as children, but in adulthood Carroll sometimes referred to his sisters generally as the 'sisterhood'. The 'sisterhood' were intelligent women who were generally acknowledged to share a strong sense of duty and family inter-dependence. They did a great deal of charitable work, all had a good sense of humour and were fond of children. In later life, he regarded their home in Guildford as his home, too, and he spent a good deal of time there.

The two oldest sisters were Frances (Fanny) and Elizabeth, respectively four and two years older than him. Fanny was said to be sensible and capable, artistic, musical, fond of flowers and devoutly religious, with a flair for looking after the sick and helpless.

Carroll seems to have particularly confided in the second sister, Elizabeth. He told her of his joys and sorrows, and she was probably the one who mothered him most. She was extremely fond of children, and always yearned to look after babies. A touching little sheet of paper has survived on which young Elizabeth dotingly copied down some of the chit-chat of her small brothers and sisters playing in the nursery.

The third sister, Caroline, was very shy and reclusive, and many early family letters mention unspecified anxieties about her. She hardly went out, and suffered particularly badly from one of the speech defects which plagued the family.

The only one of the seven daughters to marry was the fourth, Mary. She was artistic and strongly religious. She was in her mid-thirties when she married shortly after her father's death, and a Dodgson family descendant has suggested that it may have been a relief that someone had come forward to look after Mary, leaving one less mouth to feed.[7] Mary may have had a hard life, for her husband was often ill. She obviously missed her sisters, for she returned to live with them after his death, and one of her two children, Stuart Collingwood, became the family biographer.

The fifth daughter, Louisa, survived all her brothers and sisters, dying at the age of 90. She had become an invalid, which probably gave her the leisure to pursue her keen interest in mathematics, which sometimes occupied her mind so much that she did not notice what was going on around her.

The sixth daughter, Margaret, also liked mathematics and backgammon, and helped a good deal with the Croft National School, which her father had established in order to educate local poor children. Margaret does not sound particularly unconventional, but the youngest daughter, Henrietta, certainly was. By the time Henrietta was middle-aged, she had managed to inherit and keep enough money to set up a modest household independently from her sisters, although she did remain in close touch with everyone. She moved to Brighton, where she lived with an ancient maidservant and a menagerie of cats.[8]

Tall and gaunt, Henrietta generated several family stories about her eccentricities. There was the portable stove she brought along when visiting relatives, to enable her to fry sausages in her bedroom. There was the time she once became so involved with singing hymns on the train with fellow passengers that she missed her stop, and on another occasion she accidentally took an alarm clock to church one day instead of her prayer book. Carroll often visited Henrietta in Brighton, and he sometimes took his young friends along, too. One such was Katie Lucy, aged 17, who noted in her diary, 'I like her. I think she is like him.'[9]

Of the four brothers, Edwin, the youngest of all the children, felt called to become a missionary and spent time in Africa and Tristan da Cunha. His work was at times very hard and discouraging, and his descriptions of his extremely difficult life in Tristan make it clear that, for Edwin, human love and pleasure were not part of his self-denying life plan. He never married and his last years were spent as an invalid.

The third son and seventh child, Wilfred, was lively minded, humorous and clever. He loved the outdoors and rejected academia, breaking from the family clerical tradition to become an estate manager. He was a successful businessman, married his childhood sweetheart in 1871, and had nine children.

The second son and sixth child, Skeffington, had difficulty with academic work, and was forgetful and emotional. He married late in life after a rather turbulent clerical career, and settled in Vowchurch, Herefordshire. There, he lived as an impoverished vicar, pursuing his passionate hobby of fishing. He was often teased for his eccentricity by his rustic parishioners, but his wife was charming and clever and the family was very happy. He was a strict but beloved father to his three surviving children.

The fact that only three of the Dodgsons' eleven children married has sometimes attracted comment, but this is not necessarily a sign that the family had issues with the idea of marriage. Carroll and Edwin both had jobs that made marriage difficult, and the girls probably did not meet enough people or socialize enough for all of them to find husbands. Like the vast majority of young women of their class, they had a very restricted existence. They could not attend university, nor have careers. If of marriageable age, they could not go out alone to make friends outside the extended family circle, nor speak to men they did not know. Carroll never danced, and always avoided dancing, so it is also possible that there were family restrictions on this form of social entertainment.

An aged neighbour, speaking at the time of Carroll's centenary celebrations in the 1930s, knew the daughters before 1868, when they would have been in their twenties and thirties, and remarked on how plain their clothes were and how self-sacrificing their lives. As one family descendant wryly observed after considering their photographs, they seem to have been dressed in 'last year's curtains, with room allowed for growth!'[10]

Apart from Carroll, who earned his own living, the Revd Dodgson supported all his children during his lifetime, and scraped enough money to leave a trust fund to allow the sisters to live together after his death with modest financial independence. For them, as for any women with minds and means of their own, marriage was not necessarily much of an attraction. A wife had to surrender everything she owned or earned to her husband and put herself under his control. So apart from the prospect of motherhood – a mixed blessing – their father's consideration of them meant that there was no practical need for the sisters to marry.

Despite, or perhaps because of the lack of outside contacts, the siblings' closeness and interdependence meant that none of them ever needed to feel lonely, unwanted or out of place, so there would be little reason to marry for companionship. There was always someone to remember their birthdays, always someone to share a joke with or drop in and see, and always someone with whom to spend Christmas. Even Edwin wrote long, long letters to his family as he battled the windy deprivations of Tristan, and the sisters faithfully copied these long letters out and circulated them for other family members to read.

After his father's death, Carroll was to work extremely hard trying to aid Edwin in his plan to resettle the islanders. He helped Wilfred settle into a career, and Skeffington's problems were a recurring theme in his life. He spent a good deal of time dealing with his sisters' financial and legal matters, and helped all his relatives – particularly the female ones – with countless other practical details. But although he was always the leader of this little band of siblings, the first surviving glimpse of him as an individual comes in a letter that he wrote to Fanny and Elizabeth in 1844, when he was 12 years old.

Carroll had just gone to boarding school in Richmond, Yorkshire, his first attendance at school. Education was not compulsory in those days, and his financially-pressed father had tutored him at home throughout his early childhood. So, though he was not in the least socially deprived, Carroll had been denied the experience that most people soon acquire, of making a group of school friends at a young age, and standing on his own feet among them.

Richmond School was small and reasonably humanely run, but it would not have been surprising if Carroll, on the very edge of adolescence, suffered during his first time away from home. Yet he did not. He seemed to accept that he was part of a group here, too, and settled down quickly and well. In his letter, he sent his sisters a long list of the children that he liked (there were, apparently, none that he did not like) and he described the chief games they played, 'foot-ball, wrestling, leap frog, and fighting'. He had suffered the trials to which new boys were usually subjected, and described them in some detail. They were not savage, and he was sanguine about them: 'the boys play me no tricks now', he concluded cheerfully.[11]

Many early and mid-Victorian schools offered their pupils a huge degree of freedom; or, as we would now see it, gross lack of supervision. Richmond School, as Stuart Collingwood noted approvingly, was run on the old 'free' system. It was so different from more modern schools, he added, where 'the unfortunate masters hardly get a minute to themselves from sunrise till long after sunset'.[12]

Carroll seems to have enjoyed the freedom. His sisters told Collingwood that he had been a typical boy in his love of climbing trees and messing about in ponds, and in the relaxed atmosphere of the school he would have been allowed to roam. He lived in the family home of the headmaster, Mr Tate, and got on well with his children, keeping in touch with them for years afterwards.

Tate ('my kindly old headmaster', as Carroll was later to remember him) sent a closely observed and highly positive assessment of the boy to his parents. 'He possesses, along with other and excellent natural endowments, a very uncommon share of genius.' he wrote, going on to describe Carroll as 'gentle and cheerful in his intercourse with others' and 'playful and ready in conversation'. [13] The letter obviously pleased Carroll's father, for he kept it all his life.

Sadly, Carroll was much less happy at his next school, where he was sent at 14. It was the famous public school Rugby, in Warwickshire, and he remained there for three years. It was not a minute too short for him.

Rugby School had been greatly improved by the remarkable Dr Arnold only a few years before Carroll arrived. Arnold had removed many of the worst excesses of violence and brutality for which the school had previously been notorious, and Rugby was at that time probably the best and most progressive public school in the country. That does not mean, however, that it provided an environment that anyone today would consider to be remotely good, or even acceptable for their children.

In mid-19th century England, young gentlemen's schools trained them for the tough and hard life they might well have to endure, either at home or overseas. Hardship and abuse, far from stunting their tender personalities, was considered to be positively *good* for them. A typical example of what one could expect at a contemporary public school is given by the Devonshire doctor J W Ley, who was born the year after Carroll, in 1833. Dr Ley described how the boys in his school were left unsupervised at night, when the inhabitants of two of the dormitories would converge with twisted bolsters upon a third dormitory of younger children who would 'anxiously and timorously be awaiting their approach.' They would, he recalled, be carried off, tossed in blankets up to the ceilings, stripped and spanked, drenched with cold water, and various other indignities would be inflicted on them. Once, the bullied little boys took their revenge. Using ropes, bolsters, and knotted soaked towels, they reduced the chief bully to pulp, his shirt in ribbons, his face almost unrecognizable. Everyone ended up with black eyes, bloody noses and torn mouths. Finally, the teacher intervened, and added to the carnage by beating all the boys thoroughly with his cane.[14]

Dr Ley, as an old man, wrote a newspaper column of humorous reminiscences, and he delightedly recounted this horrific event as a splendid example of boyish fun. He was entirely in tune with his times in that it did not occur either to him or his editors that his readers might have the slightest reservations about sharing his pleasure.

The status or cost of a school often bore little relation to how well the pupils were nurtured. Sexual abuse, often of the most disgusting kind, was taken for granted, and violence was endemic. At Eton, in 1825, just 19 years before Carroll went to Rugby, the 13-year-old brother of the humanitarian Lord Shaftesbury was beaten to death in a fist fight. The boy's father did not prosecute because the fight had been conducted according to standard fist fighting rules.

Set against this tough background, Rugby School in Carroll's time was not bad but, according to Rouse's *History of Rugby School* (1898), boys often vandalized each others' rooms, and drunkenness was a perennial problem. Beating with a cane, both by masters and older boys, was commonplace, and Collingwood confirms that the general system of victimizing and tormenting younger boys would have been endemic in Carroll's day.

Looking back on his schooldays at the age of 23, Carroll mused in his diary that, 'I cannot say that I look back upon my life at a Public school with any sensation of pleasure, or that any earthly considerations would induce me to go through my three years again.'[15] Nevertheless, he was no sissy. His boyish words to his sisters show he considered fighting a 'game', and, in fact, wrote Collingwood, 'even though it is hard for those who have only known him as the gentle and retiring don to believe it, it is nevertheless true that long after he left school, his name was remembered as that of a boy who knew well how to use his fists in defense of a righteous cause' – that is, the protection of smaller boys.[16]

One of Carroll's major objections to Rugby was the unkindness of the bullying, and his continuous protectiveness towards the helpless would be a marked characteristic for the rest of his life. On visiting Radley School, around a decade after he had left school himself, he approvingly noted that each boy had his own wooden cubicle to sleep in at night:

... a snug little bed-room secured to himself, where he is

free from interruption and annoyance ... This to little boys must be a very great addition to their happiness, as being a kind of counterbalance to any bullying they may suffer during the day. From my own experience of school life at Rugby I can say that if I could have been thus secure from annoyance at night, the hardships of the daily life would have been comparative trifles to bear.[17]

Carroll singled out little boys as the main sufferers from 'annoyance'. As Dr Ley's account makes clear, younger boys were the main target of older bullies. It was, as Collingwood points out, the bad discipline maintained in the dormitories at Rugby that made even the nights seem intolerable, 'especially for the small boys, whose beds in winter were denuded of blankets that the bigger ones might not feel cold'.[18]

Carroll's remarks, above, about 'annoyance at night' have been interpreted to suggest that he was a lonely, bullied misfit who was sexually abused. There is nothing to support the idea that he was lonely or more bullied than anyone else, and no evidence one way or the other about sexual abuse. If he had been abused, he certainly would not have been alone, as a blind eye was turned to abuse by both boys and masters, who believed that boys would generally grow out of their homosexuality and get over any abuse inflicted upon them.

Carroll's love of learning (which he would retain throughout his life), had been developed at home by his father but, even so, his studies at Rugby were a trial to him. He made some progress in his school work, he wrote, but none of it was done *con amore*, and he spent a good deal of time in writing out 'lines' as punishment.[19] He did not enjoy organized sport, which must also have made life difficult, and it seems highly possible that Rugby was the place where he was first exposed to the stammerer's worst nightmare of having to read aloud in front of a group, and likely sustain their mockery. That was something which his home tuition never inflicted on him, and his affectionately remembered Mr Tate no doubt spared him.

Carroll kept no diary during his three years at Rugby, and he was not a person to dwell on negative experiences. Yet he must have had a robust character. He won prizes and plaudits, and inspired his headmaster to write to his father, 'I must not allow your son to leave school without expressing to you the very high opinion I entertain of him ... of his abilities and upright conduct ... During the whole time ... his conduct has been excellent.'[20]

The picture which thus emerges of Carroll is of a boy with considerable reserves of toughness and concentration beneath a sensitive exterior. He was a boy, too, who developed ways of dealing with aggressive members of his own sex without breaking down, and kept his eye firmly on what he wanted to achieve.

When he became an adult, he seems to have retained these qualities. There is no record of his having been pushed around in adult life. He was never afraid of speaking out, and there is no suggestion anywhere that he showed or felt physical fear. The journal of his one and only trip abroad, written when he was 35, goes into much more detail than his other diaries, since he seems to have written it for family members to read on his return. He travelled across Europe to Russia, and, his account of the trip shows him to have been strongly assertive and not prepared to be bullied, even when in a strange land in which he did not speak the language.

In one incident, he argued with an abusive cab driver who was refusing to accept a previously negotiated price of 30 kopeks, and demanding 40 instead. Having given him 30 kopeks, Carroll reported that he then asked for the money back. On receiving it, he returned it to his purse and counted the man out 25 kopeks. 'In doing this,' he noted, 'I felt something like a man pulling the string of a shower bath – and the effect was like it – his fury boiled over directly and quite eclipsed all the former row. I told him in very bad Russian that I had offered 30 once, but wouldn't again. ...'[21]

His correspondence with the illustrator Harry Furniss, who attempted to dominate him, is more amiable, but it is worth reading for Carroll's extraordinarily clever, gentle but steely success in forcing Furniss to back down completely.[22]

So it seems that Carroll dealt effectively with his male contemporaries and was protective towards younger children. He was close to his group of siblings, and they loved and admired him. He also had good relationships with his aunts and uncles. His sweet-natured aunt Lucy Lutwidge had long been concerned with her sister's children, and came to look after the family on their mother's death. Carroll's letters to her show that he got on well with her and felt relaxed in her company.

His favorite uncle, Robert W Skeffington Lutwidge, played an important part in his life. 'Uncle Skeffington' provided a positive bachelor role model, showing Carroll how to play the kindly uncle and how to relish an unmarried existence. He and Carroll had a one-to-one closeness that the busy Dodgson household may not have provided, and there were striking similarities between the two men. Both were deeply religious, and both were extremely fond of mathematics. Both adored gadgets; it was Lutwidge who introduced Carroll to photography. As a government Commissioner for Lunacy, he inspected asylums, and mental disorder was one of Carroll's own lifelong interests. The two men had long talks about family issues, and, despite the 30-year age difference, they socialized together, going out to concerts and plays.

So, did Carroll also get on well with his parents? It is surprisingly hard to find information about this. Not many details of his relationship with his mother have survived. She took a conscientious interest in his religious education. She kept a log of his progress in a book that was divided into sections that included 'Religious Reading: Private', and 'Religious Reading with Mama'. It was said that her religious faith was at the centre of her life – something often said, too, about Carroll. One of the few references he made to her in his childhood letters was to ask his sisters to tell their mother that his only fault had been 'coming in one day to dinner just after grace'.[23]

Mrs Dodgson had a gentle, sweet and contented nature, and her children said that she never shouted. She was not, perhaps, very imaginative, being apparently happy to live a life of quiet dullness – her life, she once confided to a relative, was exactly as she had always wanted it to be. She was preoccupied with the details of daily life; as well she might have been, with a family of 13, not to mention servants, pupils and visitors, to look after on a limited income.

It may have been that because she had such a large family, and worked so hard to do the best for them, she was unable to take as much of a personal interest in each well-loved child as that child might have wanted. Carroll treasured all his life a letter she wrote to him when he was small and she was away from home visiting relatives. Although it is a sweet and loving message, there is something a little sad about it too. It suggests an affectionate child with a deep need to communicate, writing many letters to his beloved mother and perhaps not receiving enough personal attention in return. 'I have used you rather ill in not having written to you sooner ...', runs part of the letter, continuing:

All your notes have delighted me, my precious child, and show me you have not quite forgotten me. I am always thinking of you, and longing to have you all around me again more than words can tell. God grant that we may find you all well and happy ... give [your brothers and sisters] and all my other treasures including yourself, 1,000,000,000 kisses from me with my most affectionate love, I am sending you a shabby note but I can not help it ...[24]

The letter, although genuinely affectionate, is not that long, and does not say much that is specifically about him. Yet it was so important to the little boy that he wrote threateningly on the back, 'No one is to touch this note, for it belongs to CLD. Covered in slimy pitch, so that they will wet their fingers.'[25]

Carroll's work as a whole suggests that he may have had some issues about mothers and sons, and these can perhaps be traced back to the difficulty he probably had in getting individual attention from his mother. It cannot have been easy for him to accept. Many people who knew Carroll remark on his gentleness. Fewer, though, comment on his jealousy. The early biographer Langford Reed spoke privately to some of Carroll's surviving friends and reported that Carroll had had something of a problem with jealousy, although Reed did not go into details.[26]

Carroll's flashes of anger and rage were occasionally glimpsed by others but were usually well controlled. It is interesting that a portion of this rare jealous anger is associated with the subject of mothers and sons. One cannot look at his works of fiction and make glib assumptions about exactly what he meant, but nevertheless, nowhere in Carroll's huge output is there a single realistic portrayal of a good and loving – or even a remotely convincing – relationship between a mother and a son.

He depicts doted-upon mama's boys with particularly withering scorn. In 'The Blank Check',[27] a skit upon the financing of new building in Oxford, the various luminaries of Christ Church are presented as unappealing little boys fawned over by a stupid and ignorant mother. An elaborate piece of juvenilia, 'Crundle Castle' centres almost entirely on a spoiled boy who is the apple of his mama's eye and the bane of everyone else's life.[28]

Even more unappealing – in fact downright unsettling – is the relationship of My Lady and her beloved little son Uggug in Carroll's late books *Sylvie and Bruno* (1889) and *Sylvie and*

Bruno Concluded (1893). The grim portrait of a cloying mutual relationship ends with Uggug being confined forever in a cage, transformed into a monstrous porcupine-like beast. His glaring appearance (conveyed in artwork closely supervised by Carroll) is oddly reminiscent in its brutal madness, of Goya's Saturn, who devoured his children. Worse than this, Uggug is loveless; nobody wants him. He is covered in prickles, shut up in a cage, and everyone is going to hate him forever. No jealous infant could be crueler than the elderly Carroll in savaging this beloved mama's boy. In contrast, the young hero and heroine of the book do not have a mother at all, even though they have a father. Their mother is omitted, as though she never existed, and the boy's older sister takes her place.

This replacement of a mother by an older sister is also a not uncommon feature of Carroll's work. It can be seen in *Alice in Wonderland*, where Alice recounts her adventures to an older sister, not a mother. In Carroll's long juvenile story *Sidney Hamilton*, the family scene also lacks a mother figure, even though Carroll's mother was alive and well at the time. An older sister again takes the mother's place. After her naughty brother runs away, young Lucy Hamilton busies herself with the 'domestic duties' that would normally be the province of the mother. Just as Carroll's surviving letters are to his sisters and not his mother, in his story it is Lucy, not her mother, who presides over the dinner table and worries about the missing boy.[29]

Carroll never seems to have got over his jealous emotional confusion about mothers; it may be that he was not even consciously aware of it. The surviving letters and diaries for the whole of his life refer to his feelings for his mother just once – in a letter congratulating his sister Mary on the birth of a son. The letter shows he loved his mother, although, as so often with Carroll, the actual words he uses suggest a situation without actually saying a great deal about it:

My dearest Mary,

I must write one line to *yourself*, if only to say – God bless you and the little one now entrusted to you – and may you be to him what our own dear mother was to *her* eldest son! I can hardly utter for your boy a better wish than that!

Your loving brother[30]

While Carroll makes a few idealized references elsewhere to mothers and their children in general, apart from this instance, in his letters and diaries his mother hardly appears to exist.

The lack of mothers in Carroll's work is not often remarked upon, but the brutal, domineering female figures that also occur from time to time in his work have attracted speculation from commentators as to whom they might be based upon. These include the Queen of Hearts in *Alice in Wonderland* and My Lady, who holds a position of power in *Sylvie and Bruno*. They are sometimes, on no evidence, assumed to be maternal figures, but these bullying women run to a type that seems absolutely nothing like Carroll's mother was said to be. Large, coarse and stupid, they love or hate with savage irrationality, and do not care how much damage they do. They could perhaps resemble some of the uneducated servants who would have had control of Carroll and his siblings when Mrs Dodgson was not available.

Most children of Carroll's class and period spent a great deal of time with nursemaids. It had to be that way, for if children of a large family were to be well cared for, plenty of people needed to be involved. Servants to a perpetual curate in a remote village in the 1830s were unlikely to be intellectually sophisticated and probably could not even read or write. Not much is known about the Dodgsons' servants but, perhaps significantly, an unpublished family letter refers to one nursemaid, Louisa, who left when Carroll was four. She is described as horrible, cold hearted and selfish.[31] This was very strong language by contrast with the almost uniformly gentle and positive tone of the other surviving letters.

This 'cold hearted' woman had charge of the highly sensitive and affectionate little boy in his earliest years. Her replacement, Jane, was described as loud, arrogant and conceited, but at least to the children she was kind, mild and sensitive.[32] Whatever his own experiences may have been, Carroll strongly objected to nursemaids in general, as he wrote to a Mrs Blakemore in 1877: 'I should like the whole race of nurses to be abolished: children should be with their mother as much as possible, in my opinion.'[33]

Whatever his ambivalence about mothers and female caring figures, Carroll had no such difficulties in his portrayal of fathers. The older-younger man relationships he created, from Father William to the father in 'Jabberwocky', were sometimes lively and ridiculous, and frequently rather edgy, but they were always emotionally alive. Even the bossy papa of *Sidney Hamilton*, at whom the youthful Carroll cocked a mischievous snook as he sends him 'to bed in a state of mind bordering on insanity', is only being so ridiculous because he cares so deeply about his naughty oldest son.

In everyday life, Carroll probably clashed with his father. He was self-willed, as he admitted himself. To his friend Dora Abdy, he jokingly wrote:

> Among the host of virtues which, as you are no doubt aware, form the *background* of my character ... a <u>readiness to adopt suggestions</u> (when they happen to coincide with my own inclinations) is one of the most marked – so prominent, in fact, that my biographer will fail to do justice to it, unless he devotes a whole chapter to the subject ...[34]

A self-willed boy coming up against a strong-willed father will result in conflict, and so it seems reasonable to assume that there was some. It must have been resolved well enough for Carroll to remain on decent terms with his father, who entrusted him with the supervision of his younger brothers and continued to welcome him home in the vacations.

Surviving family letters suggest that Mr Dodgson, like his wife, adored his children. Unlike his wife, he left numerous letters which testify to his deep personal interest in them as individuals. An entire collection of letters to his second son, Skeffington, survives,[35] and the paternal personality which emerges is dependable, clever and lively – as well as being very much in control. Descriptions of him suggest that Carroll inherited his father's storytelling ability and high intelligence.

In fact, Revd Dodgson was, by Victorian paterfamilias standards, highly emotionally expressive. Young Skeffington had various mild social and intellectual problems, and was continuously struggling to keep up. His father's letters were uniformly encouraging and compassionate. Perseverance was one of Skeffington's virtues, and when, after interminable effort, he finally struggled through his exams, his father wrote him a long, joyful letter which included the comment, 'The great Dr Arnold drew … a living picture of such a character as yours, and wound it up with the striking words, "I could stand hat in hand before such a man."'[36] It was wonderful praise for a youth who must often have faced failure, and it is no less joyful than the letter Revd Dodgson had written to Carroll about his brilliant examination results not long before.

As the oldest son, of course, Carroll had a special relationship with his father. Revd Dodgson had strong views about what his offspring should do with their lives, and most professional jobs were gained through the 'old-boy' network of recommendation and introduction, into which it was hard for outsiders to break. To find good positions for his sons, their father was obliged to undertake a round of asking his friends and acquaintances if they could help. Carroll followed his example when he became head of the family, helping his younger brothers to sort out their careers, and shouldering financial responsibility for his sisters where necessary.

As the bank account and the few examples of surviving correspondence between Carroll and his father show, Revd Dodgson expected his eldest son to take care of his brothers' money while they were at university. The increasing sharing of financial responsibility for his brothers and sisters must have been an important aspect of Carroll's relationship with his father as he grew older. Another letter that his father wrote to him gives an interesting insight into their early relationship. Written when Carroll was just eight years old, it shows that his father was prepared to take considerable trouble composing a long letter to amuse his child, and he had clearly also brought him a present. After describing an amusing scene of increasing chaos in obtaining the gift, it ends with a flourish: '... At last they bring the things which I ordered, and then I spare the Town, and send off in 50 wagons, and under the protection of 10,000 soldiers, a file and a screw driver and a ring as a present to Charles Lutwidge Dodgson, from his affectionate Papa.'[37]

When his father died at the age of 68, Carroll, according to Collingwood, fell into a kind of depression from which he thought he might never recover.[38] Some commentators have conjectured that Carroll was thrown into despair because his father's death removed his chance to rebel against all that the older man stood for. It has also been suggested that the death condemned Carroll to endless guilt because he had not become the person his father had wanted him to be.

There is no evidence that either was the case. For sure, he did not always obey his father, but then, few grown-up men do exactly what their father says. He may well have been jealous of him at times, since a tendency to jealousy was, as already noted, one of his personal characteristics. However, there is no record that either man felt anything other than normal parental or filial love. Another and more practical aspect of his distress may have been the only too obvious facts that not only must he now bid farewell to his devoted, hardworking and protective father, but that a huge burden now lay upon his own shoulders.

His father's death would have obliged Carroll to shoulder responsibility for all his adult brothers and sisters, all of whom were jobless, unmarried and had become homeless. The family home of 25 years was being dismantled as the rectory was prepared for its new incumbent. It must have felt as though the ground had been snatched away from under the whole family's feet, not just his own. Of course he did his duty, but the shock must have been immense, and the weight of responsibility enormous.

At the time of his father's death, Carroll was writing *Through the Looking-Glass*, the account of how Alice becomes a queen, which for the psychologically inclined may suggest something of the horror of how it feels to become a responsible adult. In the book, Alice is pleased at first to become a queen, as she has anticipated all along:

> … she turned to run down the hill: 'and now for the last brook, and to be a Queen! How grand it sounds!' A very few steps brought her to the edge of the brook. 'The Eighth Square at last!' she cried as she bounded across,

> and threw herself down to rest on a lawn as soft as moss, with little flower-beds dotted about it here and there. 'Oh, how glad I am to get here!'

Unfortunately, the badgering and pestering of the other queens gives her little freedom to enjoy her imposing new role, so when they fall asleep, Alice escapes into a dream-within-a-dream – or thinks she does. But it is all an illusion: she does not escape. As the focus of all eyes, she becomes increasingly frightened as she is expected to take charge, yet everything around her is disintegrating into a revolting and unpredictable mess. She is crushed and squashed ('You would have thought they wanted to squeeze me flat!') and finally, as the nightmare rises to its height, she screams, 'I can't stand this any longer!' and starts shaking one of the queens almost to death.

For Alice, it was a dream. For Carroll, writing about Alice's experiences Through the Looking-Glass in whatever time he could spare, daily reality as the new head of his family was undoubtedly a quick-moving procession of unfamiliar tasks. He had to take the lead and cope alone, with all eyes upon him. There was no escape, and never would be again.

Viewed in this context, there is also a certain resonance in Alice's farewell to the kindly old White Knight, immediately before she becomes a queen. The old man takes his leave in a way that always seems poignant.

> 'You've only a few yards to go,' he said ... 'and then you'll be a Queen – But you'll stay and see me off first?' he added as Alice turned with an eager look in the direction to which he pointed. 'I shan't be long. You'll wait and wave your handkerchief when I get to that turn in the road! I think it'll encourage me, you see.'
>
> 'Of course I'll wait' said Alice: 'and thank you very much for coming so far – and for the song – I liked it very much.'
> 'I hope so' said the Knight, doubtfully. 'But you didn't cry as much as I thought you would.'
>
> So they shook hands, and then the Knight rode slowly away into the forest ...

The White Knight cannot be stated to be Carroll's father (or anyone real – he is fiction), but, like any fictional character, he must reflect fragments of his maker's inner feelings and preoccupations at the time. He is similar to the comical older men or father-figures in Carroll's juvenilia, and is the only character in either book who ever cares about Alice or tries to look after her.

This, then, is about the sum of what we know about Carroll's childhood, youth and education, and about his relationships with his family. About his own feelings during this period, we know little; he wrote diaries as a teenager, but these have all disappeared. He apparently had some problems during his adolescence, which is hardly surprising or unusual. It would be interesting to have an idea of what those problems were, but he is not recorded as having said or written anything about them, just as he almost never mentioned his childhood. The letters which the family chose to preserve were cheerful, clever, companionable and upbeat.

The only brief and fragmentary first-hand recollections of him as an adolescent appeared long after his death. They were contributed by aged residents of Croft-on-Tees who had obviously hardly known him. Racking their memories, they called to mind a polite young man who studied while lying full length beneath an acacia tree in the garden, and who visited old ladies and enthusiastically ate their girdle-scones (a type of pancake). Nobody could remember discussing anything with him.

Collingwood is tellingly coy about the subject of Carroll's adolescence. He informs his readers that it was 'necessarily less interesting', although he does not say what it was less interesting *than*. It would certainly have been interesting to *us*, and it is also interesting to see how Collingwood tries to explain his decision not to discuss it without actually revealing what it is he is refusing to talk about:

We all have to pass through that painful era of self consciousness which prefaces manhood, that time when we feel so deeply and are so utterly unable to express to others, or even to define clearly to ourselves, what it is we do feel. The natural freedom of childhood is dead within us, the conventional freedom of riper years is struggling to birth, and its efforts are sometimes ludicrous to an unsympathetic observer. In Lewis Carroll's mental attitude during this critical period there was always a calm dignity which saved him from these absurdities, an undercurrent of conscious- ness that what seemed so great to him was really very little.[39]

What his words mean is anybody's guess. And so our knowledge of Carroll's youth ends in clouds of mystery deeper than those with which it started. Currently available records offer no other clues, and no indication of what happened between Carroll's return home from Rugby and his departure for Christ Church, where he would spend the rest of his life.

Six of Carroll's seven sisters and his outnumbered youngest brother Edwin. They have been posed to show that they are examining a new book. The photograph was taken at the Rectory, Croft-on-Tees, 'the old home we have known for five-and-twenty years' as Carroll described it.

2

'You can do Arithmetic, I trust?'

Oxford Life

Yet what are all such gaieties to me
Whose thoughts are full of indices and surds?
– *Double Acrostic, 'There was an Ancient City, Stricken Down'*

Carroll spent his life as an Oxford mathematics don, and his professional and recreational work in mathematics is part and parcel of the picture of him as a human being. Numbers – anything and everything about numbers – formed a thread running through his life and were an integral part of how he saw the world.

The sparse recorded family memories of his childhood show that his love of numbers dates from his early childhood. Collingwood describes him, when a little boy, showing his father a book of logarithms with the request to 'Please explain'. His father told him that he was too young to understand about logarithms, yet he insisted 'But, please explain!'[1]

As an adolescent, he was concerned with various quirky issues relating to measurement of time. In the family magazine *The Rectory Umbrella*, he ponders whether a clock that has stopped completely is, logically, better than a clock that is five minutes slow, since the stopped clock will *always* tell the right time twice a day. 'You might go on to ask, "How am I to know when eight o'clock does come?"' he jokes. The answer was, he said, that '… when eight o'clock comes, your clock is right. … keep your eye fixed on your clock and the very moment it is right, it will be eight o'clock. "But – " you say. "There, that'll do, reader. …"'![2]

He was also preoccupied about when exactly a day changes into the next day on its passage around the Earth. He went on to propose a fixed international date line, an idea finally taken up in 1884. He was a persistent young man, and it seems he must have dwelt very often on this matter of when a day begins, for Collingwood wryly recalled many years later that the difficulty of answering this apparently simple question had 'cast a gloom over many a pleasant party'.[3]

Carroll lived up to his early promise and showed a good deal of mathematical ability during his schooldays. At the end of his first year at Rugby School, for instance, he came first in mathematics in the lower fifth form, and in his second year he won second prize for mathematics in the annual general examination and first prize in the mathematics division for the half. In 1848, his mathematics tutor at Rugby, Robert Mayor, told Carroll's father, 'I have not had a more promising boy at his age since I came to Rugby.'[4]

The next stage was obviously university. Christ Church, Oxford, had been his father's college, and his father was keen for his oldest son to follow in his footsteps. Accordingly, just before his 19th birthday, in January 1851, Carroll went up to Oxford to further his mathematical studies.

The city which first met his youthful gaze was a very different place from the sprawling and in parts rather dingy built-up area of today. Mid-nineteenth century Oxford, although wealthy and imposing, was decidedly rural and compact, circular in form and measuring about 3 miles across. It consisted of two spacious streets which intersected in the centre of town, and boasted a large market place and magnificent stone bridge. Above all, the whole area was physically dominated by the colleges, 'several of which stand in the streets and give the city an air of magnificence', as the Revd James Barclay observed in his gazetteer of 1810.

Margaret Fletcher, the founder of the Catholic Women's League, was the daughter of an Oxford don, and spent her childhood in the city. She does not seem to have met Carroll, even though she was there when he was in Oxford, but her autobiography gives a fascinating view of the city in the mid-nineteenth century. She recollected that it was 'countrified and quiet … almost innocent of traffic … with grass growing in the streets in the Long Vacation'. There was an almost stately atmosphere, with women moving slowly in their rustling, voluminous crinolines, and dons walking together in pairs 'to distant horizons, so intent on their discussions that they seemed unconscious of their surroundings'.[5]

The railway had only just arrived to connect Oxford to other parts of Britain. Of course the line which carried the filthy, clanking engines did not run close to the colleges, but had been directed to the other side of the river, well away from the ancient centre. When Carroll took his long, donnish walks across the surrounding countryside, he would have climbed the dusty road up to Headington Hill, and turned at the top to see a magical, vista of ancient towers rising from the meadows below: a fairy-tale view which had hardly changed in centuries. He might have exchanged a few words with the local children who brought their cows to feed on the road's grass verges, or picked the wild flowers that grew in the hedgerows. Less pleasantly, at certain times of year, he might have caught the all-pervading stink of the fish lying stranded and dying in the water meadows around the colleges as the annual river floods receded for the summer. He might also have worried about the cholera that was ravaging many of the unsanitary old houses which still lined the streets.

No diaries and few letters exist to give his very first impressions of the place, but he obviously did well in his studies. He obtained a first class honours degree in mathematics in 1854, and in 1855 he was appointed as a mathematics lecturer, moving in as a resident of the college and starting to acquire his own students. On 24 April 1855, the 23-year old triumphantly recorded in his diary that 'Leighton sent me £5 fee for last term's coaching – this is the first earned money I ever received – the first that I can fairly call *mine.*'

He had every reason to feel pleased with himself, but disillusion began to set in before he had been long in his new job. Grand, wealthy and aristocratic it may have been, but Christ Church was snobbish and somewhat old-fashioned in its attitudes. What is more, its mathematical record had been undistinguished for many years. Indeed, it was very different from any modern university college. A bustling hive of academic excellence Christ Church may now be, but that was not the case in the early and mid-nineteenth century.

As the college most favoured by the hunting, shooting aristocracy, the Christ Church of Lewis Carroll's late teens and early twenties was dirty, noisy and teeming with the undergraduates' dogs. Carroll remembered years later how there had been around 70 dogs running about the place day and night.[6] No pampered pets, these dogs were as undisciplined as their masters often were, and the old dean's verger was often found outside the chapel with a stout whip, with which he flogged dogs that tried to follow their masters into chapel.

Old Dean Gaisford, who was running the place when Carroll arrived, was a classical scholar who did not interest himself much in college affairs. Many of the wealthy undergraduates and their families saw university simply as a rite of passage, a place they had to go before they got on with their real tasks of running their country estates or working in the colonies. They were preoccupied with horses and their social lives and they found studying tedious and tiresome. Although they were kept under strict discipline of a type we would think more appropriate for schoolchildren, there was a good deal of wild behaviour and vandalism. On one occasion they are reported to have vandalized the college buildings, burning some of the old benches and tables, and on another occasion they caused an explosion which created a small ravine in the quad.

This was not the kind of atmosphere which Carroll particularly enjoyed, and it was not long before the studious young lecturer was writing in his diary that he was 'weary of lecturing, and discouraged ... it is thankless, uphill work, goading unwilling men to learning they have no taste for.'[7] However, he persevered. After gaining his MA in 1857, he became a Senior Student, (or Fellow as it was known in other colleges) in 1858. He thereby gained a small income, but most crucially, he was then entitled to stay at the college for the rest of his life, provided that he fulfilled certain conditions. The two most important of these were that he should remain celibate, and that he should be ordained a minister of the Church of England before four further years had elapsed. Both these conditions, of course, had a major effect on his life.

The curriculum which Carroll was expected to teach was routine, although it covered a good deal of ground. Some interesting new mathematical work was being done on the continent of Europe at the time, but little news of it reached Christ Church, and there is no sign that Carroll was aware of it. His method was to cling to old approaches and refine them in detail. Mostly, he led the undergraduates through elementary geometry and algebra, writing treatises and textbooks on topics which now attract little attention.

In fact, some of his critics maintain that he never did anything of note in his mathematical career, and the mathematician Warren Weaver has even pointed out several gaps in his basic knowledge.[8] Yet his professional work was not undistinguished. In the realm of ordinary mathematics he made some minor discoveries in determinants, and Weaver concedes that his interest in logic was leading him into interesting directions when he died. In 1894 he developed a proof on the interpretation of conditionals which uses a 'truth table', a concept which did not come into general use much before 1920. In this Carroll had made a real discovery, and yet so uninterested was he in the bigger picture that he did not publicise it at all. Furthermore, the Carroll Diagram he developed is a superior and more flexible version of the Venn Diagram, and it has now, in the 21st century, been introduced into the British school curriculum.

Despite his feelings of boredom and discouragement, too, several of the textbooks he created for his students went into numerous editions and did well. Whether the students enjoyed working from the textbooks was another matter. Carroll's notable and lifelong difficulty in 'seeing the wood for the trees' often manifested itself as a love of hopeless complexity. It is a trait particularly demonstrated by his *Guide to the Mathematical Student*, published in 1864.

This book consists of a list of mathematical topics together with suggestions for the order in which they should be studied. It is arranged in 26 subject areas, which are sub-divided into over 400 topics. References to over 2,000 examples are listed, and he intended that the student using it 'should turn to the Syllabus for each reference, and work two or three examples in the subject there indicated ... of course passing over all references to subjects he has not read'. At the end of each day's work, the student was supposed to mark the point that he had reached. It was an extremely good idea in theory, but in practice it was just the sort of finicky and methodical project that Carroll himself delighted in but others often found hard to take. The book must have represented countless hours of hard work; but though it is entitled 'Part I' no further parts were ever written – or requested.

Unfortunately, Carroll's love of elaborate rules and fixed plans did not help make his teaching attractive to the undergraduates. In mathematical logic, he liked to follow every step of an argument from the beginning to the end with strict precision, an approach that has been described as using a sledgehammer to crack a walnut-sized problem. This painstaking methodology also made it hard for him to keep up with the amount of work he had to do, and his diary shows that in the early days he sometimes felt overwhelmed by the tasks he had set himself.

His greatest difficulties, however, seem to have been in managing his undergraduates. These may have been quite serious, and are hinted at in the biography that H L Thompson wrote of Dean Liddell in 1899. Dean Liddell, Alice's father, had arrived to take charge at the college soon after Carroll began his lecturing job, the old dean, Dean Gaisford, having died in June 1855. It seems that Liddell's arrival was not eagerly anticipated (Carroll recorded unenthusiastically in his diary on 7 June that '*The Times* announces that Liddell of Westminster is to be the new Dean: the selection does not seem to have given much satisfaction in the college.').

In describing the period directly after Liddell's arrival at Christ Church, Thompson notes that the new dean was much occupied and bothered about 'a tutor' who could not control his men.[9] There is ambiguity about whether Carroll was officially a tutor at the time (though he does refer to himself as one), but reading his existing diary entries for the few months after the dean arrived, it is obvious even from this unemotional record that he could not keep control of the men, and his terse recollections have a slightly nightmarish quality.

In fact, Carroll's own record of the very beginning of this period is no longer available. His diary from September to December 1855, the very first months of Dean Liddell's incumbency, survived his death, but went missing while in the care of his family. So nobody now knows the exact details of what happened to him during those first weeks; though the record after the diary resumes is bad enough.[10]

In January 1856, when the next surviving diary volume begins, Carroll was returning to Christ Church after the Christmas vacation, and he summoned 60 men to attend a meeting about his Mathematical Lecture. He recorded that only 23 turned up. He told the rest of the men to report to his rooms, but none of them did. He sent for them individually, to no avail. The next day he called on the dean, and it was agreed that the idle men should be reported to him. On 25 January, when Carroll sent for the men again, they came; but they were clearly reluctant, and several of them insolently failed to turn up for his lectures in the next few days. Clearly, he had a problem; but at this point his personal self-censor came into play. On 29 January, he wrote that, 'In future, I shall record all matters connected with the Mathematical Lecture in a separate book.' And that is the last we hear of it. The separate book was not preserved by his family.

The sorry truth is that he was never able to control unruly groups. He had tried a little teaching to classes of poor children, and enjoyed it at first, but even there quickly became discouraged. He did not approve of beating and abusing pupils, which was the fashion at the time, and his gentleness may have seemed like softness to them. His relatively high-pitched voice and his speech hesitation probably added to the difficulty of dominating groups either of children or adults.

At Christ Church, he could not avoid dealing with rude, rebellious and snobbish young men. He was not much older, and considerably less wealthy, than many of them, and his stammer provoked laughter and teasing even among his own contemporaries. But he kept his feelings to himself, coping with his unpopularity by being curt and remote with his undergraduates, so that, consequently, his teaching was described as 'dull as ditchwater'. According to a persistent rumour, some undergraduates even raised a petition in protest at being taught by him, and even as late as 1931 his unpopularity was not forgotten. Sir Herbert Maxwell, a Conservative MP, wrote to *The Times* in that year to recall that from nearly 70 years earlier he remembered 'the lean, dark-haired person of Charles Lutwidge Dodgson' and the 'singularly dry and perfunctory manner in which he imparted instruction to us, never betraying the slightest personal interest in matters that were of deep concern to us.'[11]

It seems puzzling that someone so imaginative, communicative and original could have so failed to inspire. Perhaps Carroll's shyness and acute sensitivity caused him to defend himself with the donnish dryness and remoteness which eventually came to characterize his public image. Perhaps he just decided he didn't care about thick-headed undergraduates, for to the few who were interested in learning he was unstinting in his help. His peculiar and imaginative humour would have been better suited to a more supportive environment, or a more studious atmosphere, for, just as with the storytelling, he blossomed when faced with a receptive and appreciative audience.

Fortunately, he was to do extremely well as a teacher when, in the 1880s and 1890s, after his retirement, he began to teach logic at Oxford High School for Girls. There, he had girls listening to him – and girls who wanted to learn, too: very different from jeering male undergraduates. Ethel Rowell, who later became a mathematician, recalled that when Carroll stood at the desk in the sixth form room and prepared to address the class, she thought he looked very tall, serious and formidable. As he continued, though, he relaxed. In the all-female atmosphere, his facts became more fanciful and his fancies became more fantastic, she recalled. After some time, he spotted her talent and enthusiasm, and she was delighted when he finally offered her private tuition. 'As the subject opened out, I found great delight in this, my first real experience of the patterned intricacies of abstract thought,' she wrote. But more than this, she added, 'he bestowed on me another gift of aspect more gracious. He gave me a sense of my own personal dignity. He was so punctilious, so courteous, so considerate, so scrupulous not to offend, that he made me feel that I counted.'[12]

Another student in the Oxford classes remembered that 'the girls adored him, he entertained them with written games on the blackboard. He was perfect with children, and there were always tribes of little girls attached to him. He made everyone laugh.'[13]

Just as he enjoyed teaching a receptive and polite audience all his life, so Carroll's personal curiosity about the magic and puzzles of numbers themselves never failed. Many of his letters to other dons or intellectuals are concerned with mathematical matters, and joking references to mathematics occur in many letters which he wrote to people who had no professional interest in the subject at all. In 1878, for example, his friend Edith Denman mentioned to him that she liked figure-drawing better than he did. His reply was characteristic:

> There is a rashness, which I can only deplore, in your assertion that I cannot be as fond of figure-drawing as yourself! The point cannot be satisfactorily settled till we have measured the two fondnesses by the same unit. Now the unit of pleasure (which I suggested years ago, and which Society hasn't yet adopted!) is 'the pleasure felt in eating one penny-bun in one minute.'
>
> Please to estimate the pleasure which you get from an hour of figure-drawing, using that as a unit, and then we can compare numbers: my number is 235. Trying to settle it without a unit is like arguing about two rooms, each saying, 'I'm sure this room is the hottest!' without ever referring to a thermometer ...[14]

Although he is not known to have socialized with progressive mathematicians, nor belonged to any of the mathematical societies of his time, numbers were always on his mind. He dwelt on them in idle moments and during wakeful nights, and nearly always had a little mathematical problem or idea on the go. Many of these ideas crossed the boundaries between mathematics and play, and his friend and colleague T B Strong noted that he was particularly interested in transforming predictability into surprise; he loved curiosities and apparent contradictions and double meanings.

Strong remembered how interested and perplexed Carroll was in the idea that a sum worked out accurately with figures should fail when it came into contact with details of fact. As an illustration of this, Strong quoted a problem about building a wall, which Carroll sometimes asked his students to explain. The problem goes something like, 'If it takes ten men five days to build a wall 100 yards long, how long would it take 10,000 men?' When the mathematical answer was worked out and given, Carroll would retort that it was mathematically correct, yet it was *not true*. In real life, he would say, most of the workmen would not have got within a mile of the wall.

Carroll's natural tendency to playfulness came increasingly to the fore as he grew older. By the time he was in his late forties, he had mostly given up trying to inspire his undergraduates, but he decided to try and communicate some of his feelings about mathematics to the general public in a palatable form. His book *Euclid and His Modern Rivals* (1879) is probably the most extraordinary piece of mathematical literature ever written. In it, Carroll investigates the increasingly beleaguered cause of Euclidian geometry in the form of an opinionated play.

By the late 1870s, Euclidian geometry was badly out of date, but it was still widely taught and Carroll was devoted to it. Euclid of Alexandria lived around 300 BC. Versions of his *Elements of Geometry* had served mankind well for 2,000 years, but by the late 19th century contemporary mathematicians were realizing that his system had flaws. New approaches to mathematics – and to geometry – were surfacing throughout Europe, but they were passing Carroll by.

Euclid's 'rivals' of the play's title were, in fact, merely alternative ways of interpreting the original Euclidian texts compared with the traditional way of doing it. So the book would not have been of any use to someone wishing to examine new approaches to geometry, although of course it covered the various methods of teaching Euclidian geometry, and it also devoted serious attention to the technical matter of equivalents to Euclid's Fifth Postulate: *If a straight line crossing two straight lines makes the interior angles on the same side less than two right angles, the two straight lines, if extended indefinitely, meet on that side on which are the angles less than the two right angles.*

The subject matter may seem as dry as the biscuit which the White Queen presented to Alice, but Carroll's treatment of the topic is delightful. In his book, he casts Euclid as a ghost who visits the wryly-named examiner Minos, and discusses with him the worth of each 'rival' interpretation compared with his own original. Euclid disappears at the end of Act I. "'If you had any slow music handy, I would vanish to it: as it is –" *Vanishes without slow music.*' In Chapter 2, Herr Niemand ('Mr Nobody') enters in the train of his own meerschaum's cloud of smoke, to enter into some donnish jokily mathematical discussions.

The play was a brave and interesting effort, although it could not hope to hold back the tide of modern mathematical thinking. It is probably unperformable – except for mathematicians – and its original approach was no doubt meant to catch a reader's attention rather than hold a real live audience.

There is more mathematical humour in many of Carroll's notes and pamphlets, such as one he wrote about his thoughts on running the Christ Church Common Room. Here, he commented that the consumption of Madeira wine over the past year had been zero, and added that:

after careful calculation, I estimate that, if this rate of consumption be steadily maintained, our present stock will last us an infinite number of years. And although there may be something monotonous and dreary in the prospect of such vast cycles spent in drinking second class Madeira, we may yet cheer ourselves with the thought of how economically it can be done.[15]

Even in the driest expositions, his sense of humour would flicker through. One chapter of a later, unpublished manuscript entitled 'Grills', offers his thoughts on the geometry of crossing parallel lines. Carroll probably intended to use the chapter in a book he was planning, and omitted it because there are some mistakes in the calculations, but the studious reader may also be startled to come across a section in the manuscript which reads: 'I grant you that the Diagram is a ghastly one – as ghastly, perhaps, as is to be met with in the whole range of Pure Mathematics. Still you know, it was my *duty* to draw it. England expects every man to do his duty. And I love England. The conclusion is obvious.'[16]

As Carroll grew older, his attention turned away from mathematics and towards the study of symbolic logic – a means of checking the validity of arguments based on syllogisms. These days symbolic logic has been largely dropped in favour of modern logic, which is used to define the foundations of mathematics. Yet symbolic logic remains an interesting mental discipline in its own right. It is Ancient Greek logic (which Carroll had studied as a young man as part of his classical education) expressed in mathematical symbols. Syllogisms consist of two or more 'premises' or statements, which lead to conclusions, one of the more famous examples being that presented by Aristotle in the 4th century BC, in which the two premises:

All Greeks are men

and
All men are mortal
make it possible to conclude that
All Greeks are Mortal

However, in symbolic logic, just as in mathematics, Carroll tended to be interested in issues of specific detail, rather than the overall picture. Carroll and T. B. Strong corresponded at great length about a number of logical issues, but Strong complained that his attempts to raise the subject of the relation of words and things was a failure, as Carroll simply declined to write upon it.

One of Carroll's great interests in later life was in developing logic as an entertainment for young people, and he spent a great deal of time on this. He wanted to help his readers to increase their powers of clear thought, he said, to see their way through arguments and make sense of what they read in the newspapers and what they heard from the pulpit. 'Sift your reasons well,' he urged, 'and make sure they prove your conclusions.'[17] In this worthy cause, he developed a *Game of Logic* (1886) which was designed specially for older children. He used it both with what he referred to as his 'child-friends' and also when he took logic classes at Oxford High School for Girls.

The *Game of Logic* has been reprinted many times, and is available in modern editions, but Carroll took exceptional pains to make the original volume attractive and enticing. It was bound in bright red, a colour which he felt particularly appealed to the young, and its title swirls across the front in gold. A small envelope inside contains a small board and attractively coloured counters. He had canvassed his lady friends on the most suitable colours for these counters, and had finally decided on dusky pink and grey. (It is a colour combination he particularly liked, since he also yearned to dress his actress friend Isa Bowman in those shades, which he considered more 'ladylike' than the brighter outfits which she favoured herself.)

The design on the game's board resembles a squared-off Venn Diagram – and in fact is an improvement upon it, having eight regions to the Venn's seven. The syllogisms are expressed in words, with the options to transfer them to symbols later. The game was intended to aid a young person learning with a teacher, so the instructions need to be read carefully. But once the original idea is grasped, the game is interesting, and it is made more enjoyable by the comic or ridiculous premises which Carroll deliberately used to add a dash of entertainment for his young audience. For instance,

No bald person needs a hair-brush
No lizards have hair

All wise men walk on their feet
All unwise men walk on their hands

From the premises

All dragons are uncanny
All Scotchmen are canny

he derived the reassuring conclusion that

All dragons are not-Scotchmen

and

All Scotchmen are not-dragons

'Symbolic Logic, Part I' takes the study of logic to more advanced levels, and some of the examples Carroll offers here are positively baroque:

No shark ever doubts that it is well fitted out
A fish, that cannot dance a minuet, is contemptible
No fish is quite certain that it is well fitted out, unless it
    has three rows of teeth
All fishes, except sharks, are kind to children
No heavy fish can dance a minuet
A fish with three rows of teeth is not to be despised.

Carroll probably got the idea of using entertaining and comical mathematical examples from his own childhood. At school, he had used Francis Walkingame's *The Tutor's Assistant*, a very popular work which had originally been published in 1751. Although constantly revised, the 1840s editions of the book (which Carroll would have used) contained many little Georgian dramas, such as:

A man overtaking a maid driving a flock of geese, said to her, 'How do you do, sweetheart? Where are you going with these 30 geese?' 'No, sir,' said she, 'I have not 30; but if I had as many more, half as many more, and 5 geese besides, I should have 30.'

It is a resounding put-down to the man's chat-up line, and there are more mathematical maids on the following page of the book, where:

A gentleman going into a garden, meets with some ladies, and says to them, 'Good morning to you 10 fair maids.' 'Sir, you mistake,' answered one of them, 'we are not 10, but if we were twice as many more as we are, should be as many above 10 as we are now under.'

Carroll went a step further than Walkingame in the 1880s by creating a group of mathematical short stories, collectively entitled *A Tangled Tale*, in which each tale encompasses a mathematical problem. These stories feature, among others, two boys and their teacher, Balbus, ('The Stammerer'in Latin) and the teenage Clara and her eccentric aunt, Mad Mathesis. The surreal flavour of the stories can be conveyed by a couple of quotations, as when two knights in the first story, 'Excelsior' are toiling up a hill:

> And on the dead level, our pace is – ?' the younger suggested, for he was weak in statistics, and left all such details to his aged companion.
>
> Four miles in the hour,' the other wearily replied. 'Not an ounce more,' he added, with that love of metaphor so common in old age, 'and not a farthing less!'

In the story 'Oughts and Crosses', Clara explains to her aunt that she's told the little ones at tea-time that:

> The more noise you make the less jam you will have, and vice versa. I thought they wouldn't know what vice-versa meant, so I explained it to them. I said 'If you make an infinite noise, you'll get no jam; and if you make no noise, you'll get an infinite lot of jam.' …

Carroll's stories appeared between April 1880 and November 1884 in *The Monthly Packet* periodical. He invited readers to send in solutions, which they did under a variety of imaginative pseudonyms. He then commented on the solutions and their reasonings, showing a characteristically deft ability to pinpoint the woolliness of some of the replies: '… it is interesting to know that the question 'answers itself' and I am sure it does the question great credit; still, I fear I cannot enter it on the list of winners, as this competition is only open to human beings …'.[18]

After writing ten issues of *A Tangled Tale*, he quit. He seems to have become bored with the series, although he took his leave elegantly and politely, claiming that his characters were 'neither distinctly *in* my life (like those I now address) nor yet (like Alice and the Mock Turtle) distinctly *out* of it.'[19]

His puzzles by no means always involved mathematics. 'Puzzles from Wonderland' appeared in 1870 in *Aunt Judy's*, a children's magazine, and it offers riddles set within rhymes. Some are very easy, and have something in common with crossword puzzle clues, or even Victorian cracker jokes, such as:

> Dreaming of apples on a wall,
> And dreaming often, dear
> I dreamed that, if I counted all, –
> How many would appear?

The answer, of course, is 'ten', since he dreams 'of/ten'.

More challenging are some of the probability problems from *Curiosa Mathematica Part II: Pillow Problems*, of 1893, a work which was aimed at filling the time on sleepless nights. One such problem was the following:

> A bag contains one counter, known to be either white or black. A white counter is put in, the bag shaken and a counter drawn out, which proves to be white. What is now the chance of drawing a white counter?[20]

More intriguing is the matter of the number '42'. Carroll was supposed to be particularly interested in that number and, for years, mathematicians have been finding examples of it throughout his works. Some of the 'findings' are obvious, such as when the King of Hearts announces in the *Alice in Wonderland* court scene, 'Rule Forty-two. *All persons more than a mile high to leave the court.*' In Carroll's long ghost poem 'Phantasmagoria', the narrator reveals his age in the first verse as 42, and in 'The Hunting of the Snark', the only rule quoted is No 42. Furthermore, the baker in that poem, who was famed for 'a number of things' had 'forty-two boxes all carefully packed'.

Certain 'findings' of 42 involve the most tortuous numberplay. Others, though, are both accessible and genuinely thought-provoking. In his book *Lewis Carroll in Numberland*, the mathematician Robin Wilson goes so far as to say that Carroll seems to have had an obsession with the number 42. *Alice in Wonderland* has 42 illustrations, he observes, and the trial title page for *Through the Looking-Glass* shows that Carroll also anticipated having 42 illustrations for this (although in fact he ended up with 50).

Also in *Wonderland*, Alice recites some apparently nonsensical times tables after she has followed the White Rabbit underground, and these turn out to have an unexpected link with 42: "'Four times five is twelve" says Alice "and four times six is thirteen and four times seven is – oh dear! I shall never get to twenty at that rate!"' It sounds like nonsense, but in fact Carroll was counting each calculation on a different base. Therefore, 4 × 5 equals 12 on base 18; 4 × 6 = 13 on base 21; and so on. It goes all the way up to 4 × 12 = 19 (on base 39). And sure enough, Alice never does get to 20 by continuing this way, because 4 × 13 = 20 does not work on base 42.

Perhaps the most extraordinary use of the number 42 is when the White Queen says, "'Now, I'll give you something to believe. I'm just one hundred and one, five months and a day.'" Edward Wakeling, editor of Carroll's diaries, and also a mathematician, has worked out that since the story was specifically set on 4 November 1859, when Alice was exactly seven-and-a-half (Alice Liddell's birthday was 4 May 1852), then the White Queen, taking account of leap years, was exactly 37,044 days old at the time when she spoke. The Red Queen, being a member of the same chess set, was, of course the same age as the White

Queen, giving the two queens a total combined age of 74,088 days – the sum of 42 × 42 × 42!

As well as playing with numbers, Carroll loved playing with words. He was extremely clever at saying exactly what he meant, yet not meaning what he appeared to say. Consequently, his writing often repays close examination to tease out the real meaning – and so, it seems, did his conversation. If a mother offered her hideous baby for admiration, he once remarked, one should exclaim in an admiring tone 'Now *there's* a baby!' and all honour would be satisfied.

Carroll was also particularly fond of acrostics, a kind of word-play which was very popular with Victorians, apparently including Queen Victoria herself. In its simplest form, the acrostic poem is based on a word or phrase, known as a column-word or column-phrase. The first letter, syllable or word of each line of a simple acrostic-poem spells out the column-word or column-phrase. A good example of a simple Carroll acrostic is an inscription he wrote in a book called *Holiday House* which he bought as a gift for Lorina, Alice and Edith Liddell for Christmas 1861. Here are the first eight lines of his verse, the initial letters of which spell out the word LORINA:

> Little maidens, when you look
> On this little story-book,
> Reading with attentive eye
> Its enticing history,
> Never think that hours of play
> Are your only HOLIDAY ...

Carroll sometimes seemed almost to be inspired by the limitations of the acrostic form, and several of his acrostics, like that of ALICE PLEASANCE LIDDELL in 'A Boat Beneath a Sunny Sky' (*Through The Looking-Glass*), are also precise and evocative poems in their own right.[21] However, he also relished the task of creating more technically difficult acrostics, and some of these are very clever – and not a little obscure. They include double acrostics in which each verse is a riddle and the puzzler must figure out the two 'column-words' which relate to the entire poem and whose letters in order begin and end each riddle's solution.

A little known example is 'A Day in the Country', which Carroll wrote in 1866, a year after *Alice in Wonderland* first appeared. It was probably done to amuse country friends whom he was visiting, for Carroll liked to create poems to entertain people he liked. Since it tells the story of a failed photographic session, he may have been photographing his friends, too.

The poem (given in full below) has never been fully solved, although some of the clues have been deciphered. Note that the first two verses give the two vertical column-words, each of which has eleven letters. The first column word (in this case PORTMANTEAU) gives the initial letters of the horizontal solution-words, the second column word (in this case PHOTOGRAPHY) gives the final letters of these horizontal words. The other verses give clues to the meaning of the horizontal solution-words. These horizontal words can be of any length, as long as they start and finish with the appropriate letter.

> Come, pack my things, and let the clothes
> Be neatly brushed and folded well:
> The friends I visit all suppose
> That I'm a perfect London swell.
>
> [PORTMANTEAU]

> I wield a magic art, whose skill
> Would make you open both your eyes:
> And any friend of mine, who will,
> I'm ready to immortalise.
>
> [PHOTOGRAPHY]

'But is there water?' I demand,
  'Water in limitless supplies?'
They say ''Tis ready to your hand,
  And in prodigious quantities.'

[PUMP]

'Our long-legged Johnnie shall attend:
  He'll fetch it for you at a word.'
I said 'My worthy long-legged friend,
  You're very like a monstrous bird!'

[OSTRICH]

'Arrange the group! Our eldest boy
As Shakespeare's lover shall be dressed;
  And it shall be his sole employ
To roll his eyes and thump his chest.'

[ROMEO]

'He *has* such genius!' says Momma.
  'He got the fortieth prize at Eton!
In tragedy he's best, by far –
  As Hamlet he can *not* be beaten

[unknown, but must begin with T and end with T]

'And don't forget to write below
Some neat Shakespearian quotation –
The picture'll strike our friend, I know
  All of a heap with admiration!'

[unknown but must begin with M and end with O]

'But is it really *here* you mean
  To group the family together?
You really *must* devise a screen –
  The sun will bake us brown as leather!'

[ASSEMBLING has been suggested]

'Tis done! This happy English home
Is now immortalised securely:
The great historian of Rome
Could not have done it half as surely!

[unknown but must begin with N and end with R]

But evening now drawing on,
So for today we'll give it up:
The light, you see is nearly gone –
But come indoors and take a cup

[TEA]

'Our larger cups are broken all,
So this must do – it's made of chiney.'
'Indeed,' said I, 'it's very small:
I never saw a cup so tiny!'

[EGGCUP]

I've taken pictures bad and good:
But that, I think, was worse than any
The great Logician never could
Have proved it worth a single penny!

[unknown but must begin with A and end with H]

They tell me it is turning green –
All change, I'm sure, will be a blessing:
For never, never was there seen
A thing so hideous, so distressing!

[UGLY] [22]

Carroll's interest in word puzzles also extended to making up
parlour games involving words. The easiest was Doublets, which
involved turning one word into another of the same length, by
changing a letter at a time. It is a game which is still played

today, and, as with Scrabble, the words must be found in a standard English dictionary, and proper nouns are not allowed. Carroll's examples included:

Make the DEAD LIVE:

DEAD
lead
lend
lent
lint
line
LIVE

Turn MICE into RATS:

MICE
mite
mate
mats
RATS

Most of Carroll's friends and family seem to have enjoyed doing these word games, and he also delighted in teasing his friends with riddles and puzzles. In general, however, his daily life as a mathematics don in Christ Church was regular and uneventful, and it became more so as he grew older. His friend Strong remarked that, '... any account of his life that is truthful, must be in some measure disappointing ... [because] the life of an Oxford don is for the most part ... not rich in incidents that are likely to attract the general reader. ...'[23] What Strong was too polite to say was that Carroll's colleagues and friends in the college sometimes found him very difficult to deal with, particularly in later life. Carroll eventually all but shunned the company of many of his colleagues, and his natural fastidious-ness, contrariness and love of detail were transformed over the years into an exasperating fussiness which became only too well known in Christ Church.

'He was the most prolific malcontent' proclaimed Michael Sadleir, who was steward of Christ Church during the last years of Carroll's life. Sadleir did not exaggerate. In later life, Carroll did not try to make himself agreeable to his colleagues day-to-day. No less than 48 of his surviving letters complain either about omissions or negligence on the part of the college servants, or, as Sadleir more accurately described them, 'minor inconveniences affecting his own comfortable life'.[24] These topics included the way his cauliflower was cooked, the exact time of postal collections and the amount of milk sent up to him in the mornings.

His fussiness was noted and sometimes resented in places other than Oxford, too. One of the churchwardens at the church which Carroll attended at Eastbourne remembered how angry Carroll became at the size of the hassocks in the church, and recalled that a specially large hassock had to be made for him to kneel upon. The vicar at Eastbourne also chimed in with a memory that Carroll used to rent two pews in the church – one for him and one for his silk top hat.[25]

Yet despite all his many complaints about Christ Church, there is no doubt that Carroll's life there was also extremely pleasant. Not for him were the day-to-day chores which bedevil the average modern bachelor. Nowhere is the comfort and even cosiness of this later life of his more clearly shown than in a letter which a good friend, Walter Watson, wrote to his daughter in February 1882, when Carroll was 50. Mr Watson was staying with Carroll in his Christ Church rooms for a few days, and he describes living arrangements resembling those in a large and pleasant hotel, with everything to hand.[26] The letter is particularly interesting because it is almost the only surviving indication of what it was like to live with Carroll, and gives a picture of the Christ Church domesticity that formed the background to his personal and professional life for so many years.

At about 7 am, Watson told his daughter, he and Carroll were roused by the sound of water being transferred to a bath. At 8 am they attended chapel for about half an hour, and then Carroll went through his papers or a newly arrived bookseller's catalogue, while Mr Watson read quietly. At 9 am came a cooked breakfast with coffee; after that, Carroll worked in silence till noon, leaving Mr. Watson contentedly to his own devices. Mr Watson did not mention lunch (Carroll is known to have had only a snack at lunchtime), but after taking letters to the post, he and Carroll would repair to the Common Room to read the papers. After that, Carroll would work in silence again till about three, and then the two men would take a companionable walk of about two hours in the surrounding countryside.

Between five and seven, Carroll worked again. Then the men went to dinner in the hall, where there was a huge fire in the grate. Latin grace was said, and the academic caps (or 'mortarboards') were brought in after the meal for the dons' progression to the Common Room. In the Common Room, they partook of wine and desserts which were laid out on a large table, and chatted with friends and colleagues. Returning to Carroll's rooms, there was tea at 9 pm, and then Carroll would write until late.

Looking at Carroll's daily life overall, there were many disadvantages to his Christ Church existence. In particular, he suffered social and sexual restrictions which to modern eyes seem cruel and emotionally damaging. His visitors were always scrutinized by the porters who guarded the gates, and he could never be truly alone. Yet for all that, his life in the ivory tower also had a calm, settled and positively courtly atmosphere which many a modern academic might envy.

As a young man Carroll was rather good looking. His friend Gertrude Thomson described him as having a sensitive face, 'dreamy' eyes and a finely modelled, beautifully formed head. In 1863, Carroll asked Oscar G Rejlander to photograph him, the result probably the most famous picture of Carroll in existence.

'Nose in the middle, mouth under'

The Human Body

'He has been curing himself, you know: he's a very learned doctor. Why, he's actually invented three new diseases, besides a new way of breaking your collar-bone!'

'Is it a nice way?' said Bruno.

'Well, hum, not very,' the Warden said …

Sylvie and Bruno

Lewis Carroll was very interested in the ways and workings of both the human body and the human mind. Always interested in medicine, he had taken the trouble to learn about and practice homeopathy, and was particularly fascinated by the effects of the mind on the body. Artistically, he cared little for landscapes or still lifes, but he closely supervised his illustrators' depictions of the human form, and his comments on them are penetratingly sharp and observant. He loved to look at human beauty, particularly female beauty, and had, as he once mentioned to an illustrator, a passion for symmetry.

Yet there is a paradox at the heart of his love of harmonious beauty and symmetry. His own body was notably asymmetrical, and a friend, the artist Mrs E L Shute, remembered that his face had two very different profiles. His left eyelid drooped, his left shoulder appeared higher than the right and the corners of his mouth did not match. These characteristics hardly show in photographs of him, but they gave him what the mathematician Ethel Rowell affectionately recalled as his 'own particular crooked smile'.[1] In addition, his stance was excessively upright, he had a quick, abrupt and slightly unsteady gait, and he was deaf in one ear. All this, together with his stammer, must have presented a general physical impression that was vaguely off-balance. Yet it was a pleasant one, for his crooked smile was described as tender, whimsical and ironic, and his manner had considerable charm – when he felt like being charming.

Carroll's movements were quick and his general demeanour was said to be very alert. He was dark haired and very pale, with light blue-grey eyes that were said to notice everything. Although his hair became iron grey in later life, it remained thick and wavy. All his life, he shunned bushy whiskers and kept to the slightly Bohemian, long haired, clean-shaven appearance that had been popular in his youth.

His mouth was slightly compressed when in repose, and some people considered him handsome. Indeed, photographs show that as a young man he was rather good looking. His friend Gertrude Thomson described him as having a sensitive face, 'dreamy' eyes and a finely modelled, beautifully formed head.[2] So lyrical, indeed, were her descriptions of Carroll that some commentators have wondered if she was in love with him.

His asymmetry did not handicap him or affect his health. He was deft in his movements, and healthy enough for his favourite walk at the age of 55 to have been 18 miles in four and three-quarter hours.[3] It is not known whether there was a physical reason why he carried himself so extremely straight – as if he had a poker down his back, as Alice Liddell unkindly remarked in her little memoir – with the result that his top hat was forever slipping off the back of his head.[4]

An old lady who remembered him well copied his unusual gait for the benefit of the 20th-century biographer John Pudney, who described it as resembling someone wading through very long grass.[5] This stiffness and awkward gait may not have been a lifelong peculiarity, however, as it has been speculated that it was caused by the synovitis of the knee from which Carroll suffered later in life. The Carroll of the many reminiscences that date from the later part of his life was in many ways a very different man from the one who wrote *Alice in Wonderland*.

Nothing exists to suggest what caused this slight asymmetry and no family documents have come to light which refer to it. Yet in poetry and fairy tale, in comedy and legend, oddly-shaped people are often villainous, silly or magical. It is something that would not have escaped anyone as devoted to fantastical literature as Carroll.

He was of medium height and seems to have been pleased with his very slender figure. He was not anorexic, as has sometimes been claimed, for he appreciated what he ate, but he took little more than the minimum necessary to preserve health. As a young man he was remembered as bringing along plenty of cakes on outings, but in later life he would sometimes survive on a light breakfast, followed by lunch consisting only of dry biscuits, or a slice of melon with ginger, with either a two-course supper at night or simply more fruit.

He did enjoy the occasional brandy snap – a thin and brittle sweetmeat made of butter, sugar, syrup, flour, ginger and brandy – but as he grew older, he began to disapprove of 'greed' – along with so many other things of which he disapproved. The young actress Isa Bowman was not impressed by this trait of his, and always remembered how he would take her on long walks and allow her just one rock-cake as a reward at the end of it.

Most of his photographs show him wearing well-pressed, well-fitting clothes, although his white clerical tie tended to straggle at times. In a different world, he might have enjoyed fashion. One of the earliest, pre-clerical photographs shows a decidedly dandyish youth with a large cravat, a checked waistcoat and a jacket which contemporary fashion plates confirm was in the very latest style. Fascinated by visual appearances, he also took a real interest in the clothes worn by his friends, both on stage and in the genre photographs he created during his photography years.

Carroll spoke carefully and enunciated clearly, and his voice was quiet and high in pitch. To William, the brother of Dante Gabriel Rossetti, he gave a strong impression of 'a certain externalism of polite propriety', and his manner of speech was often described as dry or donnish. However, Gertrude Thomson said the donnishness disappeared instantly in private, and he had a very pleasant, ringing laugh, although it was rarely heard.[6]

Most of the photographs that exist of him were taken with longish exposures that could not capture fleeting expressions. As a result, they make him look solemn, soulful or even rather depressed. In later life people remarked that he often looked forbidding, but this grave demeanour would instantly fall away and his whole manner would change when he smiled or laughed.

Some idea of how he appeared in life can be gathered from a group of lively sketches which the celebrated caricaturist Harry Furniss did when Carroll was in his fifties. Although less well known than the photographs, these sketches are much more expressive. Needless to say, they were done without Carroll's knowledge or consent. Furniss was a brilliant draughtsman, and excellent at catching likenesses. Like all Victorian cartoonists, he drew in an essentially realistic and well-finished style compared with most modern-day caricaturists.

Carroll hired him to illustrate a couple of books, but Furniss, a mischievous man, seems to have decided to sneak some satirical sketches of the reclusive author with the aim of making money from them later – which he did. They are apparently the only pictures to have survived that show Carroll as he was towards the end of his life, and they suggest a man with considerable vitality, and a certain eccentricity. He looks as if he is living amiably in a world full of his own fascinating thoughts, and the closeness with which he holds a book in one of the drawings suggest that he may have been short-sighted. The most rarely reproduced of the sketches, and the most illuminating, shows Carroll in three-quarter length: very thin, self-possessed, alert, and with the left shoulder higher than the right. The face, in profile, is smiling – and it's a merry and slightly tricksy smile.

Carroll was notoriously shy of publicity, something that may have been associated with his attitude to his own appearance, for he seemed rather sensitive to comments about it. This is shown in a recollection by his actress friend, Isa Bowman, who wrote:

> I had an idle trick of drawing caricatures when I was a child, and one day when he was writing some letters, I began to make a picture of him on the back of an envelope. I quite forget what the drawing was like – probably it was an abominable libel – but suddenly he turned round and saw what I was doing. He got up from his seat and turned very red, frightening me very much. Then he took my poor little drawing, and tearing it into small pieces, threw it into the fire without a word.
>
> Afterwards, he came suddenly to me and saying nothing, caught me up in his arms and kissed me passionately. Now the incident comes back to me very clearly, and I can see it as if it happened but yesterday – the sudden snatching of my picture, the hurried striding across the room, and then the tender light in his face as he caught me up to him and kissed me.[7]

The word 'passionate' refers to high emotion, not sexuality. So did Isa's innocent drawing perhaps portray features of Carroll's appearance – the asymmetry, perhaps – that he preferred to ignore? In later life he refused to give photographs of himself if he thought they would be seen by anyone but the recipient. He, who loved taking photographs of others, said that he detested the feeling that just anyone could have his picture and look at him.

Children always found him approachable and kindly, and they nearly always took a positive view of his appearance. Most of the criticisms of his appearance and demeanour come from colleagues with whom Carroll did not enjoy socialising. The literary biographer William Tuckwell described how Carroll, an 'unalluring personage' seemed to see nobody and speak to nobody as he strode in an unfriendly way about the streets. In fact, Tuckwell hardly knew Carroll, relying on comments from those who had had more to do with him, but those he spoke to must have portrayed him as a man who made college life discordant. Tuckwell also describes Carroll's appearance as 'grave and repellent' – 'repellent' here in its older sense of 'unapproachable'.[8]

Carroll was also capable of staying silent for long periods, with the result that some people hardly noticed him at all. Mark Twain met him once, and remembered of him that he was interesting – but only to look at, for '… he was the stillest and shyest full-grown man I have ever met except "Uncle Remus"'. Throughout a brisk conversation that was taking place, Twain went on, 'Carroll sat still all the while except that now and then he answered a question. His answers were brief. I do not remember that he elaborated any of them.'[9]

Carroll's silence in unfamiliar company may have been due in part to his stammer, which became worse in unfamiliar or stressful situations. Although his lifetime saw the introduction of the telephone and recording machine, no sound recordings exist of him, for one of the things known to have tormented him most was the physical affliction of his speech defect. An early Carroll biographer, Roger Lancelyn Green, confessed that he was himself a stammerer, and in his sympathetic portrayal of Carroll he described what a terrible burden it is, and how 'dreadfully' the sufferer is cut off from other people. In his fascinating book *Knotted Tongues*, the author Benson Bobrick also considers the difficulties of many well-known stammerers, including Carroll. Bobrick describes the experience of stammering as similar to holding a phone conversation when hearing a fractionally delayed echo of one's own voice, and describes in detail the anguish of having one's primary means of self-expression out of control.[10]

To other people, Carroll's stammer seemed fairly mild and did not matter a great deal. But it mattered very much to Carroll himself, for he spent a great deal of time, effort and money on trying to cure it. He once said that those who did not suffer from 'hesitation', as he called it, could not really imagine what a drawback in life it was.[11]

In his day, nobody had any real idea what caused stammering. It is now thought to be a result of a slight neurological malfunction that makes it hard for the sufferer to coordinate the huge number of tiny factors that enable intelligible speech. It can be worsened by anxiety, either the sufferer's own, or the anxiety of parents who try to correct speech too early in their child's development. A tendency to stammer or stutter is thought to be inherited, and it does seem as if this was a factor with Carroll. His parents were first cousins, and most of their children had speech difficulties of various types.

Carroll's problem was hesitation and 'blocking' on certain consonant combinations, and its degree of severity was affected by how he was feeling. When he was tired, stressed or had to meet people whom he did not want to chat with, his stammer was far worse than when he felt enthusiastic or relaxed. By contrast, it never seemed to stand in his way when he was keen to make a good impression. His letters are full of descriptions of how readily he engaged with others when his enthusiasm overcame his reticence.

In 1859, for instance, he told his cousin William how he had decided to call at the house of his literary hero, Tennyson, whom he had met two years previously. Citing what he airily told William was the 'inalienable right of a freeborn Briton' to make a morning call, he made his way to the poet's house. A servant directed him over to Tennyson, who was taken by surprise and (in a pleasing glimpse of domesticity) was mowing his lawn wearing, according to Carroll, a broad-brimmed 'wide-awake' hat and spectacles.[12] In this fashion, Carroll had edged himself into the circles he admired, stammer or no stammer.

Carroll rarely held forth upon his innermost feelings, and it was only the amount of time, money and effort he spent on trying to resolve his hesitation that reveals what a problem he found it in his everyday life. His friend Margaret Mayhew recalled with real regret how hard she had found it, as a teenager, to suppress her giggles at hearing him speak in public, but May Barber, an Eastbourne friend, described his problem with sympathy and precision:

> [It was] rather terrifying. It wasn't exactly a stammer, because there was no noise, he just opened his mouth. But there was a wait, a very nervous wait from everybody's point of view; it was very curious. He didn't always have it, but sometimes he did … he'd suddenly stop and you wondered if you'd done anything wrong. Then you looked at him and you knew that you hadn't, it was all right. You got used to it after a bit. He fought it very wonderfully. …[13]

Like many other stammerers, Carroll found reading aloud far more difficult than normal everyday conversation. When he was reading, he could look ahead and see difficult words coming up, and this immediately made him anxious. He eventually managed to deal with the problem of public speaking by memorising the main points of what he was going to say, for fortunately he had an excellent memory right up to the end of his life.

After his ordination as deacon, he became particularly upset if he hesitated while preaching, or reading from the Bible, because he hated the idea of making people laugh at the word of God. Ina Liddell, older sister of Alice, offered a particularly unpleasant recollection of his difficulties in this area, as she looked back in 1930. 'He stuttered badly at times,' she told the biographer Florence Becker Lennon. 'As the Students were, in those days, allowed to choose a senior Student to read the lessons in Chapel, they always chose him for the lesson 13th Chapter of the Acts of the Apostles 9th verse, where Saul's name is changed to Paul and it was a long time before P-P-P could be got into Paul.'[14]

In 1861, that teasing must have been fresh in Carroll's mind, for in that year he paid his first visit to James Hunt, a speech therapist. Hunt lived at Ore, near Hastings, on the south coast. He was one of the most celebrated 19th-century authorities on stuttering and stammering, and is estimated to have treated about 1,700 patients in his short lifetime. He made a clear distinction between stammering and stuttering. The stammering patient, he said, found it hard or impossible to make some elementary speech sounds, and had a hesitating, often convulsive delivery, but no repetition of the initial sounds. By contrast, what Hunt called 'stuttering' involved repetition of initial sounds and muscular contortions, as the sufferer found it hard to enunciate syllables, words and sentences. Carroll was a stammerer by this definition, thereby disproving the truth of one of the hoary old tales that is sometimes told about him, that he referred to himself as 'the Dodo' because he was repeating the first syllable of his name as a stutterer might.

Hunt's therapy was based on his belief that the 'discipline of the vocal and articulating organs under an experienced instructor' – that is, himself, or his father, Thomas, also a speech therapist – provided a solution to speech difficulties. The Hunt system carefully analysed the exact form of the speech defect, the manner of breathing and the use of the lips and the tongue. By patient and repetitive re-training, Hunt boasted that he taught the patient to speak consciously in the way that other men spoke unconsciously. He picturesquely reminded sufferers that nature had fitted them for speech, and so he would aid them to 'replace nature on her throne'.[15]

Carroll told his sister Mary that Hunt's system helped him. He did not say whether he personally liked Hunt, but since Hunt was a racist even by Victorian standards, a supporter of slavery and a critic of missionary work, it is unlikely that he did.

Hunt died in 1869, and Carroll does not refer to his speech therapy again until 5 June 1872, when he wrote in his diary that it may be a day 'of the greatest importance to me'. He had been to Nottingham and heard a Dr Lewin lecture on his system to cure stammering. Sadly, that came to nothing, and soon afterwards, in July 1873 Carroll approached James Hunt's brother-in-law, Henry F Rivers, who had taken over Hunt's practice after his death. Rivers was running classes for stammering schoolboys, and Carroll, who was then 41, wrote to ask if the boys had gone away: 'On that depends my idea of coming for a day or two. I feel rather too (let us say) "middle-aged" to care to join a class of boys'.[16]

Having established that he did not have to consult Rivers in company with boys, Carroll asked him if he could help him with the sounds he found particularly difficult, '… my difficulties with "p" in such combinations as "impossible", "them patience", "the power", "spake", which combinations have lately beaten me when trying to read in the presence of others, in spite of my feeling quite cool, and trying my best to do it "on rule".'[17] 'These failures', he added, 'have rather deferred the hope I had formed of being very soon able to help in Church again, for if

I break down in reading to only one or two, I should be all the worse, I fear, for the presence of a congregation.'[18]

He obviously liked Rivers, and quickly became friendly with him and his wife. After the initial meetings, his diary mentions many social get-togethers with the Rivers family as well as consultations, and he recommended Rivers to various friends. His surviving letters to Rivers are light and joking in tone yet there are unmistakable undertones of distress. In late 1873 he wrote to ask Rivers for another meeting, saying he was 'in a bad way' for speaking, and felt deeply discouraged. 'I actually so entirely broke down, twice lately, over a hard "C", that I had to spell the word! Once was in a shop, which made it more annoying; however it is an annoyance one must make up one's mind to bear, I suppose, now and then – especially when, as now, I have been rather hard worked. I expect you would pronounce me now *decidedly worse*, both in reading and speaking, than I was …'[19]

Shortly afterwards, he wrote to Rivers again: 'Thanks for advice about hard "C", which I acknowledge as my vanquisher in single-hand combat, at present. As to working the jaw more, your advice is within my power, generally: but as to the direction to "keep the back of the tongue down", *in the moment of diffi-culty*, I fear you might almost as well advise me to stand on my head!'[20]

In 1874 he paid for his sisters to attend Rivers, with satisfactory results, and he told Rivers that he had been speaking far better, and felt greatly comforted. So impressed was he that he came up with another potential patient for Rivers. This was an undergraduate in straitened circumstances called Rees, whom Carroll hoped Rivers might treat for a reduced fee. Rivers did not exactly jump at the chance of offering his services cheap, but Carroll persisted, and eventually, he got Rees taken on at a special price. After that, he and the undergraduate practised reading aloud together and helping each other with their pronunciation.

It seems that Carroll had hopes that he might achieve a real cure, but after the late 1870s, references to Rivers in his diary also die away. Rivers had helped, but obviously not enough. By 1890 Carroll was confessing to a Miss Alice Cooper that he could not give an address at her school: he found the prospect of public speaking too formidable with his speech defect. After his death, a Voice Cultivation Machine appeared as Lot 198 in Brooke's auction catalogue of his possessions. No further details survive, but it may have been an Ammoniaphone, a commercially produced device which claimed to relieve coughs, asthma and throat or chest problems as well as improve the voice.

No doubt Carroll read as thoroughly about the oppressive problem of stammering as he did about other physical matters. His intense interest in medical matters was sparked when he was in his twenties at the dramatic sight of a colleague falling to the ground in an epileptic fit. He realized that he was unable to help, and was inspired to learn more. In the course of doing so, he attended St Bartholomew's Hospital to view an operation being performed upon a man with an abcess below the knee joint.

In those days operating theatres were blood-and-sawdust places, with no attention paid to hygiene. The operating rooms resembled a 'theatre', even down to the gallery where spectators could gather and watch operations. John Flint South, an eminent early 19th-century surgeon once commented that spectators would stand 'packed like herrings in a barrel, but not so quiet' with those in the back rows continually pushing those in front of them out of the way and yelling 'Heads, heads!' because the heads of the surgeons sometimes interfered with their view.[21] The surgeons wore filthy bloodstained, pus-smeared clothes, and the entire spectacle must have been disgusting. Carroll obviously expected it to be so, but he later observed in his diary that he had not found the operation quite as bad as he had anticipated. At least the patient had not suffered, for

the operation had been done under the influence of chloro-
form, which produced at first convulsions and then a stupor.
The surgeon told the onlookers that 3 inches of the man's bone
was destroyed, and he went on to amputate the leg above the
knee. Carroll recalled:

> The whole thing lasted more than an hour. I fully expected
> to turn ill at the sight, and be forced to go away, and was
> much surprised to find that I could bear it perfectly well. I
> doubt if I could have done this, had the man been suffering
> pain all the while, but it was quite evident that he felt
> nothing. This is an experiment I have long been anxious to
> make, in order to know whether I might rely on myself to
> be of any use in cases of emergency, and I am very glad to
> believe that I might. Still I don't think I should enjoy seeing
> much of it.[22]

Over the years, Carroll put together a huge library of medical
books, many of which were later bequeathed to a doctor
nephew. Unfortunately very little information exists about this
collection, for Carroll's own catalogue of it has disappeared, and
the books were destroyed some years later in a fire at St Mary's
Hospital, Paddington.

As well as reading about medicine, Carroll took pains to
obtain hands-on experience of treating others. In particular he
nursed, visited and sat with the sick – something which would
have been expected of the women of the family, but not necessarily of the men. He was happy to keep his favourite Uncle
Skeffington company when he was ill with facial erysipelas
in January 1872, and noted that he could be useful not only in
reading and writing for him, but also in keeping him company.

He also helped to nurse his dying godson Charlie Wilcox
in the early 1870s. He was sensitive to the needs of invalids, and
turning melancholy thoughts towards laughter was one of the

things he characteristically did in all situations. His efforts with Charlie included making up 'The Hunting of the Snark', which lightly and humorously transforms the horror of oblivion into something less terrible.

His attempts to sooth and cheer were not always appreciated, however, since tact does not seem to have been one of his nursing skills. Between 1888 and 1892, he went to some trouble to visit a paralysed young woman called Louie Taylor, who was distantly related to him by marriage. He gave Louie's plight considerable thought, and even made her a device so that she could read books more easily while lying in bed. Louie's actual complaint was vague, however, and Carroll was unable to stop himself from suggesting that she might be able to move about more if she put her mind to it. This remark infuriated her so much that she told him to stay out of her life forever; a command which he received with wry dismay. [23]

Even though he never studied medicine formally, Carroll also enjoyed looking after other people as a homeopathic practitioner. He owned several books on homeopathy, boxes of homeopathic medicines were among his possessions when he died, and his diary sometimes tells of occasions when he administered homeopathic remedies. He also recommended homeopathy to his brother Edwin when Edwin went off to be a missionary abroad.[24] He himself generally used conventional doctors, although for a while he did use a homeopath friend of his, Edward Shuldham, for minor complaints. It seems he did not trust Shuldham's diagnoses very well. He consulted him for an oval patch of pink on his skin, which shone as if it had been varnished, but then rejected Shuldham's verdict of ringworm and diagnosed it as erythema and treated it himself. After that, his only other recorded foray into homeopathy was when he visited a Dr Burnett in late 1888 and took madder in water, night and morning, to treat eczema, varicosis, and a disordered spleen.

Carroll's interest in homeopathy may have led him to avoid taking too many strong and potent medicines. That is something which may, paradoxically, have improved his health, since in those days drugs which are now known to be dangerous were in constant use. Sherlock Holmes famously injected 7 per cent cocaine; and nobody thought worse of him for it, because both cocaine and morphine were then thought to be essentially harmless.

Opium in the form of laudanum was another popular drug that was often used to help with pain, reduce irritation, check sweating and induce sleep. If gin was the 'mother's ruin' of the lower classes, then laudanum was the bane of the menopausal middle-class lady. Not only was it dispensed without prescription, but it could be made at home by anyone willing to gather up a few basketfuls of withered poppies and spend an hour or two preparing them into a dose, which was then mixed with sugar or alcohol to make it palatable. If an antidote was needed, then a dubious mix of potassium bromide and spirit of ether was recommended.

Although Carroll is now something of an iconic figure for psychedelic drug users, there is only the tiniest shred of evidence that he ever took laudanum, morphine, cocaine, magic mushrooms or indeed that he sampled any mind-altering drugs at all. In the Harry Ransom Center at the University of Texas, is a jotting on the obverse of a sheet of paper on which Carroll has written about one of his favourite topics, 'Where the day Begins'. It appears to be a recipe involving 2 grams of opium, plus camphor, divided into ten pills. Very short, it is undated, and may have been for him, or for someone else.

Carroll's general health was excellent, something he probably owed partially to the care taken of him by his mother and father when he was young, and the habits which they passed on to him. He died a few days short of his 66th birthday, but his brothers and sisters all survived infancy and lived to a good age, dying between the ages of 71 and 90 years old. His mother's letters when her children were small show how carefully the Dodgson parents sought the best medical care when their children were ill, and did everything possible to preserve their health. To have 11 children survive was most unusual at that time, when cholera was rife, knowledge of disease prevention was scanty and most families lost at least one child and often many more.

Asiatic Cholera was the scourge of the mid-nineteenth century, and Carroll and his contemporaries would always have had the fear of cholera at the back of their minds. Anxiety about the spread of the disease can be seen in Dodgson family letters written during Carroll's childhood, for it had arrived in nearby Sunderland from India in 1831, and, during the following years it spread inexorably outwards from there. Cholera was fostered by filthy living conditions, but doctors were not aware of exactly what caused it or what to do about it. The Dodgson family lived in an isolated house, which had its own water supply and sewage arrangements, so they rarely encountered the foul air and disgustingly polluted living conditions of cities. The children were mostly educated at home, so they probably did not mix much with others who may have been less clean.

Carroll did, of course, suffer the usual childhood ailments during his infancy and youth. His worst childhood illness seems to have been an attack of something called 'infantile fever', which has not been identified by modern doctors, but which left him with permanent deafness in one ear. Dr Selwyn Goodacre, a Carroll expert who is also a GP, has hypothesized that as a result of the fever, Carroll probably got otitis media, a common middle ear infection which, if untreated by modern medication, can result in hearing loss.

At the age of 17, Carroll contracted whooping cough. This is usually a disease of childhood, but because he was nearly an adult, it hit him hard. Not only did it increase his deafness in the right ear but the cough lingered for five months. For some of that time he was boarding at Rugby school, where conditions were far from comfortable, and this cannot have helped his convalescence. Indeed, Dr Goodacre conjectures that the lingering whooping cough led to the complication of bronchiectasis, a localized infection of the lungs which may have predisposed Carroll to lung trouble later in life. He certainly suffered throughout his life from bronchial attacks, and ultimately died of pneumonia as a complication of bronchitis.

Dr Goodacre also suggested that Carroll might have had mild chronic pyelonephritis, as he had repeated attacks of ague, sometimes with cystitis and backache.[25] If so, then it never developed into anything serious.

Carroll also remarked occasionally of his sufferings from neuralgia of the face. There is a droll account of his efforts to obtain relief from this in the journal of his travels in Russia, made when he was 35, in which he describes how, in Paris, he went to a convent to buy some salve made by the nuns for what he called the 'tic-doloreux'. The nuns refused to sell him any, since according to their pious principles, the ointment was only to be given free to the poor. Carroll, ingenious as ever, hit upon the idea of asking the nuns to give him some ointment in exchange for a donation from him for the poor, 'and so the delicately-veiled bargain was at last concluded', he wrote.[26]

Not only did Carroll tend his own body (and sometimes other's ailments) with care, but he also found bodies fascinating in all kinds of ways – scientific, physical and artistic. Landscapes interested him hardly at all, and Irene Dodgson Jacques, his niece, recalled the disappointment of her father, Skeffington, when he took Carroll to a local beauty spot and found his brother impervious to its charms. On the other hand, Carroll's comments after visits to picture galleries show what an ardent interest he took in beautiful depictions of human face and form. Nearly always, this was female beauty. Carroll particularly loved pictures of children and young women (clothed or not) that combined beauty with soulfulness or gentle spirituality. He commissioned Arthur Hughes to paint *Lady of the Lilacs* for him, a head-and-shoulders portrait of a gentle young woman holding up one hand as if in benediction. Collingwood remembered him lovingly pointing out the contrasts of colour in it, and how exquisitely the girl's hair stood out against the purple lilac blossom.

Although Carroll took care not to sketch or photograph nude women himself, he did admire many such pictures very much, so long as the images were not crude or overtly sexual. There is nothing salacious in his many diary references to how much he appreciated such works as Collier's *Pharaoh's Handmaidens*, which shows three bare-breasted young women, Weguelin's *The Maidens' Race*, showing a line of graceful semi-nude women, and others of the same type. There was, it must be confessed, a certain sentimentality in his approach. In his feeling for art, as in so much else, Carroll's taste ran towards the feminine – the girly, even. He loved gentleness and harmlessness, and was repelled by coarseness and prurience.

Yet, being human, he had a certain interest in the latter, too, and his diaries attest to his efforts to draw some kind of a boundary. In 1884, he wrote that he had been to see *Nana* by Marceli Suchorowsky, a picture he had been recommended to view by a friend. Inspired by Zola's fictional prostitute, it was, according to the French critic Hugues Lebailly, most controversially displayed in a dark room, with a mirror flanking either side of the brilliantly lit easel on which it stood. The *Art-Journal*, wrote Lebailly, considered the picture to be revoltingly sensual, and trumpeted for the authorities who looked after England's morals to rouse themselves to action about it.[27]

When Carroll saw the picture, he disliked the fact that it had drapery. He always felt that using drapery suggested that there was something unseemly about God's work. In fact, he did not like the picture at all. 'It is a very life-like picture of a reclining woman, nude, except for a little drapery covering one leg from knee to foot; it would have been better entirely nude, but even so rather "French" in feeling,' he noted.[28] Although this was before the Naughty Nineties began, describing anything as 'French' was tantamount to saying it was racy. Nevertheless, Carroll had satisfied himself that *Nana* was not actually indecent, so he did not join the *Art-Journal*'s public protests. For him, *Nana* had stayed on the right side of the line.

It was not only the human body which intrigued Carroll, for he was as interested in minds as he was in bodies. He was very curious about madness and mental abnormalities, and what we might now call altered states or altered consciousness. His library included books on nervous exhaustion, the diseases of memory, the influence of the mind upon the body, sleepwalking, hypnotism and the delusions of the insane. Even though the details of so many of his other medical books went unrecorded, he is known to have owned titles that covered the rudimentary psychology of the period, for the links between body and mind were of particular interest to him. One of these titles was Sir James Paget's *Clinical Lectures*, which impressed Carroll so much that he recommended it to a doctor acquaintance.

The enormously gifted Paget was one of the foremost doctors of his day, and Carroll knew him personally, as Paget had attended his uncle, Skeffington Lutwidge, after a serious accident. The book was intended for medical students, and provides a panorama of Victorian medicine as an ever-expanding new world of scientific knowledge. It was, too, a world that was still accessible to the average intelligent person. Dr Paget's approach to medicine could broadly be described as holistic, and he affected no clinical detachment in anything pertaining to morality, with his personal voice resounding through the pages and indeed over the centuries:

I have not heard anything to make me believe that occasional masturbation has any other effects on one who practises it than has occasional sexual intercourse, nor anything justifying the dread with which sexual hypochondriacs regard having occasionally practised it. I wish that I could say something worse of so nasty a practice; an uncleanliness, a filthiness forbidden by GOD, an unmanliness despised by men.[29]

Carroll's interest in the book probably lay mainly in the chapters relating to what we would now consider to be psychosomatic subjects. Dr Paget had no background of modern psychology, of course, but several chapters of 'Clinical Lectures' deal with what might be broadly termed psychological conditions. His chapter on 'Stammering With Other Organs Than That of Speech' mostly deals with mental difficulties associated with carrying out normal bodily functions, such as urination. Other topics range from 'Nervous Mimicry' to sexual hypochondria in males, and they draw extensively upon observations of diseases then prevalent.

It can be seen how Carroll's interest in mental functioning, normal or abnormal, spilled over into his creative work. Not only is everyone mad in Wonderland, as the Cheshire Cat so memorably said, but his lengthy two-part novel *Sylvie and Bruno*, written many years later, is full of descriptions of altered mental states. However, the way that he treated the subject of mind and consciousness over the years echoes an increasing strangeness in Carroll himself as he grew older.

The 30-year-old man who told the story of *Alice in Wonderland* appears from his letters and diaries to have been lively and normal in every way. The man who finally published *Sylvie and Bruno Concluded* when he was around 60 years old, had become someone who seemed in some respects to live in a world of his own, and who had become notably eccentric.

Those who disliked him – and even some of those who did

not – found him increasingly difficult to deal with as time went on. There is no recorded suggestion that his behaviour was mad: at least, not by comparison with other Oxford dons, some of whom were almost a byword for eccentricity. Carroll's little peculiarities were in some respects less odd than, for instance, those of the Christ Church canon Dr Buckland, who frequently chose to dine on unpalatable creatures like mice and earwigs (he considered mole one of the nastiest dishes he had ever eaten, he said, but bluebottle was nastier still).

Roughly from 1880 onwards, unmistakable signs of eccentricity began to appear in Carroll's behaviour. It is well attested that he continued to function competently within his own social setting, and his capacity for logical thought was as good as ever even at the end of his life. He was working on his system of symbolic logic almost till the day of his death, and logicians have no quarrel with its competence, nor mathematicians with the mental puzzles he took such pleasure in devising. Nor does anyone seem to have shrunk from him or found him personally disturbing. He had many, many friends and he had no difficulty in making more. Children adored him, and his social behaviour, time and again, was described as courteous, gentlemanly, considerate, gentle and kindly. Yet it is hard to read some of his writings of later life, in particular his peculiar preface to *Sylvie and Bruno Concluded* without a feeling of puzzlement, even concern.

In this rambling discourse, Carroll goes into detail about the peculiar mind-states of the characters in the story. He asks the reader to hypothesize that his story could take place *if* fairies existed, and *if* they were sometimes visible to human beings, and *if* they were sometimes able to assume human form, and also *if* human beings 'might sometimes become conscious of what goes on in the Fairy-world'. He assumes that this awareness would involve actual transference of the non-material 'essence' of self, and compares it with the state of mind found in Esoteric

Buddhism – presumably the 8th-century Japanese variety, and not Madame Blavatsky's controversial theories which had then been circulating for some years. He then describes human beings as being capable of various psychical states:

(*a*) the ordinary state, with no consciousness of the presence of Fairies;

(*b*) the 'eerie' state, in which, while conscious of actual surroundings, he is *also* conscious of the presence of Fairies;

(*c*) a form of trance, in which, while *un*conscious of actual surroundings, and apparently asleep, the subject (that is, his immaterial essence) migrates to other scenes, in the actual world, or Fairyland, and is conscious of the presence of Fairies.

Fairies, Carroll blithely continues, were also capable of having corresponding mental states in relation to being in contact with humans! He went on laboriously to tabulate all the passages in each volume of the story where each mental state occurred, stating which character was involved, noting the relevant page numbers and whether the mental state was (a), (b) or (c), as well as further details, almost impossible for the average reader to understand. .

This bizarre approach to what is, after all, a made-up story, as well as the chaotic nature of the whole work, almost suggests that, by then, something had happened to change Carroll himself. He may have been suffering some kind of mild and indefinable mental damage; a lesion of the brain, perhaps, which set him onto a path of slight difference, and perhaps made him less aware of the impression he was making on others.

Dorothy Furniss, daughter of the illustrator Harry Furniss, wrote amusingly about her late father's tribulations with Carroll's eccentricities in later life. Furniss is often criticized for poking fun at Carroll, but correspondence such as this suggests that sometimes Furniss may have found it easier to laugh than to cry. At one stage, Dorothy recalls, Carroll wished Furniss to draw a creature which looked like a spider but sat cross-legged like a tailor. He wanted the creature to be,

> '... portrayed front view and full faced because some writer says that the full face of a spider, as seen under a magnifying glass, is very striking. Could you find one in some book of entomology, or look at a live one?'
>
> After a day spent sketching spiders and endeavouring to give them 'just that human touch' required by the author, the artist wrote in despair that it was an impossibility to depict a spider sitting cross legged like a tailor ...[30]

After Furniss protested, Carroll offered a sketch of his own, offering the opinion that 'a creature, mostly human, but suggestive of a spidery nature, would be quite accurate enough'. In increasingly surreal vein, he added that the spider was deeply love-stricken, and was 'in the midst of a "declaration", quite unaware that the young lady is out of hearing! Would not that be a subject for pity? ... I meant him to be laying his hand on his heart: but his chin got in the way ...'.[31]

In fact, Carroll is known to have had some kind of physical brain problem. It was mentioned explicitly for the first time on the last day of 1885 when he had a mild attack, diagnosed as 'epileptiform', which left him with a headache for 10 days or so. His interest in mental strangeness, particularly epilepsy, had developed long before this first recorded incident, and several entries in his diary describe occasions when he witnessed or helped with people who had epileptic fits, starting with the colleague whose fit had inspired him to improve his medical knowledge. As his fascination for medical matters grew, he witnessed a number of fits diagnosed as 'epileptic'. In 1875, he reported in his diary that he was able to help a stranger who had collapsed in a fit, since he himself was by now 'quite experienced in dealing with that kind of fit'.[32]

It is conceivable that Carroll unwittingly experienced epileptic 'auras' himself earlier in his life, and that it was this which helped to inspire his interest in madness and with fitting. However, if any such attacks did occur, they must have been slight, for he only became ill enough to cause real concern in 1888. At that point, he fainted, and after that he felt ill for some considerable time.

Carroll originally believed epilepsy was a form of insanity, as he wrote in his diary of 6 April 1876. This was a widely held view at the time. Many people believed it was caused by masturbation, but Carroll had read so widely on medical subjects that he probably did not. At any rate, he was relaxed about that some years later, in 1891, when referring to the matter to his friend Edith Blakemore. Nonetheless, his family have tried to censor material in his diary relating to his 'epileptiform' attacks, even though it is not clear precisely what these attacks were. Victorian treatments and diagnoses were necessarily more primitive than today's, and there was, of course, no access to modern diagnostic technology or tests, so a good deal of what went on inside body and brain was a mystery. For that reason, contemporary diagnoses of Carroll as 'epileptic' cannot be relied upon.

It is also difficult for any modern doctor to make comments on a long-dead patient, but all references and descriptions of the brain symptoms in Carroll's letters and diaries were collected together and presented in 2008 to Dr Yvonne Hart, a consultant neurologist at the Radcliffe Hospital, Oxford with a special interest in epilepsy. Dr Hart also considered the famous incidents of macropsia and micropsia (growing larger and smaller) which occur in *Alice in Wonderland*, and which have also been compared to symptoms of temporal lobe epilepsy. Her report appears in full in the Appendix to this book.

Although she warned that any definite diagnosis was impossible, Dr Hart concluded that Carroll probably had migraine. She was more doubtful about the epilepsy because of the lack of independent observation of his attacks. She also pointed out that some doctors believe that epilepsy and migraine are linked.[33]

As far as migraine is concerned, Carroll is known to have read (and probably owned) *Nervous or Sick Headache* by Dr P W Latham. This book detailed some of the migrainous symptoms from which he suffered, and suggested treatments for them, which included the building up of the system with iron, cod-liver oil and, rather alarmingly, strychnine! No other information about the physical state of Carroll's brain has been forthcoming. He himself does not seem to have been overly worried about his visual migraine symptoms, and, apart from his eccentric behaviour at times, he coped well with his life.

As he grew older, Carroll began to take an active interest in preserving his physical health. He increased the amount of exercise he took, adding to his normal habit of walking everywhere by going for long, solitary walks in the countryside (which he timed), and also using Whiteley Exercisers, a kind of strengthening device for the muscles. He continued to eat sparingly, and although 5 feet 10 inches in height, did not rise appreciably over ten-and-a-quarter stone – 144 lb (65.3 kg). His ascetism did not, apparently, extend to alcohol, for he was knowledgeable about wine, and his lunch, in 18th-century style, consisted of sherry – or, if the mischievous Harry Furniss is to be believed, several sherries – and a biscuit. He is even reported to have carried his own flask of sherry with him on social calls, but this was probably just another manifestation of his increasing eccentricity rather than a desperate need to have sherry with him at all times.

Not long before his death, his doctor pronounced him a thoroughly fit man. But just a few days before his 66th birthday,

One of the earliest, pre-clerical photographs shows a decidedly dandyish youth with a large cravat, a checked waistcoat and a jacket which contemporary fashion plates confirm was in the very latest style.

'This strange wild man from other lands'

Love and Sex

'... against the door of the room three strong men were leaning, vainly trying to shut it – for some great animal inside was constantly bursting it half open, and we had a glimpse, before the men could push it back again, of the head of a furious wild beast, with great fiery eyes and gnashing teeth ...'

Sylvie and Bruno Concluded

Lewis Carroll, living in a secretive age, was considered reticent even by his friends. He belonged to a private, self-contained family, and after his death many personal documents that had been in his family's keeping mysteriously disappeared. His diary does not mention his romantic yearnings or needs. Yet even though most of the material about his personal life has been destroyed, this does not mean that he had none. Is it possible, so long after his death, to get a glimpse of it?

In the earlier part of the 20th century, Carroll was often presented as virginal, sexless or, at the least, highly repressed. In 1932, the biographer Langford Reed made a good deal of Carroll's 'split personality' although he was genteel enough not to speculate about Carroll's sexual life in print. After interviewing several of those who had been Carroll's child-friends, he concluded that Carroll must have been one of those 'super-sensitive and over-refined people to whom the very idea of physical familiarity was abhorrent', and he compared Carroll with an old maid or a nun.[1] Some years later, Carroll's niece, Menella Dodgson, told an acquaintance that, from her memories of him, she could not imagine Carroll married because no woman could have dealt with his exact and fastidious ways.[2]

In later life, he was, indeed, a quaint old bachelor, and there are numerous tales of his gentle eccentricities. One of his grown-up child-friends recalled how delighted he was with a special kettle he had designed for making tea in the best possible way, which he boasted of to her 'in the most ingenuous manner' every single time she visited.[3] Yet in truth, Carroll was far from being a maidenly nun-figure who was ignorant of sexual matters. He may have given that impression to the casual observer, but, on closer examination, one of the most nun-like aspects of his life was the number of women who surrounded him.

His views on physical life were better informed, even more outré, than those that many men of his background held in his own day. He strongly disapproved of pornography, and yet he owned books that covered sexual and physical matters as frankly as was then legally possible. These included Alexander Walker's *Woman Physiologically Considered as to Mind, Morals, Marriage, Matrimonial Slavery, Infidelity and Divorce*, which includes discussion of polygamy, infidelity, concubinage, and prostitution, and William Acton's famous treatise on prostitution, the standard 19th-century work on the subject. He also owned medical texts covering many aspects of sexuality, such as Dr Paget's book (described in Chapter 3), and books that considered social aspects of sexuality, such as William Dixon's startling observations on free-thinking religious sects, *Spiritual Wives*, which includes events that would seem noteworthy even by modern-day cult standards.[4]

Carroll also read about polygamy and unconventional types

of marriage; he owned a copy of *Plain Home Talk* by Dr Foote, whose frank ideas on free love as well as birth control, dress reform and Utopianism, were way ahead of their time. In fact, some of the material Carroll sought, such as Michael Ryan's *The Philosophy of Marriage and its Social, Moral and Physical Relations*, although certainly not pornographic, was extremely candid. He asked his American illustrator Arthur Burdett Frost if he could obtain this and a couple of Ryan's other titles in America, obviously being under the impression that they were not available in England.[5]

Carroll would sometimes visit his artist friends in their studios and see them at work, but his diary is so laconic about them that his liberal-mindedness has often gone unremarked. In April 1865, for instance, he recorded a visit to Dante Gabriel Rossetti thus: 'We went ... to call on Rossetti. We found him at home, and his friend Swinburne also in the room, whom I had not met before. He showed us many beautiful pictures, two quite new, the bride going to meet the bride-groom (from Solomon's Song), and Venus with a back-ground of roses.' The critic Hugues Lebailly has pointed out that one of the pictures Carroll admired during the visit was Rossetti's *Venus Verticordia*, the eroticism of which made it difficult for Rossetti to sell.[6] Carroll does not tell us what he made of the scandalous Swinburne, but he did go out and buy a first edition of his notorious *Poems and Ballads*.[7]

As his bank account shows, Carroll could be almost reckless in private, even though he kept up an impenetrably prudent front in public. His friend Gertrude Thomson described how his donnish manner would utterly disappear when he was in informal surroundings; and his scornful comments about 'Mrs Grundy', the fictitious moralizer, show how little he cared what conventional people thought of the way he was obliged to live his life. 'Oh, Edith, I wish you could come and stay here a bit!' he wrote to Edith Rix in 1888, when she was in her twenties.

I believe the "Mrs. Grundy" risk might be altogether avoided by simply arranging 2 or 3 visits to be paid consecutively, Eastbourne to be one. Then, when Mrs. Grundy calls, and asks for you, she will simply be told, "She is away, paying a round of visits." The miserable old gossip will hardly be inquisitive enough to say "and what particular house is she at just now?" or, at any rate, if she *is*, she will deserve to be snubbed![8]

So, despite the apparent emptiness of his emotional life from this distance in time, closer examination suggests that he did manage to fill the spaces after all. What is more, during his moralistic later years, he demonstrated a well-honed and effective knowledge of how to win over girls in their teens and grown-up women, as well as children. Several descriptions exist of his technique, which was based on presenting the potential friend with interesting aspects of himself that he wished her to see, and allowing her to respond if she wanted to do so. It was a gentle, skilful extension of his storytelling or dramatic technique. If she did not wish to get involved, nothing was lost; if she did react, a friendship usually developed. The start of his lifelong friendship with a Mrs Bennie (described in full in Chapter 8) demonstrates how he used this technique, intriguing her sufficiently to make her put in the effort to pursue his company. The account of his first meeting with Gertrude Thomson shows the same mind at work.

Miss Thomson was a respectable and independent young lady artist of a type starting to emerge towards the end of the century. She produced charming pictures of children, fairies and cherubs. An early photograph of her depicts a bright, untidy young woman, ornamentally clad in fur, feathers, embroidery and jewellery. A later, more sedate photograph has her with an elaborately elegant hairstyle and dressed in dark ruffles. She was talented, unconventional and scatty.

Miss Thomson first met Carroll in June 1879 when she was in her late twenties and he was 47. He had seen her pictures, liked them, and wanted her to draw for him. He suggested they meet in the South Kensington Museum to discuss the matter. Miss Thomson forgot, however, to tell Carroll what she looked like, and, since it would have been unseemly for her to approach an unknown man, when she reached the museum she wondered what to do. However, punctually at the appointed time, she saw a 'tall, slim figure' with a 'clean-shaven, delicate, refined face' arriving with two little girls (the well-dressed child chaperones showing, to Victorian eyes, that he was a respectable man). The man glanced swiftly about, and then 'bending down, [he] whispered something to one of the children; she, without a moment's pause, pointed straight at me. Dropping their hands, he came forward with that winning smile of his ... and said simply "I am Mr. Dodgson; I was to meet you I think?"' Astonished, Miss Thomson asked him how he had recognized her. '"My little friend found you," Carroll replied. "I told her I had come to meet a young lady who knew fairies, and she fixed on you at once." Then he added: "But, I knew you, before she spoke."'[9]

Miss Thomson, the fairy painter, was delighted by this charming story, which flatteringly emphasized her fairy-like credentials. Closer examination of her tale, though, suggests that there was more to it. No child could have instantly and unaided picked her out of the crowd. But Carroll knew that she had not asked how she should recognize him – though since she was waiting with a portfolio at the appointed time, he could easily spot who *she* was. Rather than approaching her directly, he had spun the unusual idea of asking the child to spot a 'young lady who knew fairies'.

He had (as he said) already recognized Miss Thomson. So the child, having no idea what a 'lady who liked fairies' looked like, would have automatically pointed out the woman at whom Carroll was gazing. The path was then free for him to approach Miss Thomson with a 'winning smile' – that is, with full eye contact – bypassing the awkwardness that would usually have attended a meeting between strangers of opposite sexes. Furthermore, he could involve Miss Thomson in the charming, wholly improbable yet respectable suggestion that she had been instantly, attractively recognizable to him. No lies were told, for she filled in all the gaps herself. Within days, he was writing to her, 'Are you sufficiently unconventional (I *think* you are) to defy Mrs Grundy and come down to spend the day with me in Oxford?'[10] Of course, Miss Thomson was.

Carroll's light-handed skill at controlling how others responded to him can also be seen in how he won over 17-year-old Charlotte Rix. She wrote a letter to her mother describing how, as a friend of her father's, Carroll had turned up at her boarding school to take her out for the day. She had never met him but, once again, there was no stiff and awkward start to their conversation. To her amazement, his first action on meeting was to turn her round and look at her back.

'I wondered what on earth he was doing, but he said that he had been made to expect a tremendous lot of hair,' Charlotte reported to her mother. Lots of hair was a great sign of beauty in those days, so this remark, like his comment to Miss Thomson, was surprising, personal and flattering. Immediately it set them upon closer and less formal terms. He then told the gratified Charlotte that 'he was surprised to see that she [the principal] would let the young ladies go out with any gentleman that called, without even coming to see that they *looked* respectable. ...' Although polite enough to report to her mother, this comment was guaranteed to raise the emotional temperature, which – as the rest of the letter makes clear – Charlotte herself was stoking up. The description she goes on to give of the outing shows how Carroll managed to set up a little mutual admiration society in which he gave her a good time and she played the part that he wanted her to play. 'Mrs Grundy', despite Charlotte's relatively advanced age of 17, was kept at bay.[11]

Did Carroll's ability to charm – which is mentioned by several people and which he was aware of himself – have sexual undertones? He must have obtained emotional satisfaction from it, since these and other descriptions indicate that he took the trouble to hone his skills. There was no reported impropriety, and his genuine horror of sin probably means there really was not any, at least later in his life, and certainly not with teenage girls like Charlotte.

What there was, was gossip. He attracted a large female retinue, and Mrs Grundy's tongue never stopped wagging in relation to Carroll and women. From at least his twenties, when he was supposed to be chasing Alice's governess, right until the end of his life, he was dodging tittle-tattle. The older he became, the more lady friends he acquired, and the more obtrusive the gossip became.

He countered it partly by presenting himself to his fellows as a man who was no threat to their sheltered womenfolk, and who could be welcomed without anxiety into their family circles. His unmarried status and his love of children's company conveyed to Victorians the idea that he was a person who had chosen not to be sexual.

He was only in his forties when he began to tell people that he was too old to pose a moral threat to respectable women. A letter he wrote to a Mr Alderson in 1884 when he was 51 asking if he could take out his 22-year-old daughter Helen shows the line he adopted:

> As yet I do not know if you would sanction any such expe-
> dition, without other chaperon, but ... I am an entirely
> confirmed old bachelor who is now well over 50 ... so why
> should Mrs. Grundy object to my having what is so pleasant
> to me, the friendship of my child friends? So many of my

friends … have allowed me to chaperone my quondam child friends – at all ages from 15 to 25 and upwards. …"[12]

Carroll was extremely fit and looked young for his years, but by constantly telling people he was 'old' he was making the point that he could at last be trusted to take out un-chaperoned young women (whom he ostentatiously referred to as 'child friends' – children compared to him, that is). He could also enjoy the personal liberties, including loving kisses, which so many of them seemed pleased to grant him.

As he grew older, large numbers of his letters were to or about women. Some are charming, some positively flirtatious. To Marion Miller, aged 18, he wrote:

My dear May.
Here is the photo. Looking at it, however, it is not much of a substitute for the live May. I wish you would come back again: I need not point out how cruel it is of you to be away so many weeks while I am here, for no doubt you are already feeling a little ashamed of your heartless conduct … [13]

While to 22-year-old Edith Lucy he wrote, 'My dearest Edith, Why *will* you insist on my beginning so, [i.e. calling her 'dearest'] when you know what a lot of Ediths I know … and how awfully hard it is to decide which of them is the dearest!'[14] It is no wonder that the theatrical designer Laurence Irving noted that the ageing Carroll was seen by some in Oxford not as the nun or spinster figure of Langford Reed's imagination, but as a 'greying satyr in sheep's clothing'.[15]

There was no shortage of young women willing to go out to the theatre, art galleries, on long walks, to tête-à-tête meals and on lengthy outings with him – outings they would never normally have gone on alone with other men. Even today, a middle-aged man who accompanied so many young women would probably cause comment, as would his very cordial tête-à-tête meetings with married women.

With his lady friends, however, Carroll set his own moral limits and stuck to them rigidly. Within these moral limits, he did what he liked. What other people made of him was up to them; but he deflected a good deal of criticism honestly enough by emphasizing certain ultra-moralistic views that became a feature of his later life. There seems to have been no irony in his loud protestations against 'ungodly' stories, and he manifestly meant the angry letters he wrote to theatre proprietors who allowed 'indecency' in their plays. Isa Bowman was echoing a general sentiment when she said, 'He was the purest-minded and cleanest living of men, intolerant of anything in the slightest degree coarse.'[16] His protestations conveyed the message in no uncertain terms that he was an intensely moral man.

So Lewis Carroll, the inveterate caricaturist, made himself into a caricature of Victorian primness, and thus deflected a great deal of attention away from what he did. Crucially, his genuine and longstanding love of little girls made him seem much more appropriate company for women than a man with an 'eye for the ladies'; and however eccentric it made him seem, he was not going to allow anyone to forget it.

Unsurprisingly, sarcastic, fanciful and downright catty gossip began circulating around Oxford about him in this respect. Carroll's young women, it was ironically said, would react with delight to gifts of little toys and packets of pear drops that he supposedly gave them. His entourage became well known, and Laurence Irving no doubt spoke for many observers when he said that Carroll's lady friends' 'affectation of whimsies long past, and now, to flatter their author, kept up with desperate *naivete,* [was] embarrassing, if not a bit macabre'.[17]

Yet Irving also remarked that Carroll, ever-puzzling, was patently innocent of any intent to harm anybody. So his mother, then a young aspiring actress, was allowed to meet him despite all the gossip which buzzed about the kindly and, apparently, unworldly don.

A letter that has only recently come to light casts a bright beam of illumination on this intriguing aspect of Carroll's life. A year after his brother's death, Wilfred Dodgson wrote to the periodical *Literature*, a precursor of *The Times Literary Supplement*. Arguably the most worldly of the Dodgson siblings, Wilfred complained that Isa Bowman, in her just-published memoir, was presenting herself uniquely as Carroll's adopted niece.

Wilfred, on the contrary, felt that Isa was very far indeed from being unique. He wrote that his brother had 'almost a mania' for 'adopting' nieces. He followed this with the bombshell announcement that Carroll had often told him that he 'adopted this avuncular position with a view to the time when his "nieces" began to grow out of their teens'. At this point they could 'no longer be treated with anything like intimate affection except by "uncles" and such-like relations,' wrote Wilfred. There were at least *fifty* women who fell into this category, he added, before continuing, 'I know of [a] very charming married lady who says that one of the conditions she made when she accepted her husband was that she might continue to be kissed by 'Uncle Charles [Carroll].'[18]

Carroll's nephew-biographer Stuart Collingwood, writing his book for the general public, also went so far as to mention briefly Carroll's many lady friends. Indeed, he admitted that *most* of his uncle's friends were 'ladies', and remarked that Carroll had a 'Bohemian', that is, an unconventional, side.

These comments show that the family believed in Carroll and were prepared to stand by him in public – even though in private there is evidence that there was some concern about the gossip that circulated about him and women. Most of this gossip entirely escapes modern readers, since in print it was heavily underplayed and veiled in euphemistic Victorian style.

One very interesting example occurs in a conversation reported by Carroll's friend Gertrude Thomson in her reminiscences marking Carroll's death.

Miss Thomson was unusual in that she was *not* one of Carroll's ex-'little girls' but an openly grown-up woman friend. She wished to celebrate her close friendship with Carroll – and also to inform the world exactly what their relationship signified. In her memoir she describes how she and Carroll once went to sketch the children of an extremely conventional lady. This lady waited till Carroll had departed before initiating a woman-to-woman talk with Miss Thomson.

'I hear that you spent the other day in Oxford with Mr. Dodgson?' she said, ' … It's a very unconventional thing to do.' Miss Thomson replied that she and Carroll were 'both unconventional'. The lady then responded that Carroll was 'not at all a ladies' man – a confirmed bachelor', to which Miss Thomson retorted that she herself was a 'lady bachelor'. As the conversation progressed, she said she became so angry at the woman's impertinence that she could hardly contain her temper.[19]

This conversation seems somewhat mystifying to a modern reader, although Miss Thomson clearly did not feel she needed to spell anything out to her Victorian audience. The 'unconventionality' referred to an unmarried man and woman openly spending the day together (including alone in his rooms) without an accompanying chaperone, thereby advertising their liberated social views. This behaviour was not unknown in the 1880s among progressive-minded folk, but it could have harmed Miss Thomson's own marriage prospects, had she wished to marry. So the lady was warning Miss Thomson that Carroll would never marry *her*. He would go around with her and give people the impression they were a couple, but in the end he would not tie the wedding knot.

Miss Thomson was known in her own circle for not wishing to marry, and she found the woman's remarks very offensive.

Later in her memoir, to emphasize her point, Miss Thomson reports how, when she had been attending the theatre with Carroll, someone had sent her a note marked 'Mrs. Dodgson'. Carroll jokingly remarked, 'Well, we are certainly labelled *now!*' Indeed. And, 'How we laughed!' Miss Thomson defiantly told her readers.[20]

The gossip which circulated about Carroll also explains why so many of the young women who were close to him make the point in their recollections of how young and childlike they were. It also suggests why other women asserted that he was usually only interested in little girls and that *they* were the exception. It made everything in the whole scenario seem so much more innocent.

Several references to her own unfeasible youthfulness are found in the 1899 book by Isa Bowman about which Wilfred complained. Isa was undeniably close to Carroll, and stayed with him, unchaperoned, for weeks at a time. Carroll confessed to a friend that she was the only young lady he had felt happy living with for longer than the traditional 'honeymoon' month: a risky remark if ever there was one. Gossip about Isa was rife. When she was nineteen, he was writing to her, 'I'm still exactly "on the balance" … as to whether it would be wise to have my pet Isa down here! How am I to make it weigh, I wonder? Can you advise any way to do it?"[21]

His 'pet''s photographs show her to have been slim, dainty and pretty: quite the 'stunner'. However, in her book, she persistently implies she was younger than she really was, even to the point of lying about it and referring to herself as 10 years old when she was in fact around 13 when they first met.

Although the acting profession had become more respectable as the 19th century went on, it still had a rather racy reputation even at the end of the century. Those of Carroll's contemporaries and friends who were tolerant and easy going were willing to believe that Isa was not his mistress. But merely having a pretty young lower-class actress to stay, being on close and familiar terms with her (she was heard to address him as 'Goosie'), and making the sort of fuss of her that Carroll did, was a truly startling thing for a man in his position to do. It is hardly surprising that Carroll's friends often glossed nervously over the subject.

Sometimes, too, people were genuinely confused. Ruth Waterhouse, who knew Carroll as a little girl, recalled how he was very much interested in the 'little Bowman girls ... especially in Isa':

> ... he was very anxious that I should meet her, but of course she was on the stage and he was afraid my parents might object. You must remember that this was sixty years ago when actresses occupied a very different position to what they do now ... So, in order that my parents might see for themselves what a very nice little girl Isa was, he invited them to meet her at dinner ... Later my mother said that as a dinner party it had not been a great success but she and my father had enjoyed it and been very much amused. ... You can see it all – Mr. Dodgson, never very happy in the society of grown-ups, the poor shy little girl of twelve, and my parents (both of them very good company) doing their best to make themselves agreeable.[22]

Carroll's diaries reveal, however, that he only met Ruth, then aged 10, when Isa was a 'nice little girl' of 18. Ruth had been mystified by Isa's reluctance to play games with her, and seems not to have realised she was not the child she was introduced as. Ruth's parents, Mr and Mrs Gamlen, were no doubt amused at having dinner with the reverend and his 'stunner', whom they had to pretend was a child. They probably never told Ruth the real story.

Others, primmer or less good-natured than the Gamlens,

were more concerned at this dizzying display of walking on the edge of social acceptability. They felt Carroll risked overstepping the mark. Carroll's sister Mary, married to a clergyman, wrote him a distressed letter about his many friendships with women in 1893. Mary's letter has disappeared, but Carroll's detailed response has often, bizarrely, been quoted to 'prove' that Mary fretted about his friendships with little girls. If only, as Mary might have said today. The women referred to were 27 and 23 years old, and Carroll wrote, 'I don't think it at all advisable to enter into any controversy about it. There is no reasonable probability that it would modify the views either of you or of me. ...'

He then went on to criticise gossips, adding:

> The only two tests I now apply to such a question as to the having some particular girl-friend as a guest are, first, my own conscience, to settle whether I feel it to be entirely innocent and right, in the sight of God; secondly the parents of my friend, to settle whether I have their full approval for what I do.
>
> You need not be shocked at my being spoken against. Anybody, who is spoken about at all, is sure to be spoken against by somebody, and any action, however innocent in itself, is liable, and not at all unlikely, to be blamed by somebody. If you limit your actions in life to things that nobody can possibly find fault with, you will not do much![23]

He had worked out to his own satisfaction that he was morally in the right, and so he was not prepared to curtail his activities. His frequent meetings and outings, including a weekend jaunt with the married 30-something Constance Burch, continued to raise eyebrows, not least those of Mr Burch, perhaps, since he called on Carroll not long afterwards.[24] Carroll's diary does not record what they talked about.

He noted his outings with women down in the briefest and

dullest of ways in his diary, and just a few descriptions survive to bring them to life. One, written to a beloved child-friend called Enid, describes an extraordinary day Carroll spent with 23 year-old May Miller. That he could write about it to a 10-year-old, knowing her mother would almost certainly read the letter, shows how confident he was in his own moral rightness. It also gives a glimpse of the irresponsible fun he could offer his lady friends when he felt like it.

He told Enid how he and May took a steamer from Eastbourne to Brighton to visit Carroll's sister Henrietta. On the way, just for fun, they deliberately got themselves drenched by the rough waves that slopped over the side of the boat. It was, Carroll told Enid, like being slapped by a large warm blanket. Not surprisingly, on reaching Brighton, they were soaked to the skin, so, skipping the visit to Henrietta, they returned to Eastbourne. There, they went to Carroll's rooms, and May changed into the maid's outfit while her own clothes dried. Then the two of them had a tête-à-tête dinner together in the evening. 'And she did look so pretty in the maid's Sunday-gown!' Carroll commented to Enid.

'"What stupid little adventures!"' I hear Enid muttering to herself. Well, I can't help it, my pet. These are *true*. If I were to invent some, why they wouldn't be ad-ventures, you know. They would be in-ventures, which is quite a different thing …'[25]

It is well known that Carroll never married. Could it be possible that he remained a bachelor in order to leave the way clear for his adventures with numerous young ladies? Whatever the larger picture, it is unlikely to be straightforward.

In practical terms, marriage had always been difficult for him. Sworn to celibacy while he stayed at Christ Church, his heavy family responsibilities and the lack of family money would have made it hard for him to abandon his job and its secure income. For various reasons, to be discussed in later chapters, it was difficult for him to become a vicar – the usual procedure for men in his position who wanted to marry. What is more, marriage would probably have brought even more dependants. Carroll had seen his father burdened with 11 children, including seven sisters, the responsibility for whose welfare had now been passed to him. Bachelor life at Christ Church, for all its faults, offered ample free time to pursue his own ideas without the distractions of a wife and family. As he had so very many close relatives, loneliness was the least of his problems.

Yet this is where we come up against one of the startling contradictions that bedevil the study of Carroll. If he was so charming and so at ease with women, if he had so many loving lady friends, why did his diaries in earlier life never refer to women whom he thought interesting or attractive? The special days (ones that he said that he 'marked with a white stone' usually represented happy times with children, interesting excursions, or meetings with important people – not meetings with women. Where are the love affairs, the infatuations? Where are the private musings which one might expect from a man who was so adept at dealing with women and who enjoyed their company so much?

The missing diaries from his teens and into his early twenties may have been franker than his later ones, but they have gone. He is also known to have kept separate notebooks for some matters omitted from his main adult diary, such as the matter of the mathematical lecture referred to in Chapter 2. Few such notebooks survive and, for obvious reasons, nobody knows what was in the missing ones; we can only guess.

The adult diaries are circumspect. Delicate matters, when mentioned at all, are referred to obliquely, as though he feared his words might be read. He barely mentions his feelings on the death of his beloved father, for instance, even though he later described this event as the greatest sadness of his life. In 1866, he dined twice with his Uncle Skeffington and, 'on each occasion we had a good deal of conversation about Wilfred, and about A.L. – it is a very anxious subject.'[26] He never said any more about this, and despite much conjecture, nobody has ever discovered who 'A.L.' was.

So it is more than possible that any notes on his private feelings or intimate personal life were kept in a form which has not come down to us, while the diary, cross-referenced and written up from notes, was maintained to record more mundane matters. However, there are enough hints and suggestions over the spread of Carroll's writings to make the case that he had at least one love affair, and that, far from being a joy for him, it was a disaster, and affected the way he lived the rest of his life.

According to Collingwood, Carroll started writing his diary when he was nine years old,[27] but the earliest surviving volume dates from 1855, when he was 23. The early adult diaries indicate that at this time, like many young men, he wanted to have an interesting life, and broaden his horizons. He was establishing his career, and he hoped to meet celebrities, create art, and write something worth publishing.

His letters to family and friends are full of lively humour and quaint details, illustrated with comical pen-and-ink cartoons. They contain little of the moralism and none of the eccentricity of his later life, and show him to have been cheerful, smart, energetic and receptive. He saw the funny side of life, and eagerly collected curious trifles and new ideas.

A marked change occurred during his late twenties. His diaries are missing between 1858 and 1862, and almost no letters remain from that time. When the diary resumed in 1862, Carroll was 30, and the diary's emotional tone is markedly different from before. It is more sombre, and anguished prayers for forgiveness from sin appear from time to time. He gives no details of what this sin was, but he pleaded with God to, 'help me to live to Thee. Help me to overcome temptation: help me to live as in Thy sight: help me to remember the coming hour of death. For of myself I am utterly weak, and vile, and selfish.

Lord, I believe that Thou canst do all things: oh deliver me from the chains of sin. For Christ's sake. Amen.'[28] A few weeks later he added, 'Mar. 13. Amen, amen.'

These and other similar prayers were not primarily impassioned outpourings of inner feelings. He did not treat his diary as a confidante. The prayers probably mark his spiritual progress in rejecting whatever his sin was. He would have renewed them on the dates when he added 'Amen'.

He never expressed despair of this type in any other surviving diaries, even though as a rector's son he had been raised to consider his sins. He was naturally inclined to be positive, not negative, but this time he apparently could not resolve his difficulty. Since other documents show that his problem was not financial or familial, it could have been religious, sexual, emotional or a mixture of all three.

If sexual, it did not torment him before the break in his diary record; so what was then delicately termed 'self-abuse' was probably not to blame. Few men who had been through public school at that time could have remained innocent of that particular 'sin'. Religion had bothered him for a while, and religious concerns had been expressed vaguely before, yet nothing he had previously written displays the sense of corrosive guilt and shame of these particular entries.

It has also been suggested by some commentators that the prayers were to do with little girls. Yet although he liked children's company, he never expressed the slightest concern or anxiety about his feelings for them at any stage of his life. He was always glad to have children's company, and had at the time been just as concerned with 'handsome' little Harry Liddell as with Alice Liddell or her sisters.

So what clues exist to suggest what chastened him so much? Stuart Collingwood did not want to dwell on unhappy matters in his admiring chronicle. Yet, in throwaway remarks, Collingwood did touch gently on difficulties which readers (including

Carroll's friends) may themselves have remembered. The gentlemanly Collingwood might have expected that any decent chaps who knew of past problems would take the hint and keep quiet.

His most intriguing remark refers to a collection of Carroll's serious poems, *Three Sunsets*, which was published in the 1890s. Its most emotional and heartfelt poems were written during the diary 'black-out' period of 1858–62. Collingwood wrote: 'One cannot read this little volume without feeling that the shadow of some disappointment lay over Lewis Carroll's life. Such I believe to have been the case, and it was this that gave him his wonderful sympathy with all who suffered.' A 'disappointment' would usually mean a sadness in emotional life, and Collingwood urged his readers to hold back and not 'lift the veil' on this. He expressed the hope that Carroll had forgotten his pain in Paradise.[29]

All this aroused some interest at the time, and some of the poems in the book do suggest sadness and disappointment. It is tempting to see them as straight autobiography, but they are not. Poetry uses imagery, allegory and fancy to convey its meaning, and autobiography is what it says. They are not the same. Yet Carroll's works at this time do offer a repetition of certain ideas and themes, showing that particular issues were indubitably on his mind during this difficult period. These themes are both unusual and consistent, and for this reason it is worth considering how they could have related to his life.

The title work of *Three Sunsets* was first published in 1861 and revised almost immediately. It originally had the curious title 'Dream of Fame', ironically picking up a reference in *Idylls of the King* by Carroll's favourite poet, Tennyson: 'Man dreams of fame, while woman wakes to love.' In Tennyson's poem, Merlin stupidly loves the treacherous Vivien. He reveals to her his secret charm, and is viciously betrayed:

And shrieking out 'O fool!' the harlot leapt

> Adown the forest, and the thicket closed
> Behind her, and the forest echoed 'fool.'

Carroll's long poem describes a man falling passionately in love with a woman, being deprived of her, and becoming so obsessed that he loses all dignity and emotional connection with normal society. Above all, he loses the mental independence which characterises his 'manhood, strength and pride', and behaves instead like a lovestruck loser. He ultimately dies a stupid and pointless death.

The poem is not at all sympathetic to the man. He is weak, because he has allowed his feelings to overwhelm and destroy him. Yet Carroll's description of how it feels to be instantly love-smitten by the woman in the poem is precise and oddly poignant, and suggests that he knew what it felt like.

> He saw her once, and in the glance
> A moment's glance of meeting eyes
> His heart stood still in sudden trance
> He trembled with a sweet surprise. ...

Later in the poem, when the man realizes he cannot have his beloved, Carroll observes that only *children* will accept this deluded and bereft creature as he roams around like some grieving animal, daydreaming obsessively about his love, 'half in Fancy's sunny trance/and half in Misery's aching void.'

Another poem, 'Stolen Waters', was written just a few months later, and this tells of a man being degradingly seduced by a tempting and immoral woman. Although Carroll does not refer to Tennyson's *Idylls* in this poem, the first half of the poem exactly echoes the theme of Merlin's downfall. The main character, like Merlin, is entranced by the woman's apparent beauty and sweet words, and, like Merlin, stupidly reveals his secret heart to her. Like Vivien, she betrays him. He flees, and becomes so disconnected from God that he ceases, night-marishly, to feel like his real self. (Carroll wrote this within weeks of telling the original story of *Alice in Wonderland* which is also famously concerned with problems of identity.) Even-tually, the disoriented sexual sinner comes across a beautiful, innocent little girl with long, golden hair who offers him a revelation of redemption.

First, she is seen full of life. In the next verse, she is dying, with patient resignation. In the third verse she is viewing the lifeless body which has taken 'her' place in the world. She herself has reached the Kingdom of Heaven sinless and undefiled: she is an angel. The poem's narrator feels his human heart returning at this revelatory vision. He decides he will shun evil and spend his time with children in the future, no matter how mad people think he is.

By contrast, the 'Stolen Waters' of the poem's title refers to a prostitute, and comes from Proverbs, Chapter IX:

16. Whoso is simple, let him turn in hither; and as for him that wanteth understanding, she said to him,
17. Stolen waters are sweet, and bread eaten in secret is pleasant.
18. But he knoweth not that the dead are there; and that her guests are in the depths of hell.

Originally printed in the magazine *College Rhymes* in 1862, 'Stolen Waters' stands out from the surrounding work because of its unusual subject matter. Obscure though it is, it was as explicit as it was then possible to be about forbidden love with a woman.

A third poem of 1868, written in retrospect, continues the theme of being unwillingly chained to sinful pleasure. Like the lover in 'Stolen Waters', the narrator cannot live either with or without his problem. Like the character in 'Dream of Fame', he yearns desperately, but cannot have. His poisoned love wrecks his life, and ruins his view of himself:

> The spells that bound me with a chain,
> Sin's stern behest to do,
> Till Pleasure's self, invoked in vain,
> a heavy burden grew. ...

He does not identify 'Pleasure's self'.

Just as in the earlier two poems, this poem also has suicidal elements. Once again the solution includes the sight of pure and innocent girls, close to God. Additionally, in this case, a mother-figure also appears in a dream. And again, Carroll sees the female child and pure-minded femininity as an antidote to Sin.

Crucially, too, the problem in all these poems is with *love*, not just sex. It was the irreconcilable conflict between good and evil which tormented this deeply religious man: the conflict between purity and impurity, and whether one made the personal choice to live in a moral or an immoral way. The vast underworld of sex outside marriage in Victorian England was of a commodity which had everything to do with money, much to do with class and little to do with love. Yet 'Stolen Waters' and 'Dream of Fame' suggest a genuine *love*, a painful, one-sided and degrading *love*.

> Oh, blind mine eye that would not trace
> Oh, deaf mine ear that would not heed-
> The mocking smile upon her face,
> The mocking voice of greed! ...
> True love gives true love of the best.
> 'Then take' I cried, 'my heart to thee!'
> The very heart from out my breast
> I plucked, I gave it willingly. ...

The poems consistently express a confusion about how one may dare to love sexually outside marriage, since impure and forbidden love may condemn one to both a worldly and an eternal hell. In a more practical sense, a man in Carroll's position with a secret girlfriend – particularly one that he paid – would risk exposure or blackmail. Any scandal would taint innocent family members, or friends who continued to be in touch with him.[30] Marriage to such a woman would be out of the question even if legally possible.

Yet there is more. People usually get over bad love affairs, however difficult those love affairs may have been at the time. But Carroll was tormented by the horror of his 'sin' for many years, and references he made in later years suggest that he was affected by it for the rest of his life. Falling in love with, or even fornication with, immoral women was sinful, but it was not a major sin – not like, for instance, flouting the Ten Commandments. Much as it may upset some Carroll fans to consider it, the possibility exists that Carroll was tormented by the idea of a more serious sin than fornication.

Then as now, there would have been married women around who wanted the excitement of a lover – the flattery, the fun and perhaps the gifts that went along with it. An inexperienced, celibate and romantic young man would not have been so very difficult to ensnare. A case has been made by Karoline Leach that Carroll could have been having an adulterous affair,[31] but her notion of Mrs Liddell as the other party makes little sense. Leach suggests that the idea of adultery is backed up by Carroll's two separate diary quotations of Psalm 51 in connection with his sin – the psalm is David's broken-hearted plea for forgiveness for his adultery with someone else's wife. Carroll himself also referred in his diary to his 'corrupt affection', which suggests that something about his love, either for God or for someone else, was essentially wrong.

Years later, too, in August 1885, Carroll wrote mysteriously to his friend Mrs Feilding (who had suggested he write a religious book for children), that 'I may perhaps some day try to write such a book for children as you want. But I feel much about it as David did about building the Temple.'[32]

To someone as profoundly religious as Carroll, committing adultery would be to flout a holy commandment and deliberately defy God. To encourage another person to embrace evil would be a major and tormenting sin. To yearn passionately to *become* evil would be utterly disorientating, going against everything in which he believed. Well might one agree with Alice as she asked, 'Who am I?' in her amoral Wonderland.

As well as writing these poems, Carroll pasted two poems by Christina Rossetti in his personal scrapbook during the mid-1860s. The first, 'Who Shall Deliver Me?', is preoccupied with agonizing feelings of sin and lonely self-hatred. The second, 'Amor Mundi', again uses the theme of a man stupidly seduced, and bitterly regretting it. The refined Miss Rossetti was presumably not writing from personal experience in this latter poem, and this is another reason why it is important to remember that Carroll's poems, too, are unlikely to be a straightforward account of something which happened in his life. What Carroll's behaviour does show is that his concerns with the intertwined issues of secret neediness, love, sex and pain, and a particular symbolism relating to these, were pushing him to express himself repeatedly at the time.

Carroll's parallel theme of little girls offering the prospect of moral redemption is not often found in poetry of the period, yet the idea is something upon which Carroll also dwelt, not only in these poems but also in other works, such as his poem 'Beatrice', of 1862. This work will be examined more closely in Chapter 6 in connection with *Alice*, but there is no reason to imagine that Carroll would have repeatedly used this concept in his small number of serious poems if he had not believed it had some relevance to himself.

During the 1860s, Carroll's diaries recorded an increasing concentration on the company of children, and this apparently led to a larger decision to embrace a lifestyle that concentrated on 'pure' little girls, as though it would somehow benefit him. By 1862, when the surviving diary begins, he was already photographing fewer celebrities, still lifes or art works. He was spending more time with children, particularly, but certainly not exclusively, his nearest neighbours, the Liddells.

In the depressions which Collingwood mentions,[33] little girls' company usually cheered Carroll up. With them, he could be loved, admired and soothed as sinlessly as was humanly possible. He could lay aside his adult male miseries by teaching them gentle games, talking to them about their dolls and toys, singing songs with them – almost as if he were a child himself.

Perhaps, with modern psychological knowledge, one may conjecture that it was in his need for the company of children over the next 20 years that he channelled intense yearnings for romantic love that were denied other outlets; that their feminine company helped him to suppress an insistent, despised sexuality of his own.

His pretty little girls innocently kissed him, held his hand and sat on his knees. He never 'romped' with them, and upsetting them was the last thing he wanted to do. So he need not feel guilty about his need for chaste physical affection from them – nor risk it escalating into anything else. If he was afraid of being seduced, he was safe, for his small child-friends could never deliberately seduce him, nor anyone. They were beautiful, but their purity was the antithesis of predatory female sexuality.

After the death of his father, when he was in his late thirties, there was a further subtle change of emphasis. As he shouldered his father's burden as head of the family, he donned ever more of the old man's upright moralism too. At this time, he seemed to decide that younger girls could sinlessly offer the sight of beautiful human bodies which he so badly wanted. As observed in earlier chapters, his intense interest in all aspects of the human body was lifelong, and even his childhood drawings demonstrated a startlingly mature and acute observation of the human form. As he grew older, his increasing preoccupation with the finer details of 'morality' began to make it difficult for him to satisfy this interest in what he felt was an unequivocally moral way.

In his unpublished essay 'Theatre Dress',[34] written when he was 56, Carroll said that men had a duty to turn away if they felt themselves being stimulated by the bodies of flimsily clad women. He did not like the look of the bony and muscular bodies of men and boys, so that left little girls' bodies as the only ones that he could view with joy and without evil.

Unfortunately, this idea has done his reputation no good in our own very different times, and his anxiety that others may fail to acknowledge his purity of intention has sometimes been taken as sign of a guilty conscience towards little girls. Seen in context, it is more likely that his anxiety was about the safety of his soul: others *must* acknowledge and validate his 'purity' to confirm that his evil and undisciplined past was behind him.

His worries occurred mainly when the 'little girls' were at or approaching the age of consent. The letters he wrote then are most often quoted today to suggest that Carroll had an unwholesome interest in children. Some make uncomfortable reading to the modern eye, but not, as we shall see, to the eyes of his contemporaries.

In the 1860s and 1870s, he photographed many children in family settings, including some nude photographs of under-sevens which he (and their families) considered perfectly virtuous. By the late 1870s, he had become considerably more moralistic than in his younger days, and had not relaxed his efforts to live a godly life. As he grew older and less susceptible, he started seeking sinless ways of admiring older female flesh. At last he himself was no longer young, and the importance of 'romance', as he put it, was fading from his life. He was now capable, with care, of taking a genuinely aesthetic view of the female body which so fascinated him.

He still never sought adult nude models, although he did possess modest drawings of adult female nudes. As a man who had mixed a good deal with artists, he would have been well aware that women who posed nude for artists were not unaware of their own charms, and there would always be the possibility of temptation or seduction so long as any spark of life lingered in the male spectator.

But unawakened young girls were incapable of deliberately tempting anyone. So if he played his own part in keeping his thoughts pure, then drawing or photographing slightly older girls would be, to his way of thinking, a celebration of God's handiwork in the most harmless and pleasant way, for 'no imperfect representations of life ... could take the place of life itself', as Collingwood put it.[35] By middle age, Carroll felt very earnestly that he had finally achieved trustworthiness. He had worked hard at it, and desperately wanted others to acknowledge it.

A correspondence has survived from 1879 between Carroll and a Mr and Mrs Mayhew about photographing their three daughters, aged 7 (Janet), 11 (Ethel) and 13 (Ruth), which shows how his mind was working – and, even more interestingly, what people thought at the time.

The Mayhews did not mind Janet being photographed without clothes, but were more concerned about Ethel, who was approaching the then legal age of consent – 12 years old. Photographing the oldest, Ruth, in any state of undress would normally be out of the question. In his first letter, Carroll asked to take nude pictures of all the children, saying, 'If I did not believe I could take such pictures without any lower motive than a pure love of Art, I would not ask it.' He continued in similar vein, but the Mayhews refused his request.

Carroll wrote again to emphasize the moral nature of his request. At the end of this letter he added, 'If Ruth and Ethel bring Janet, there is really no need for her [Mrs Mayhew] to come as well – that is if you can trust me to keep my promise of abiding strictly by the limits laid down. If you can't trust my word, then please never bring or send any of the children again. ...'[36]

The Mayhews' response is lost, but his next letter said:

After my last had gone, I wished to recall it and take out the sentence in which I had quite gratuitously suggested the possibility that you might be unwilling to trust me to photograph the children by themselves in undress. And now I am more than ever sorry I wrote it ... For I hope you won't think me very fanciful in saying I should have no pleasure in doing any such pictures, now that I know I am ~~not thought fit for~~ [sic] only permitted such a privilege ~~except~~ [sic] on condition of being under chaperonage. I had rather do no more pictures of your children except in full dress: please forgive all the trouble I have given you about it.[37]

That was the end of the correspondence. He was bitterly upset at not being trusted.

Any modern reader might imagine that the Mayhews would steer decidedly clear in future of any middle-aged man who got so heated about photographing their young daughters nude. But actually, a few years later, they all made it up, and Carroll became friends with the youngest Mayhew daughter, Margaret, aged about 10. What is more, in the early 1950s, Margaret wrote a brief memoir about the incident for the biographer Derek Hudson. This is what she wrote:

My mother raised no objection to my youngest sister, aged about six or seven, being photographed in the nude or in very scanty clothing … but when permission was asked to photograph her elder sister, who was probably then about eleven, in a similar state, my mother's strict sense of Victorian propriety was shocked and she refused the request. Mr. Dodgson was offended and the friendship ceased. …

She goes on to describe how Carroll's friendship with her family revived via a mutual friend. To her joy her parents let her spend some 'unforgettably wonderful' times in Carroll's company. The quarrel was never mentioned, but after she grew up, she read the letters of which parts are quoted above. She felt they showed 'how essentially kind and courteous and punctilious [Carroll] was, and that he felt he must be careful in dealing with a lady of such strict Victorian principles', adding that, 'The perusal of them touched me very much.'[38]

None of this will stop many today psychoanalysing what Carroll supposedly 'really' meant from the perspective of our own entirely different culture. Nobody now can be blamed for failing to understand the ways in which other times were different from our own. But Carroll lived in pre-Freudian times when the suppression and denial of sexuality was seen as a Christian virtue, not only by himself but by many other people. To appreciate God's beautiful work in the human body was entirely acceptable, but to contaminate sinless purity with sex would be to embrace and invite the Devil into one's soul. That was something he would not do.

It makes no sense today to eliminate sex from one's life, but that was not so in Carroll's culture. Every scrap of evidence points to the idea that his little girls offered Carroll elements of the idealized romantic relationships he craved, *but without the actual sex* – and that was how he wanted it. The little girls who did not take to him – and some did find him boring, soppy or exasperating – never felt threatened. If any of them wanted to continue with him after they grew up – in the right pure spirit of course – then he felt blessed to receive sinless kisses and cuddles from real women. They had always to understand where the boundaries lay, and, to him, they must *always* present themselves as sinless 'children'. As indicated earlier, Carroll is often presented as a lifelong virgin. There is a significant possibility that he was not; but sexual relationships seem to have represented pain, shame and misery for him, and he was probably celibate for many years. There is a great deal of evidence that it was imperative for him to see himself as a good person who could master his body and live in a pure and Godly way.

In his later years, he certainly spiced his life up with as many affectionate and respectable women as he could and looked after them tenderly. He had at last succeeded in casting himself in the public mind as a prim, harmless old fellow, and accordingly gathered around himself many intelligent young ladies who were happy to kiss him. As he wrote to his friend Mrs Poole, when boldly inviting her to dine alone with him one evening, 'Child society is very delightful to me, but I confess that grown-up society is much more interesting!'[39]

The mischievous iconoclast in him loved to tease 'Mrs Grundy' about his lady friends, but that was because Mrs Grundy was getting everything wrong, to his way of thinking. Some people might gossip about the kisses he was getting in return for his love and care. Others might think he was odd – and indeed he was odd. But, as he said to his sister Mary, he had settled it in his mind, and he knew he was all right.

His unfailing kindness and protectiveness to children showed how he cared for the helpless, and since they themselves wanted his company, and since his religion was genuinely and manifestly his mainspring, he was welcome in many homes. By the end of his life, he felt at peace with himself, whatever some people think about him now, or thought of him then. As he said to Mary, '... the opinion of "people" in general is absolutely worthless as a test of right and wrong."[40]

And, as Karoline Leach perceptively remarks in *In the Shadow of the Dreamchild*, 'Crudity sometimes repelled him, but … he was … deeply responsive to the physical world around him, fascinated by and curious about the female body. Physical contact with other human beings was essential to him. To hug and cuddle and kiss a beloved gave his life warmth and meaning. He found beauty and godliness in the naked human form [and] saw the validity and morality of human relationships as defined entirely by "love."'[41]

In 1928, Alice Hargreaves, (née Liddell), sold the original "Alice" book which Carroll had hand-written and illustrated for her. There was considerable public interest in the sale, and the "Illustrated London News" magazine reprinted some of Carroll's endearingly amateurish illustrations, thereby allowing its readers to compare them with Tenniel's more famous images.

'Children are three-fourths of my life'

Children

For I think it is Love,
For I feel it is Love,
For I'm sure it is nothing but Love!

Sylvie and Bruno

Lewis Carroll made no secret of how important children were to him. His family biographer Stuart Collingwood was sure that this was entirely to his credit. He devoted two whole chapters of his book to his uncle's love of children and also dedicated the book to what were known as his 'child-friends'. The devoted nephew summed up Carroll's attitude in one word – 'Love'. 'As *he* read everything in its light' he wrote, 'so it is only in its light that *we* can properly understand *him*.'[1]

The question is, what is meant by 'love'? Carroll told very few people about his inner feelings, but he once explained to a younger colleague, Arthur Girdlestone, what children meant to him. Girdlestone had called in to Carroll's rooms one evening, and perhaps he had caught him at a vulnerable time, because he recollected that he seemed tired. But when he commented on a newly taken picture of a baby which Carroll had propped onto a reading stand, the older man brightened, and said, "'That is the baby of a girl-friend of mine.'"

'He said that in the company of very little children his brain enjoyed a rest which was startlingly recuperative,' added Girdle-stone, 'If he had been working too hard or had tired his brain in any way, to play with children was like an actual material tonic on his whole system.' Carroll went on to say that he found it easiest to get in tune with children when he was tired with other work. Girdlestone responded that he did not understand children himself, and he asked Carroll if he did not sometimes find them boring. 'He had been standing up for most of the time, and when I asked him that, he sat down suddenly. "They are three-fourths of my life," he said. "I cannot understand how anyone could be bored by little children. I think when you are older, you will come to see this – I hope you'll come to see it.""[2]

Reading Carroll's diaries in his middle age, it is easy to believe that children were indeed 'three-fourths' of his life. Particularly when he was on holiday at Eastbourne, the diary entries sometimes seem like a roll call of his 'child-friends'. They were friends whom he always took perfectly seriously; just as seriously as he took the adults in his life. Yet the extent to which he focused on them was really unusual, and few other public figures have made such efforts to obtain their company. So why were they so important to him, and what did the love of them represent in his complicated mind?

The previous chapter suggests one important reason, which is that of innocent diversion from romantic love, but it is far from being the only one. Collingwood had plenty other sugges-tions in his book. Carroll was by nature a teacher, he said. Also, children appealed to him aesthetically. In a veiled reference to the nude photographs, he added that his uncle preferred 'life as God made it' to any imperfect representations of life created by a painter. Yet, he continued, although Carroll loved the human form, the soul attracted him more.

It does not seem to have occurred to Collingwood that Carroll may also have simply liked children's company for its own sake. Carroll made no secret of the fact that adult social prattle bored him. He loathed the people he met in 'fashionable drawing-rooms, who conceal all such feelings as they may chance to possess beneath the impenetrable mask of a conventional placidity.'[3] Children's spontaneous and sincere company offered the chance to express the playfulness which was so much part of his own nature, and this was undoubtedly a part of the truth that was hidden in his remark to Girdlestone.

Both Carroll and his child friends adored toys and gadgets. He – and they – also loved jokes, humour and imaginary things: ghosts, witches, fairies, charades. The capacious cupboards in his rooms were full of treasures which his child-friends were to remember with delight. They included an early typewriter and some beautiful musical boxes, together with a mechanical 'orguinette' – a kind of home barrel organ (which worked much like a pianola) – on which he sometimes gave concerts in reverse by putting the rolls in the wrong way round.

His niece, Irene Dodgson Jacques, looking back to her childhood, remembered him sitting beside her on the carpet happily playing with a marvellous bear that opened and closed its mouth as it spoke.[4] A bat named Bob, which worked with the use of elastic bands, caused real chaos on one occasion when it 'flew' into the wrong place, something which Carroll probably enjoyed as much as the children did. He also invented novelties himself. Some were useful, like a contraption for writing in bed at night in the dark. Others were just for fun, like a gadget still in the possession of the Dodgson descendants which makes it appear as though a string is being pulled through the middle of one's nose.

Carroll also created endless riddles, puzzles and domestic games, and loved to tell stories about doll and animal characters. The gentleman in his toy-strewn college rooms was perfectly recognizable as the youth who had loved creating puppet stories for his little brothers and sisters, and the grown

man who had taken considerable trouble to make a portrait of
Tim, the well-used boy doll of his childhood.

There have been many condescending remarks made about
this characteristic of his, as though a love of childish things
somehow prevented him from being a proper adult. Virginia
Woolf thought that childhood had lodged within Carroll 'whole
and entire',[5] and in her view this was an '"impediment' which
starved him of maturity; she described him as slipping through
the grown-up world like a shadow.[6] But it is unfair to suggest
that he could not handle adult life. It is probably true that, as a
lifelong bachelor, he failed to acquire the kind of maturity that
comes from sharing life with another person, but he undeniably
saw himself as a family man. As the head of his family, he worked
conscientiously not only for his brothers and sisters but also for
many cousins and friends in a way that showed full practical
understanding of the ways of the grown-up world, even though
it was a world into which he did not always choose to fit himself.

Being with children allowed Carroll to inhabit a special
in-between realm set well apart from care and sadness, and he
felt at home in it. It is very noticeable that he offered his child-
friends some of the things that he himself would have liked
as a child, and still liked as an adult. He preferred children to
visit individually, so that he could give them personal attention,
something which had inevitably been very lacking in his own
huge family. During their visits, they, too, had nobody to focus
upon but him.

He shared their joy as they accompanied him to the glittering world of the theatre, and on their walks and expeditions
he saw the sights of the town through their fresh eyes. They went
out to tea together, and had long conversations. Sometimes they
discussed moral and religious matters, and read the Bible; the
latter only in gentle and kindly ways, for Carroll hated moralistic church-going which he felt darkened a child's bright faith.
Sometimes his child-friends put up with him talking about

mathematics. Occasionally, they even enjoyed talking to him about mathematics.

Carroll was particularly fascinated by stage children; and perhaps his interest in them ties up with what has been described as his own extraordinary sense of the theatre. Perhaps he could have been an actor himself, if only it had been possible. But of course it never would have been possible, for so many reasons, including the central fact that neither his father nor mother would set foot in a theatre. Carroll was always delighted by stage childrens' pleasure in performance, and overjoyed to see them loving their work as professional actors. The theatre was a kind of enchanted dream world of stories come to life, and his child actor friends were part of the enchantment.

His photography was, in some ways, part of this dream world. Many people who were children in the 19th century recalled how they loathed their dull, scratchy restrictive clothes, their thick stockings and their badly-shaped shoes. If Carroll too had yearned for the freedom to discard his dreary woollies and re-enter the Garden of Eden, it would have been an impossible dream. But he could please his child-friends, and please himself, by offering them something a little like Eden: the chance to exchange the hateful clothes for fanciful and colourful costumes, or innocently discard them altogether.

But if he was such a child-lover, why did he only like girls, and not boys? In fact, he did not, as is often claimed, hate all boys. He had many male friends, and he got on well with some individual boys and youths. He cared a good deal for his brothers, and he took much time and trouble to help undergraduates who needed it. Despite the large difference in their ages, as mentioned in Chapter 3, he and the undergraduate Walter Rees tackled their stammering problem together. In his twenties, he made almost a surrogate little brother of Harry Liddell. He brought Harry along on outings, thought about him, wrote about him and took a real interest in his welfare.

Another boy with whom he had a good relationship was the writer George MacDonald's young son, Greville, one of the first children to read Carroll's original book about Alice. 'He was very dear,' recalled Greville later. 'There was a toy shop in Regent Street where he let us choose gifts, one of which will remain my own as long as memory endures. It was an unpainted wooden horse. I loved it as much as any girl her doll ...'[7]

Essentially, Carroll got on with individual boys with whom he had something in common, like Bert Coote, whom he met when Coote was 10. 'My sister and I were regular young imps,' Coote recalled later, 'and nothing delighted us more than to give imitations. ... but we never gave imitations of Lewis Carroll, or shared any joke in which he could not join – he was one of us, and never a grown up pretending to be a child ...'[8]

However, the happy little world that Carroll created with children tended very strongly to the feminine rather than the masculine. Nobody has (yet) written a serious book accusing him of being homosexual or a closet transvestite, but he has been described variously as womanish, tender, gentle, nun-like, shy or like a 'mother hen'. One friend described him weeping with emotion at the sight of the sea at sunset, and the preacher H P Liddon once found Carroll sobbing like a child in a cathedral, overcome by its beauty.[9] The ostentatiously manly qualities that were so important in Victorian social life left Carroll cold, and he rejected them. He shunned whiskers, moustache and beard, and he did not crop his hair short or smoke a pipe like other men. He did not go out game-shooting, and he loathed the fishing which his younger brothers loved. He was an anti-vivi-sectionist, and he had no enthusiasm for war. Even his interest in sport was, at best, lukewarm.

This failure to enjoy hearty, manly interests often stopped him relaxing with boys. So, perhaps, did his rough and gruelling experiences in the all-boy milieu of Rugby School which had given him such a horrible three years. 'As a salmon should be on a gravel path, so should I be at a boys' school,' he once memorably remarked.[10] On the other hand, tales of fairies, pictures of pretty children, dainty outfits, light music, soft girly colours and senti- mental poetry all entranced him. He was very proud of a syrupy set of verses he wrote in *Sylvie and Bruno* which begins:

> Say, what is the spell, when her fledglings are cheeping,
>   That lures the bird home to her nest?
> Or wakes the tired mother, whose infant is weeping,
>   To cuddle and croon it to rest?
> What the magic that charms the glad babe in her arms,
>   Till it coos with the voice of the dove?
> 'Tis a secret, and so let us whisper it low
>   And the name of the secret is Love!

His pastel-coloured emotional tastes were not for everyone, and it is not entirely surprising that one of the tougher little girls he knew, Ursula Mallam, according to an unpublished family anecdote, thought that Lewis Carroll was 'soppy'.

Carroll also had a strong need for loving attention. He needed his child-friends to respond kindly and affectionately towards him, and little girls were more at ease expressing affection than boys were. As already discussed in the last chapter, Carroll believed that little girls were pure and non-sexual. They were good moral company for him, and with them he could expe- rience the tenderness he needed without descending into the nightmare of tangled love and sex.

He had a great deal of love to offer, for beneath his stiff public exterior, he was a most affectionate man. Girl after girl testified to his kindness, understanding and sweetness, and recalled how much they appreciated it. 'So gentle and kindly a nature, whose friendship enriched my childhood', remembered Ella Bickersteth. 'My parents' loved friend, as well as my adored one', said Winifred Holiday, 'We cried when he went away', recalled Dymphna Ellis. And Ethel Rowell wrote in 1943, 'For me, now forty years on ... I think my love for him is as fresh and confident as in the days when I first in my childishness signed myself to him as "your very loving friend".'[11]

Edith Maitland had a particularly touching memory of him sitting on a bench and reading her the story of the Ugly Duckling, a tale which 'made a great impression on me, being very sensitive about my ugly little self'. Carroll, typically, did not discuss whether she was ugly or not. He made sure she knew that he loved her as she was, and impressed on her how it was much better to be good, truthful and concerned with others, than pretty, selfish and disagreeable. He reassured her about her looks by calling her 'Ducky' and cheered her up by reminding her that she, too, might turn out to be a beautiful swan. How happy she was, she recalls, 'to see the well known figure in his cap and gown coming so swiftly, with his kind smile ready to welcome the "Ugly Duckling" sitting in the grass!'[12]

In all his friendships with boys or girls, it was vitally important to Carroll that the children themselves wanted to be with him. If their love was shallow or fleeting, he could deal with that; but it must be sincerely felt at the time and, as he said to his friend Mrs Richards, he did find it very sweet.[13] On the rare occasions that a child did not want to see him or be with him, he would not press the issue. When he first met Edith 'Dolly' Blakemore, she caused an enormous fuss, so he told her mother, 'I will gladly do without ever seeing her again, if only she will be happy again, poor little thing.'[14] He then offered suggestions about how to handle the over-emotional Dolly which showed genuine sympathy towards her but an equal determination not to let her set the rules. She seems to have been a strong-minded little girl, and Carroll recommended a few minutes of ignoring her when she misbe-haved: 'I wonder if you noticed, as I did, that when she thought you were not petting her quite enough, she roared a little louder to recall your attention?' he asked Dolly's mother.[15]

Eventually, the contrary-minded Dolly decided she did want to see him after all. She made him a pocket book and then began showering him with gifts. He replied to her personally, and showed how carefully he listened to her feelings by gently asking her mother to 'Please give my love and my best thanks to *Edith* (I call her so rather than "*Dolly*," believing that to be her own wish) …'.[16] And after this rocky start, he and Edith remained friends till the end of his life, when she was quite grown up.

Friendships with children also made it possible for him to bypass many of the confines of the class system which still ruled Victorian social life. Carroll did not rebel against the intensely snobbish social structure within which he lived, but he found many aspects of it stressful and tiresome. True, the class system was not as brutally rigid in his day as it had been in preceding centuries, but it was still a formidable and stuffy institution. The classes each had characteristics and customs which were distinguished from each other by countless nuances of accent, appearance, behaviour and dress, as well as by income. Anyone attempting to move between classes might find their efforts met with disapproval or even contempt from members of their own class.

Carroll slipped through the class barriers to mix with higher-class children when he chose to play the role of 'Lewis Carroll', the famous author, for their parents. Characteristically, he would not always agree to be shunted off with the children even in the grandest circles, and though he never liked being lionized, he did enjoy the mild thrill of occasionally mixing with the upper crust. In his accounts of the glittering social occasions he attended, his dislike of social chit-chat was forgotten, and he established some continuing friendships – an achievement which probably gave his family a certain satisfaction too.

Carroll's yearnings towards the stage also allowed him to move downwards in the class system towards theatrical children and their families. If they were respectable people, and not too much 'below' him, matters usually went well. Actors respected his knowledge of the theatre and his wide range of theatrical contacts, and there was always plenty to talk about. Of course, his friendliness to these 'lower' families was sometimes sniffed at by his social equals. The architect Harry R Mileham said that his cousin May was forbidden to continue visiting Carroll because 'her mother considered that the child's ear for the King's English was suffering through the rather mixed company'.[17] In other words, she felt that spending time with Carroll's stage friends was encouraging May to pick up accents and expressions 'below' those of a middle-class child.

Children of a considerably lower class than Carroll posed more of a problem. They were usually badly educated, so that their general knowledge and ability to converse would typically be well below that of higher-class children. They were sometimes referred to as the 'servant classes', as though servitude was bred into them. It was not true, but their manners were often rough, and their accents coarse. Carroll was not good at dealing with rough behaviour or rudeness in children. He was on good terms with the poor children in his father's parish, and often taught and entertained them, but, even with them, he had difficulties in keeping order when he needed to, and he did not seek very low-class children as friends.

As well as his difficulties in dealing with loud or boisterous behaviour, an equally important reason for his reluctance to befriend girls of much lower class is suggested in a letter that he wrote to his friend Beatrice Hatch. 'I should like to know, for curiosity, who that sweet-looking girl was, aged 12 ... speaking to you when I came up to wish you goodnight. I fear I must be content with her name only: the social gulf between us is probably too wide for it to be wise to make friends. Some of my little actress-friends are of a rather lower status than myself. But, below a certain line, it is hardly wise to let a girl have a "gentleman" friend – even one of 62!"[18] He was politely saying that people would assume that a gentleman would probably have indecent reasons for becoming friendly with a young girl so far outside his own social circle, and he wanted no part of that.

Carroll's diary descriptions of getting to know children are very interesting because they reveal something of how the middle-class social system operated at the time. What might be referred to as social networking in the mid-19th century depended almost entirely on personal introduction, or their presenting themselves in the appropriate social context.

Middle- and upper-class people did not tend to become friendly with strangers in a casual way. They relied upon having some point of mutual social contact to enable them to 'place' a stranger to see if they were a suitable sort of person for the family to know. Being related, however distantly, or having a mutual friend would usually be sufficient; or a stranger's title, or history of attending the right type of school or college would offer useful clues about the kind of person they were. There is a certain resonance to W S Gilbert's poem about two Englishmen being stranded together on a desert island, but never speaking in 30 years because they had no mutual acquaintances!

In this middle-class social structure, people did not always meet personally, but would sometimes call at each others' houses and leave their cards if they wished to establish or maintain a cordial relationship. They also complied with elaborate unwritten rules as to the precise degree of familiarity to show to others: whether a bow or a smile – or both – would suit a meeting in the street, for example.

Carroll detested conventional formality, and often said so, but his pattern of social behaviour conformed to the Victorian way of doing things. If he had kicked against the traces, it would have caused difficulties for him and may well have reflected badly on his family. His diaries often refer to spotting children that he thought seemed pleasant company, and then finding out who their parents were. As they were only children, he could usually smile at them or address them directly without an introduction, and he valued this human social contact. After this, he would present his credentials, or leave his card at the family home with a note to ask if it would be possible for him to get to know the children. The parents would consider his request, and sometimes they said yes, sometimes they said no. Sometimes they laid down conditions, such as that the children were only allowed to mix with people with certain religious views. Whatever their views, if they did not choose to know him, they said so, and that was the end of the matter.

For Carroll, his popularity with children was a striking social asset when it came to making adult friends. Once he was accepted on behalf of the children, the whole family, including its womenfolk, would be allowed to mix with him on a friendly basis. By the time the children grew up, he had become a familiar figure in everyone's lives. The children often lost interest in him as they got older, and, although he did not reject them, the feeling seems to have been mutual if they became conventional people to whom he was obliged to bow and raise his hat.

Today, though there is, of course, an extra element in how Carroll's friendships with little girls are perceived. The bottom line which any commentator must consider is whether there was anything untoward about them. Carroll's strong interest in little girls and his liking for portraying them nude runs directly counter to our own society's assumptions and unspoken rules. An enthusiasm for drawing or photographing children in the nude would be considered unacceptable today, and might possibly be considered a matter for the police.

It is only too easy for modern commentators to declare that Carroll's behaviour shows that he had paedophile instincts which he suppressed. But modern "'evidence' is based on the incorrect assumption that he and his contemporaries lived similar lives and held similar views to the ones we hold now – and they did not.

Yet, although it is only fair to judge Carroll by the standards of his time, not ours, he would also have been the first to agree that there is also a standard of right or wrong – 'good versus evil' – on which he must be held to account. Looking at the matter in these terms, there is not the slightest shred of evidence that he did anything out of line with pre-pubescent girls, and no indication that he had sexual feelings towards them. Taken as a whole, the documents suggest that he found late-teenage girls and grown women attractive, but that he struggled to suppress a sexual interest in them by concentrating on what he considered to be 'pure', that is, non-carnal aspects of femininity.

His reasons for yearning to be pure, considered in Chapter 4, were compatible with his celibate lifestyle. Once again, by modern standards, seeking out pure people as companions seems an odd thing to do, but it was not so in his own context and in his own times. He was a personal protégé of Pusey, who believed that virginity was the highest state of life. Many of his colleagues and friends, such as H P Liddon, were known to prize chastity as a high ideal. He was also, of course, sworn to celibacy himself.

Rather than being a closet paedophile, it seems that the intensity of Carroll's pursuit of little girls reflects the extent to which he sought an antidote to his feelings for women. With his loving child-friends, he could obtain loving, beautiful, feminine company which was neither tempting nor 'sinful'.

Those who are still convinced that he must have been a closet paedophile, suggest that his kindness and protectiveness was merely a public face, a kind of 'grooming' of children. In private, they presumably therefore think, he would have been different. Again, there is no evidence for this. Not one single recollection of any child indicates that he ever seemed like a threat to them or upset them: indeed, the exact opposite was true. Even more significantly, the discovery of his bank account, which he never imagined would be made public, has illuminated this aspect of his life in a way he never dreamed of.

Payments that he made show that he detested the idea of children, or indeed other helpless creatures, being abused. Privately, and without fuss, he gave financial support to an organization which caught and punished men who abused children. He also, equally privately and unfussily, contributed to many other charities which helped the helpless in other ways.

He was particularly concerned with the welfare of unprotected women and children of both sexes. Protectiveness was a personal characteristic which people remarked upon, and the way in which he lived his life also suggests that he had a horror of all forms of abuse.

When the behaviour of the Dodgson family in destroying so much documentation is closely examined, it also shows that they were confident that Carroll did not possess any disturbing material about children. They got rid of a great deal of material. The papers which Stuart Collingwood saw, and which no longer exist today, include 11 missing years of Carroll's diary – from the age of nine to the age of 23 (excluding the three Rugby years) – plus four-and-a-half years' worth of other diaries from his twenties, which cover times of religious and emotional upheaval in Carroll's life. The family also disposed of Carroll's letter register, covering tens of thousands of letters and their contents, and his photographic register, which listed details of every photograph that he took. They mutilated, erased and censored parts of the remaining diary volumes, apparently not long afterwards.

They were a very private family living in an era when privacy was greatly valued. They did not want later readers finding out anything about their family life, with its squabbles, dramas and crises, and they wished to present their famous brother to posterity in the most virtuous light possible. Yet, most significantly, in this entire gigantic welter of concealment there is no suggestion at all that the family found anything to make them feel concerned about Carroll's relationships with little girls. On the contrary, the exact opposite is the case. Collingwood's book, which spoke for the whole family, emphasized Carroll's child-friendships for all they were worth, taking two full chapters to do so. This intensely religious family also took pains to preserve and publicise as many papers as possible that dealt with Carroll's love for little girls.

Furthermore, after Carroll's unexpected death, his brother Wilfred spent several days going through Carroll's possessions while clearing his rooms. If these had contained anything at all – letters, pictures, photographs – which gave rise to the slightest moral concern about Carroll's relationships with children, Wilfred would undoubtedly have insisted that the child-friendships be downplayed immediately.

So his family knew him intimately, they knew many of his secrets, they wanted to protect his reputation and their own – and they uniformly acted as if there was everything to be proud of about his close friendships with children.

Still, the idea that Carroll was in some way predatory towards young children has become well established. The growth of his image is a subject which has been examined in a number of recent books, and it is therefore necessary, and fascinating, to take a brief look at how this 'paedophile' aspect of Carroll's image has evolved.

No suspicions were raised about him and his relationships with his little friends by anyone who knew him, either during his lifetime or after his death. On the contrary, most children remembered him with affection. Even those who did not take to him – and there were some – merely found his puzzles and riddles uninteresting. Nobody seems to have thought him creepy; nobody was made uneasy by him.

The development of the negative image of him began about

30 years after his death, when Freud's works had been translated and become fashionable in intellectual circles. This was a time of intense rebellion against the Victorian past, and Freud's ideas were one of the ways in which the sunshine was let in on the numerous secrecies and repressions upon which the Victorians had determinedly drawn the blinds. In this atmosphere of exposure, Lewis Carroll was among many once-revered figures that were up for grabs.

A M E Goldschmidt's '*Alice in Wonderland* Psychoanalysed'[19] appeared in 1933, and was probably the first shot to be fired at the 'St Lewis Carroll' image. This essay made the odd assumption that because the original Alice story was impromptu, the version written down months later, and then rewritten for publication, could be scientifically labelled as 'free association' and analysed accordingly in Freudian terms.

It was known that Carroll was a highly religious lifelong bachelor who presumably had no sex life and who had been inspired by little Alice Liddell to write his famous story. Therefore, according to Goldschmidt's posthumous psychoanalysis, falling down the rabbit hole was not a literary device to get the fictional Alice into another world, but was a symbol of the sexually-frustrated Carroll wishing to have sex with the real Alice. The door with the golden key was no longer a simple means of getting her into the garden, but a symbol of coitus. It was obvious to Goldschmidt (although not necessarily to anyone else) that Alice's growing and shrinking meant that she represented a tumescent and detumescent penis.

Goldschmidt either did not know, or else simply disregarded, the fact that Carroll's impromptu stories usually wove in themes or incidents that were particularly relevant to his audience at the time. Perhaps Alice had joked that she might like to scramble down a rabbit hole that day. Perhaps she had tripped in a rabbit hole and fallen over. Nobody knows, and *still* nobody knows which of the ideas in his story arose from Carroll's own mind, and which arose from casual remarks from those around him, or incidents which had befallen them that day.

More analysis followed, and then more. The Cheshire Cat represented Carroll's emotional detachment from sex, it seemed. Alice supposedly ignored the large doors in her dream hall because she represented Carroll and the doors represented women. And so on. Some of this work is now hard to read without laughing, but once the idea had been broached that Carroll had abnormally sinister tastes and emotions, then this *soi-disant* science was able to 'prove' anything that people felt like saying about him.

The fact that these Freudian analyses look primitive now does not mean, of course, that they looked ridiculous then. Freud's approach was revolutionary and did signify a genuinely new way of approaching human beings. Psychoanalysis was then crude and in its infancy, and this was the period during which the idea of Carroll as 'abnormal' took root.

It might all have been forgotten in time, except for two things. One was the well-intentioned but unwisely secretive attitude of certain members of the Dodgson family towards Carroll's papers, which fanned the flames of the idea that he had something to hide. The other is the 'snowball' effect, in which an idea – in this case, Carroll as pervert – gains a momentum of its own and begins to seem self-evidently true.

The Dodgson family members in charge of Carroll's papers had valiantly fought in the late Victorian era to disassociate Carroll from gossip about his friendships with women. Now, the family's destruction (or, at the least, their gross lack of care) of many important documents relating to his private life had resulted in the fact that little was available to counterbalance the focus on little girls, which by the 20th century was starting to look increasingly odd.

Early researchers, therefore, understandably searched out personal recollections from those who had been alive during

Carroll's lifetime. There had been a fair amount of gossip about him, and as with all gossip nobody quite knew what was true and what was not. Carroll was sufficiently eccentric, reclusive and famous to generate rumours and make people intrigued. From the mid-1920s onward, people who had known Carroll, or known of him, begun casting their minds back to what they remembered from all those years ago.

The gossip had been about young (and older) women, but, since he was presented as a man who was exclusively interested in children, and whose muse was a little girl, some of those looking back 40 years or more would have endeavoured to make their memories fit what they now believed to be the reality. That Carroll and his friends had bent over backwards in his lifetime to emphasise his love of children and not women would have strongly reinforced that tendency, and so it is hardly surprising that the idea took hold in the way it did.

Contemporary gossip had included rumours that he had wanted to marry one of the Liddells, probably Alice. This matter will be covered more thoroughly in Chapter 6, but even if he had wished to do this, the mid-Victorian mind would not have imagined that a grown man would have wanted actually to marry a child. He would have applied to her parents for leave to court her and, if they had agreed, there would have been a long courtship. Assuming that she remained agreeable, she would have grown to womanhood before she married. Sometimes, a suitor who found he was unable to marry one girl, would marry her sister. But 30 years or more into the 20th century, everything had changed. People now married each other for love, and those who remembered mid-Victorian courtship customs were nearly all dead.

As the years passed so the ball rolled on, gathering increasingly inaccurate information about a supposedly dull, reclusive and thoroughly peculiar personality who was scared of women and could only get along with little girls – and had sinister designs on them, too. In 1938 a Professor Paul Schilder found 'preponderant oral sadistic trends of cannibalistic character' in Carroll's works.[20] In 1947, a Martin Grotjahn wrote a long, earnest screed about the subject of 'Girl = Phallus' in relation to Carroll.[21] They were voices among many saying similar things. Carroll was being increasingly dismissed as a bore, a recluse, a pervert, a man who had no life and little personality, an unlovable man who had left no personal trace upon the world.

The now-elderly survivors who had known and loved him were ignored when they raised their voices in protest. 'They have such wrong ideas about him, that he was a recluse, and that he made friends with little girls but was too shy to talk to grown ups,' recalled Ethel Hatch in a radio talk. Gertrude Anderson added, 'Many people have said that he liked children only as long as they were really children and did not care about them when they grew up. This was not my experience …'. 'I have such vivid memories of happy times spent in his company that I am unable to stand aside without protest while he is dismissed as "dull,"' wrote Enid Shawyer to the *Observer*. 'He was always completely at ease with women,' added Ethel Rowell. But their remarks were to no avail.

Children who had been photographed nude by him also retained loyal and loving memories, but even the views of these people who knew first-hand about the reality of his nude photographic sessions were brushed aside. Beatrice Hatch, whom Carroll had photographed nude as a little girl, mourned how badly he would be missed, and, 'above all, the true affection that grows scarcer in these latter days'. Diana Bannister, the daughter of Annie Henderson, who had also been photographed nude as a little girl by Carroll, protested that her mother had been really angry at suggestions that there had been anything unhealthy in his interest in small girls.[22]

But nobody cared what they had to say.

Before long, Carroll seemed to be permanently on the verge

of checking in at Bates' Motel, with no motive too sinister to ascribe to him and nothing too outrageous to pin upon him. Some extremely strange essays, such as that by the American psychoanalyst John Skinner, became quite influential. Skinner's assessment of Carroll, published in 1947, is worth examining in a little more detail here, partly because it is still seriously quoted today.

Here is the un-edited beginning of a long nonsense letter that Carroll wrote to a little boy. In his paper, Skinner assured his readers it was 'full of rejection, with little friendliness in its tone':

My dear Bertie,

I would have been very glad to write to you as you wish, only there are several objections. I think, when you have heard them, you will see that I am right in saying "No".

The first objection is, I've got no ink. You don't believe it? Ah, you should have seen the ink there was in *my* days! (About the time of the battle of Waterloo: I was a soldier in that battle.) Why, you had only to pour a little of it on the paper, and it went on by itself! *This* ink is so stupid, if you begin a word for it, it can't even finish it by itself!

The next objection is, I've no time. You don't believe *that*, you say? Well, who cares? You should have seen the time there was in *my* days! (At the time of the battle of Waterloo, where I led a regiment.) There were always 25 hours in the day – sometimes 30 or 40.

The third and greatest objection is, my *great* dislike for children. I don't know why, I'm sure: but I *hate* them – just as one hates arm-chairs and plum-pudding! You don't believe *that*, don't you? Did I ever say you would? Ah, you should have seen the children there were in my days! (Battle of Waterloo ...)[23]

This letter is not unlike a stage 'comic monologue' of a type with which both Carroll and Bertie, a child actor, would have been familiar. It uses a rhythmic, repetitious device of saying apparently insulting things, which are then revealed as affectionately ridiculous, a style Carroll often used when writing to girls. It is clear from Carroll's references to hating plum pudding, to having '25 hours in the day – sometimes 30 or 40', and using ink that writes by itself, and so on, that he is joking throughout the letter.

However, Skinner ignored all the humour and stated that the letter was a 'clear expression of hostility towards boys', and used misleading, highly selective extracts from it to make his deadly serious point that Carroll was gravely abnormal in his attitude to boys. Skinner's ludicrous piece appeared in a respected journal and was being reprinted in serious books until quite recently.[24]

One of the greatest boosts to the image of Carroll as 'abnormal' was, unfortunately, the careful biography written by Florence Becker Lennon and published in 1947.[25] Mrs Lennon did her best to create a balanced picture of Carroll, even interviewing Lorina Liddell, Alice's sister (Alice herself was unable to be interviewed). She also conducted a long correspondence over many years with Miss F Menella Dodgson, Carroll's niece and one of the family members most closely involved with his papers.

Mrs Lennon believed that Carroll would have been 'normal' if only he had not been constrained by the unusual circumstances of his Christ Church life. Since he did not have that chance of normality, Mrs Lennon believed, he 'loved' little girls instead, even though he never actually did anything sexual about it. She portrayed him as a damaged person who had been raised with sexual repressions that deprived him of happiness and obliged him to live inside an abnormal emotional 'box'.

There is a certain amount of truth in this picture, although it is far more complex than Mrs Lennon supposed. Unfortunately, she had incomplete sources, and although she was a careful and conscientious biographer, some of the sources she did use have since been shown to be unreliable. She was also American, and did not fully understand British social attitudes of Carroll's day.

Crucially, she failed to appreciate that Carroll was the person he was largely *because* of his environment and upbringing, with all its faults and virtues. Had he been raised elsewhere – in 1960s San Francisco or 21st-century Beijing, for instance – he would have been unrecognizably different. Not only his sexual life but almost every other aspect of his life would have developed in completely different ways.

So it was entirely anachronistic for Mrs Lennon to compare him with her 1940s idea of a 'normal' man, just as there is no point in anyone now making a heavily culturally biased comparison of him with a 'normal' person of our own period and environment. He must be seen in the context of his own society. In that society he was not seen as damaged, nor sinister, nor unhappy. He was also not seen as in any way perverted.

The last letter in Mrs Lennon's long correspondence with Menella Dodgson was a reply from Menella, written in wavering handwriting by the then very old lady. Menella could not conceal the hurt and distress which she felt, and believed other Dodgson family members would feel, at the image of her uncle which Mrs Lennon had suggested.

> Why do you look for such things, because I presume it came from you or the psychologist in the first place ... And although we have not read the 4 missing diaries so can not be certain of anything, there is absolutely nothing in all the others supporting even the idea you mention ... So there we are, a suggestion based on nothing but possibilities only. And the most unlikely person too. We cannot do anything about it. The 4 lost diaries could, if they turned up, but

my cousin never hinted at it when he talked to me about them, and he had read them all. So we are quite as much in the dark as you are though knowing Uncle Charles quite well we cannot believe it to be true. Now, there will be lots written about it based on what you say, of course. You will not encourage such gossip naturally but other people will. I am sorry indeed that it has come up like this.[26]

As the 20th century wore on, more and more theories, increasingly grotesque and disgusting, grew and flourished upon this framework of Carroll as neurotic sexual deviant. Only in recent years has there been something of a revision in this view. Yet, as any public relations expert will confirm, the weirder the subject seems, the better the publicity; so, unfortunately, Carroll is unlikely to lose this image in a hurry.

Leaving the psychoanalytic studies and returning to the man himself, there is no sign that any of his relationships were abnormal, although there are hints that he did not wish to become too intimate with those outside his family. His family were very important to him; even the man most often said to be his best friend, Thomas Vere Bayne, was actually his oldest friend. Bayne's father had known Carroll's father and Baynes' family had known Carroll's family since childhood. Bayne himself was a congenial plodder with whom Carroll seems to have had little in common. They got on well, but Bayne and his life and opinions certainly do not figure much in Carroll's diaries. The two of them never, for example, holidayed together and rarely accompanied each other to social events. Carroll had many other friends of both sexes, but he did not appear to confide in them. In a way, he did not seem to need them.

Children, of course, were a different matter. He had a gift for entertaining them, he liked the things they liked, he approved of them and he was effortlessly popular with them. They did not get possessive and they did not ask him difficult questions, but they were truthful, sincere and human. They honestly loved him, and then they grew up and left him, with no hard feelings on either side, and with the door always open for them to return if they wished.

That he could enjoy their affection without feeling evil and threatened, can be seen from a letter he wrote to a young friend, Hilda Moberly Bell: 'It *is* sweet of you children, to sign your letters to me, after only *once* seeing me, as you do! When I get letters signed "your loving," I always *kiss* the signature. You see I'm a sentimental old fogey!"[27]

Since children were, as far as the Victorian mind was concerned, sexless and therefore sinless, he could have as many beautiful little child-friends as he liked. Like lovable little animals, they surrounded him with friendly warmth. As he said to Girdlestone, it was like a tonic to him. If the girls sensed any emotional neediness in his wish to be accepted and appreciated by them, they did not mind. He made their lives happy and was good to them, and most of them were sincerely kind to him in return.

of her own little sister. So the boat wound slowly along, beneath the bright summer-day, with its merry crew and its music of voices and laughter, till it passed round one of the many turnings of the stream, and she saw it no more.

Then she thought, (in a dream within the dream, as it were,) how this same little Alice would, in the after-time, be herself a grown woman: and how she would keep, through her riper years, the simple and loving heart of her childhood: and how she would gather around her other little children, and make their eyes bright and eager with many a wonderful tale, perhaps even with these very adventures of the little Alice of long-ago: and how she would feel with all their simple sorrows, and find a pleasure in all their simple joys, remembering her own child-life, and the happy summer days.

A facsimile of the final page of the handwritten 'Alice's Adventures Under Ground'. Carroll originally sketched Alice Liddell, with short, dark hair, at the end of the text. Later, presumably unsatisfied with his efforts, he pasted one of his photographs over his drawing.

'Child of the pure unclouded brow'

Alice

'Is she like me?' Alice asked eagerly, for the thought crossed her mind, 'there's another little girl in the garden, somewhere!'

Through the Looking Glass

One day (so the story goes), a shy Oxford don called Lewis Carroll took the three small daughters of his Dean out rowing on the river. They were called Edith, Lorina and Alice. The golden-haired Alice, his favourite, asked him to tell them a story. As they glided over the water, he did, and then he carefully wrote it out for her. The story became *Alice's Adventures in Wonderland,* an international bestseller. To Alice's delight, a follow-up story about her was also a great success.

It would be charming if it had been like that – but it was not. Alice had short, dark hair, cut in an unusual, almost boyish style, and by the time *Alice in Wonderland* was published, she was well into her teens, and had had little to do with Carroll for years. Far from being delighted, Alice Liddell did not own up to being Carroll's muse until she was an old woman, and that was only when she wanted the proceeds from selling the original manuscript which Carroll had given her.

The legend also continues that Carroll, supposedly shy and

awkward with women, was unusual because he could only relate properly to children. He fell hopelessly in love with the beautiful Alice as she grew older, and may even have proposed to her. (Given the perversions of which Carroll has sometimes been accused, an alternate version, these days, has Carroll as a Victorian version of Humbert Humbert with Alice as his Lolita.) Sometimes in this tale there is a story of a quarrel with Alice's family about some vague and undefined matter to do with love. And that is where the story peters out.

The fairy tale has some truth in it, of course. Alice sounds as if she was a captivating child, and Carroll was very fond of her. Although he was sociable enough with adults, he loved playing with the Liddell children when he was a young man living a bachelor existence at Christ Church.

But there is one character who never fitted into the fairy tale from the start. Alice's older brother, Harry, was Carroll's reason for becoming involved with the Liddells in the first place. He commented more about Harry in his diary than he ever did about Alice. His photographs of him show a long-faced, good-looking boy. In 1856, Harry stares pensively to one side, clad in a splendidly trimmed jacket with his tam-o'shanter resting on his knee. In 1860, aged 13, he is dressed in cricket whites with his bat propped up against him: still a boy, but only just. He gazes haughtily out of the picture with the dark and extraordinarily compelling eyes which he and his sister Lorina inherited from their mother. It is not surprising that Carroll thought Harry the 'handsomest boy I ever saw'.[1]

Before arriving at Christ Church, Carroll had revelled in his role as the well-loved entertainer of his 10 brothers and sisters. In the monastic, child-free atmosphere of the college, there was none of the lively chatter and bustle of his home, but the Dean's energetic and clever children would have offered him echoes of the family fun which he had left behind. Seeking out their company was, in the context of Christ Church, an unconventional solution to any feelings of loneliness – but Carroll always was unconventional.

It was early March 1856 when he first made friends 'down at the boats' with nine-year-old Harry. Shortly afterwards, he met Lorina, ('Ina'), aged seven, and Alice, who was nearly four. He liked them all, but it was Harry in particular who came to his rooms, accompanied him on photographing sessions and went out on excursions with him.

Of course, as Ina, Alice and their younger sister Edith started to grow up, Carroll included them too, although Harry was still the main one. The first time he took Harry and Ina out on the boat, he surprised onlookers who were not used to seeing a man taking children out without accompanying ladies. He recorded in his diary that it was fortunate that 'considering the wild spirits of the children, we got home without accident, having attracted by our remarkable crew a good deal of attention from almost every one we met.'[2]

Dean Liddell and his wife were tolerant of Carroll's unconventional visits to their family, and may even have enjoyed them. Carroll's new hobby of photography was an exciting development. Even the Dean's aged father wanted his portrait to be 'taken', and the little Liddells were among Carroll's earliest photographic subjects. Soon Carroll was on close enough terms with the family to be giving Harry a mechanical tortoise for Christmas.

When the Dean and his wife went to Madeira for several months in 1856–7, Carroll and the governess, Miss Prickett, agreed that he would help Harry with his sums. The Dean's mother immediately protested, because she feared the effects of overwork on Harry's brain. But 'as far as I can judge, there is nothing to fear at present on that score', Carroll observed dryly.[3] He continued teaching Harry, and took the boy to picture galleries, on outings and to chapel. He jotted down Harry's funny remarks, and Harry wrote to him when he was away from

Oxford. Gradually, Carroll became part of the scenery as far as the Liddell children were concerned. 'I don't know how we first knew Mr. Dodgson,' Ina recalled, many years later.[4]

Of course, in the stuffy and socially restricted world of Christ Church, nothing that was remotely unusual went unnoticed. Eventually, the unconventionality of Carroll's visits to the children attracted enough gossip to be a problem, although the problem was nothing to do with Alice. By May 1857, Carroll was remarking in his diary that, 'I find to my great surprise that my notice of [the children] is construed by some men into attentions to the governess, Miss Prickett ...'.[5] Fortunately, Miss Prickett did not seem to mind this threat to her reputation; she may already have had her eye on the landlord of the Mitre Inn, whom she later married. So Carroll continued to call on the Liddells, sometimes taking photographs, and sometimes just playing with the children and telling them stories.

His diaries between 1858 and 1862 are missing, but he continued to see the Liddells and took some good photographs of them during those years. He composed his poem 'A Sea Dirge' possibly to entertain relatives at the seaside, and said in a family letter that he had recited it to the children:

> ... Pour some salt water over the floor –
> Ugly I'm sure you'll allow it to be:
> Suppose it extended a mile or more.
> That's very like the Sea....

And he found it amusing that they indignantly told him it was 'Not true.'[6]

When Caroll's diaries resume in 1862, he was 30 years old and he was still seeing the children. This was the year in which he was to tell them *Alice in Wonderland*. Harry had gone away to boarding school, by then, so Carroll's time with the family was spent with the three next-oldest children, Ina, born 1849,

Alice, born 1852, and Edith, born 1854. Occasionally he would take them out on boat trips, either with one of his brothers, with a friend, or with visiting sisters. The expedition would include good food – a large basket of cakes, a picnic of cold chicken and salad or something similar. They would progress at a slow and leisurely pace, lulled by the splashing of their oars and the clear, piping calls of plovers that wheeled over that particular stretch of the river.

One of their favourite picnic spots was on the river bank near Nuneham House the seat of the Harcourt family. 'Here, 'rustic cottages set in masses of sylvan shade' (as an 1873 river guide romantically enthused) were clustered about the picturesque Nuneham Bridge. At other times they would make for Godstow, with its huge trees and its old riverside inn, The Trout. Sometimes they would tie the boat up, go into a field and light a fire in order to make tea.

On these sociable river trips, the grown-ups would allow the children to row, and they would all sing songs, or ask riddles. Sometimes Carroll would tell the children stories. On 4 July 1862, he first began the story of 'Alice's Adventures under Ground'. He would later rewrite this as *Alice's Adventures in Wonderland.*

Alice, looking back as an old woman, recalled how, although Carroll told them many stories, the one about her under the ground particularly caught her fancy. Perhaps that was because it was 'about' her, or perhaps there really was something special about it. In any case, Alice then begged him to write his story down for her.

Actually, Carroll's original diary entry for the day did not mention telling the story at all. He said he took the children back to his rooms after the outing to show them some 'microphotographs' and dropped them home at 9 pm. It was only in February 1863 that he went back and added a note that he had begun the story of Alice, and mentioned that he had started to write the headings out on 5 July, on his way to London on the train.

At this point the 'Wonderland' fairy tale starts to diverge even more from what really happened. In the book, the characters at the Pool of Tears famously include several who were named after members of the boating party. Carroll's real name, Dodgson, translated into 'the Dodo'; and there was Lorina the Lory, Edith the Eaglet, Alice (who of course played herself), and also Carroll's friend Robinson Duckworth, the Duck. Carroll and Alice both separately remembered how hot that 4 July had been, with a sky of 'cloudless blue'. Alice recalled that nearly the whole story had been told on a blazing summer afternoon 'with the heat haze shimmering over the meadows where the party landed to shelter for awhile in the shadow cast by the haycocks. ...'[7]

Yet the weather report indicates that the day was cloudy and cool. What is more, in one of her letters, Ina Liddell remembered that they did *not* have Duckworth with them when the story was first told.[8] She was so convinced she was right that she discussed it with Alice, who was adamant that Duckworth *had* been there. Lorina concluded, with some surprise, that her own memory must have been at fault.[9]

In fact, they were remembering different days. There may well have been clear, sunny breaks in the clouds on 4 July but at a maximum of only 68°F, the heat haze would hardly have shimmered. Alice remembered Carroll telling them many stories at various times, and so the 'golden afternoon', although undoubtedly real enough on one day or another, had become just another element in the fairy tale.

On 6 August, a few weeks later, the party made another river trip. Once again, the English summer delivered a day of glum weather – overcast skies, with rain in the early afternoon. On this second occasion, they were accompanied by Carroll's friend Augustus Vernon Harcourt, and Duckworth was nowhere to be seen. Perhaps that was the trip that Lorina remembered.

They went to Godstow and had tea, just like before, and 'I had to go on with my interminable fairy-tale of *Alice's Adventures*', Carroll recorded. That is when he probably concluded the tale of *Alice in Wonderland*; but he would probably never have done so if a game they were playing on the boat had been more interesting.

The game was called The Ural Mountains. It was a parlour game about imaginary crimes that had recently been devised by the logician Henry Sidgwick[10] In the game, one person was elected as the Judge and the other participants were divided into two teams. One team captain accused the other of some outrageous and stupid crime – the more ridiculous the better. Then, the other players argued the case.

Carroll wove information about his hearers and his surroundings into his stories, so the children's unsuccessful efforts at the boring Ural Mountains, as they floated down the river, very likely gave him ideas for the famous trial scene in *Alice in Wonderland*. If so, it is as well that it was not a better game. Otherwise they might have gone on playing it, and then the story might never have been finished; for after 6 August, there were no more river outings for quite a while. Indeed, there never was another that included a picnic at Godstow.

After this, Carroll seems to have forgotten his promise to write out Alice's adventures. During the autumn, in fact, he stopped seeing the Liddells so often, because he had fallen out with Mrs Liddell. The disagreement was nothing to do with Alice; it revolved around an incident with an aristocratic protégé of Mrs Liddell's, involving whether or not a ball should be held at the college. So on 13 November, when Carroll met Ina, Edith and Alice by chance in the quad, he noted that the little chat they enjoyed was 'a rare event of late'. And it was only on that November evening – months after the river trip – that he started to write out *Alice's Adventures*.

He may have been feeling a little low spirited. November is

a dark and gloomy month in England. Fogs and mists obscure the light, and cold winds rattle the window frames and whirl dead leaves from the trees. Other entries in Carroll's diary show that he was not happy at this time. His emotional outlet of playing with the children and telling them stories had been unavailable for a while. Recalling the pleasant summer outings and happy storytelling sessions would have seemed like a good thing to do.

The meeting in the quad had pleasing results, at any rate. The children were so glad to have his company again that they persuaded their mother not to be so cross with him, and to let them start seeing him once more. She relented, and soon they were all back on their old easy terms. By the following 10 March, Carroll was borrowing a natural history text from the Deanery to help him with his illustrations for *Alice's Adventures*. He was also back in the middle of their family life. Also in March, he showed Alice around the illuminations for the Prince of Wales's wedding, and rejoiced in the 'thorough abandonment' with which she enjoyed it. In the next few days there were more walks, and he also recorded that he ran a race with Ina, who was now a tall girl of nearly 14.

As 1863 went on, the Liddell family was having problems, and the Dean and his wife cannot have been feeling happy. At the end of May, they lost their new baby, which had been ailing, and to add to their misery, the Deanery gardens were unpleasantly vandalized. During this time, Carroll was around the edges of their lives a great deal. He was seeing the children almost continually, helping them with their school tasks, taking them to the circus and generally entertaining them.

In the middle of June, the bereaved parents had to set aside their feelings in order to entertain the Prince of Wales at an enormous event at the Deanery. Alice, Edith and Ina ran a stall at a grand bazaar which the royal couple attended. The bazaar was closed to the public when Carroll arrived there on 16 June, so he crept under the counter and joined the children on their stall, just in time for the royal arrival. He exchanged pleasantries with the prince and boldly tried to get the princess to buy one of the kittens Alice was selling. If the royal pair wondered why he was there, they did not say.

On 25 June, Carroll accompanied the Dean's family and friends on an outing with the children. Afterwards, to his amazement and delight, he was allowed to take all three girls home on the railway unescorted. Two days later, something mysterious happened between Carroll and the Liddell family – an event which has puzzled writers for years. Carroll's diary entry for 27 June 1863 reads, in part: 'Wrote to Mrs. Liddell, urging her either [the word 'either' has been crossed out, apparently by another hand] to send the children to be photographed'. The next page of the journal has been removed. Carroll later added a note about the missing page, cross referencing it with the entry on 17 May 1857, which tells of the rumours about him and Miss Prickett. And after that, there is a resounding emptiness where the Liddells used to be.

At the end of June, the Dean and his family departed for their new holiday home in Llandudno, and Carroll did not refer to them again (other than a brief meeting in October 1863) until 5 December 1863, when he coldly noted that he saw Mrs Liddell and the children but 'held aloof from them, as I have done all this term'.

Many have puzzled over what happened during the time for which the page was removed, why Carroll subsequently 'held aloof', and why things were never the same again. Gossip, as usual in claustrophobic Christ Church, was rife. The idea went around that Carroll had proposed either to Alice or to one of the sisters, and been told to go away by the parents. This rumour is confirmed by a note on the cover of a skit published some years later. In this scurrilous little play, Carroll is portrayed in thin disguise as an objector to the joint marriage of the Liddell daughters, and a contemporary note on the British Library's copy of the play states that 'D-dgs-n had been rejected.'[11]

Over the years this supposition was fed (as will be seen) by a grossly misleading statement by Ina Liddell, and blossomed into a wholly imaginary scenario in which Carroll proposed to Alice, or was turned out of the Liddell's lives for a variety of reasons which are neither convincing nor tie up with the known facts.

So what really happened?

A small piece of paper in the Dodgson Family Collection archive in Surrey gives, among other things, a brief note of the contents of the missing page of Carroll's diary. The note also refers to another missing page which mentioned Carroll's troublesome younger brother Skeffington. (A third page also mentioned, in which Carroll referred to Alice's ungracious behavior, was not removed.) The handwriting on the little slip of paper is almost certainly that of Menella Dodgson, daughter of Carroll's brother Wilfred. Menella was a hard-working and conscientious woman, and assisted her brother, Major C H W Dodgson, in dealing with the family papers in the early part of the 20th century. The part of Menella's note relating to the missing pages reads: 'L.C. learns from Mrs. Liddell that he is supposed to be using the children as a means of paying court to the governess. He is also supposed by some to be courting Ina.'

So Menella saw the missing pages of the diary before they were removed. With the knowledge of her brother, who kept the diaries in his house, she jotted down what was on the pages that she (or they together) planned to take out. We know this was so, because she did not remove the page about Alice's ungra-ciousness after all, but scribbled it out heavily instead. Menella had examined every word of the diaries. Yet, busily censoring away with her pen and scissors, she did nothing to remove the earlier reference to Miss Prickett. The repetition of *that* rumour did not concern her. The gossip about Carroll courting Ina was, therefore, the problem.

Ina was well-developed and mature for her age. Photographs of her suggest that she was the best looking of the Liddell daughters, having inherited her mother's glamorous, sultry, and almost Spanish appearance; at 14, she was also old enough to be considered eligible for marriage. She had no doubt also started developing some of what were then coyly termed 'womanly feelings'. She had been out and about a good deal with Carroll, who was only 31 in 1863; and sometimes they were not chaperoned. Even Carroll knew there was risk attached to this; he had noted himself in 1862 that she was starting to look 'too tall', as he euphemistically put it, to be out with him. How much less suitable would it have seemed by 1863 – although of course nobody would have expected a 14-year-old actually to marry. She would be 'promised' and the wedding would take place years later. Alice, at 10 or 11, would be considered too young to have serious admirers.

So is there the slightest chance that Carroll would have proposed to Ina, Alice, or any of the Liddell girls? Whatever he thought of them, the answer must be no. For a start, he never expressed the slightest inclination to marry anyone. Secondly, it was not practical for him to marry at that time. Thirdly, he was, to be frank, not the type of husband Mrs Liddell wanted for her girls.

Mrs Liddell wanted her daughters to marry well. Since girls were not allowed independence or careers, their main chance of succeeding in life was to marry someone rich. Carroll later sarcastically referred to Mrs Liddell as a 'King-fisher' – literally a 'fisher of kings' – for her daughters.[12] She wanted to do everything possible to help them to marry royalty, or aristocrats, or at the least very rich men. Carroll, although well-bred and the social equal of Mrs Liddell, was a worse marriage bet even than many of his colleagues, something of which he would have been perfectly aware. Far from having good prospects, his main prospect seems to have been the loss of his job upon marriage, since all men in his position were supposed to be bachelors.

Just weeks before, Alice's father had finally relieved Carroll of the obligation to take priest's orders. The main route out of Christ Church involved being a priest, so he now had even less chance than before of getting a good job if he quit his bachelor post. There was no family money; he would have no inheritance. How could he propose to anyone, when he could not adequately support a wife?

As Ina grew older, too, her marriage prospects would be damaged by socializing too closely with Carroll, even though he was a family friend. She did not need a reputation as the sort of girl who hung around with men, and it would have been reasonable for Mrs Liddell to point this out. A little unjust, perhaps, since she and the Dean had let the easy relationship go on for so long – but not unreasonable. Carroll no doubt agreed that the gossip was unpleasant, and so agreed to stay out of the family's way for a while so it would all die down. And this is exactly what he did.

So surely this clears up the matter? Not quite. Because it made no sense, all those years later, for Menella to *remove the page itself, yet keep a note of what was on it.* The only possible reason for her doing this could have been that she wanted to note what had been on the page – but not *exactly* what had been on it. Her note, in other words, is a censored version of what was on the missing diary page.

This missing material was almost certainly not an emotional diary outburst from Carroll. Over and over again, he showed himself to be tight-lipped about his troubles, at least as far as his diary was concerned. From early on, he seems to have had an eye on posterity – even if the posterity he had in mind was only his relatives reading his diaries after his death. He rarely went into detail about unpleasant or upsetting matters.

To the mystery of this missing information, must be added the behavior of Ina Liddell many years later, when speaking to a biographer. In the late 1920s, the American writer Florence Becker Lennon began researching her biography of Lewis Carroll. Ina and Alice were both still alive, and although Alice was too ill to be interviewed, Mrs Becker (as she was then) met Ina in early 1930. After the meeting, Ina wrote to Alice in some dismay: 'My dear!! see what I'm let in for! On thinking to myself, I think she tried to see if Mr. Dodgson ever wanted to marry you! She said he had such a sad face, and she thought he must have had a love affair. I said, "I never heard of one" and it did occur to me at the time what she perhaps was driving at!! ... I begin to tremble at what I said to her ...' Two days later, on 2 May 1930, returning to the theme in another letter to Alice, Ina continued:

> ... I suppose you don't remember when Mr. Dodgson ceased coming to the Deanery? How old you were? I said his manner became too affectionate to you as you grew older and that mother spoke to him about it, and that offended him so he ceased coming to visit us again, as one had to give some reason for all intercourse [i.e. personal communication] ceasing. I don't think you could have been more than 9 or 10 on account of my age! I must put it a bit differently for Mrs. B.'s book. ..."[13]

So, in these letters, Ina was saying that she had needed to give Mrs Becker *some* reason why Carroll had stopped visiting the family. Whatever the real reason was, she did not want to say. Instead, she told the biographer that Carroll had become too fond of Alice.

The matter might have remained there. A few scholars have puzzled over the letter, which only came to light in recent years, but have surmised nothing more. None apparently noticed *another* letter from Ina, written around the same time, now at the University of Colorado. Colorado is not a centre of Carroll studies, but happens to be the institution to which Mrs Becker bequeathed her correspondence.

In this letter of 28 April 1930, Ina told Mrs Becker, 'my childish recollections of Mr. Dodgson are very small, as we saw little of him after I was about ten or so …'. Yet as her letter to Alice just four days later makes clear, this was completely untrue. Ina was elderly in 1930, but she was not in the slightest bit dotty. Her letter to Alice shows that she was well aware *Alice* had been pre-pubescent, on account of her own age of 14. Just like the actress Isa Bowman all those years earlier, Alice's sister had pretended she was about 10 when she was close to Carroll – when she knew she was in fact older, and of an age when she would be considered eligible.

Ina continued to emphasize to Mrs Becker just how very young she really had been. A little further on in the letter, she added that she and her sisters were 'young children', underlining the word 'young'. And on 4 May, she artlessly remarked, with two exclamation marks, that '… I don't know how we first knew Mr. Dodgson! I suppose because he liked little girls!!' Just to make her point crystal clear, she added that, 'The whole story of "A in W" has no mystery!'

Then she launched into the familiar tale of the 'three little sisters' going out on the boat, and asked Mrs Becker to remove the reference to Carroll having been 'too affectionate' towards Alice. Mrs. Becker believed her unquestioningly, and used Ina's quotations as she had been asked to do.

Ina's letters raise some interesting questions, however. First, why did she lie at all? Mrs Becker was interviewing her in 1930, not 1860. Elderly as she was, Ina had not retired from the modern world. It may have been rather unconventional in the 1860s for a 14-year-old girl and her small sisters to be taken out by a male family friend of 31. It was not considered the slightest bit wrong in the 1930s, and there would have been no need to treat it with secrecy.

Secondly, by putting the idea into Mrs Becker's head that Carroll had become too fond of *Alice* rather than her, Ina was only shifting the spotlight. By 1930, the idea of Carroll being too fond of Alice sounded just as bad (if not worse) than the idea that he had been too fond of Ina herself.

Might it not be more believable that Ina had been too fond of *him*? A 14-year-old, particularly a physically mature one, is very susceptible. Grown men, particularly youngish ones, are often targets for teen dreams, as many male schoolteachers are well aware. Carroll could not suppress his playfulness – it shone out constantly when he was relaxed, and he charmed both women and children. He was witty, clever, enormously entertaining and not at all bad-looking. He was unconventional enough to run a race with Ina and he had also enjoyed little adventures with her: adventures which seem insignificant by today's standards but would not have seemed so to a sheltered mid-Victorian girl.

Just a couple of days beforehand, for example, Carroll and Ina had made their way home alone and unchaperoned with the two younger children. They had both known that this was unusual. Carroll's 25 June diary entry makes it clear that it was a notable treat for him when 'Ina, Alice, Edith, and I (*mirabile dictu!*) walked down to Abingdon-road station, and so home by railway. A pleasant expedition with a *very* pleasant conclusion.'

Carroll looked young for his age, and Ina looked old for hers, and on that trip they were doing something that usually only married or engaged couples did. Carroll obviously found it fun. What effect would it have on a hormonal teenager?

Even 65 years on, Ina clearly did not want to be questioned too closely about what Mr Dodgson had meant to her, or she to him. She wanted people to think she had been a little girl, not a young woman who had been old enough to have feelings for men. She was prepared to lie to Mrs Becker in order to deflect her attention from the truth, and her letter catches her out in that lie.

So, carefully untangling the threads of memory, secrets and lies, it seems that Ina, not Alice, was the reason for the break. And Carroll would *not* have proposed – not to her, nor to Alice – because at the time, he could not sensibly have proposed to anyone.

Strangely enough, a suggestion that Ina's feelings were involved would have been exactly the kind of thing Menella would have edited out of the manuscript in the early 1930s. She was very anxious not to upset or embarrass people who were then still alive, or their families. Ina may well have shared Menella's sensibilities, but her deliberately misleading comments were largely – though probably accidentally – responsible for Mrs Becker acquiring the idea of Carroll being fixated on little girls. It was an idea which led to a mountain of misunderstanding, and eventually caused great distress to Menella.

Carroll's friendship with the children was never resumed, although he saw the younger Liddell children briefly from time to time. Highly significantly, he was never allowed to take Ina out again, even with a chaperone, and the river trips came to a firm stop. In fact, he noted on 12 May the following year that Mrs Liddell would not let any of her daughters come out with him (even though he had not asked for Ina). 'Rather superfluous caution' he added bitterly. When he eventually presented 'Alice's Adventures under Ground' to Alice, she was 12 years old. It was November 1864, two-and-a-half years after the original trip and nearly 18 months after the fateful interview at the Deanery.

His offering was a very attractive little book, with a title page bordered by an exquisite design of blue and mauve cornflowers and pink convolvulus. Flowers like these must have dotted the golden cornfields and river banks as the party rowed along in early July. Inside the border, Carroll carefully combined ivy and foxgloves to make a design twining around the red and blue letters of the title. Interestingly, in the then widely-known language of flowers, these two intertwined plants represent the two opposing qualities of fidelity and insincerity.

No doubt the family was pleased with the little book, for they kept it out for guests to read, but it was a postscript to the friendship rather than a celebration of it. The following 6 April, Carroll saw a painting of the three girls on show at the British Institution, and commented wistfully that it was 'a very pretty picture on the whole. Ina looking a little too severe and melancholy, much as I am sure she would have looked, sitting to a stranger. ...'[14] Then there was a chance meeting with Alice and Miss Prickett on 11 May 1865, in which Alice was 'changed a good deal, and hardly for the better'. And that was about the end of the close Liddell friendship.

His little book, though, continued to occupy him. He already had the idea of making an edition for general public sale, and he began changing and expanding the text of 'Under Ground'. He removed some references to the Liddells, and also made some clever improvements, such as rewriting the original 'Mouse's Tale' in caudate rhyme – otherwise known as 'tail rhyme'. After much deliberation as to titles (he mercifully rejected 'Alice's Hour in Elfland' and several others equally bad), he entitled his book *Alice's Adventures in Wonderland*. It is notable that when considering ideas for the title, he explicitly rejected the idea of anything associated with 'morality'.[15]

In April 1864, Carroll hired John Tenniel to illustrate the book. Tenniel and Alice are now inextricably linked in the public mind, but at the time Tenniel seemed an unconventional choice of illustrator. Already 44 years old, he was established as a major political cartoonist, and he charged an extremely high fee: Carroll was a total unknown, and was paying Tenniel out of his own modestly-lined pocket. Yet Carroll's visual instincts did not fail, for, of course, Tenniel was just the right man for the job. His drawings, with pantomime-like 'Big Heads' for the more outlandish characters, gave the book its ideal blend of gravitas and buffoonery.

The firm of Macmillan & Co agreed to publish the book for Carroll. Since its foundation in 1843, Macmillan had become a highly reputable imprint with a respected stable of authors, and it had good relationships with writers, booksellers and distributors. Contrary to conventional modern practice, Macmillan expected Carroll to cover the cost of publishing, and marketed the book in exchange for a commission on sales. Although not the kind of publishing deal with which we are most familiar today, it was a common type of arrangement then, falling somewhere between modern ideas of conventional publishing and self-publishing.

Carroll supervised the illustrations and printing of all his books very closely, to the irritation of both illustrators and publishers. By the end of June 1865, 2,000 copies of *Alice's Adventures in Wonderland* had been printed by the Clarendon Press, at Carroll's expense. He was presumably pleased, although, as ever, his diary conveys little about his feelings. Unfortunately, Tenniel was not pleased at all, and complained that he was entirely dissatisfied with the printing of the pictures.

If Tenniel was not happy, then Carroll would not be happy either. On 2 August, he decided to withdraw the whole printing and get the book redone at a different printer's, Clay's. He recalled all the presentation copies he had had made, Clarendon wrote off £27 11s 0d and Carroll sold the disbound first edition copies to an American publisher, D Appleton & Co. The very few copies of this true first edition that were not sent back to Carroll are now like the Holy Grail for book collectors. Even copies of the 'second' first edition (Clay's version) go for astronomical prices.

So *Alice's Adventures in Wonderland* greeted the world, and Carroll's life would now change forever. So, perhaps, would Alice's. She would never again be free of the feeling that people might see her only as the 'girl from Wonderland' rather than her own self.

Yet there is a further mystery about Alice Liddell. Carroll made efforts to get Tenniel to draw a girl with long fair hair, in contrast to Alice's short, dark hair. His own illustrations for 'Alice's Adventures under Ground' show a long-haired girl – a girl who could therefore not be Alice Liddell.

He did intend his little book as a gift to Alice Liddell, of course. It can be viewed at the British Library and there are various facsimiles on sale. At the very end of the manuscript, it can be seen that Carroll drew a small picture frame. In it, he first sketched a picture of Alice Liddell – with short, (very) dark hair. Then, presumably unsatisfied with his efforts, he pasted one of his photographs of her over his drawing. So there is no doubt that the book was *for* Alice Liddell – but it was clearly *about* some other girl who had long, fair hair. Perhaps nobody realized the significance of this at the time. As so often was the case, Carroll left others to make their own assumptions about what he meant.

Furthermore, the 1886 facsimile edition that Carroll presented to the grown-up Alice Hargreaves (née Liddell) is most pointedly inscribed 'To Her *whose namesake* [my italics] one happy summer day, inspired his story: from the Author.' Did Alice realize, when she read the inscription, that it was not her, but her *namesake,* who had inspired the story? If she had, this might help explain why she was never particularly keen to tell the world that she was 'Alice in Wonderland'.

And who might her namesake have been?

There is no doubt that the young Alice Liddell meant a lot to Carroll, even if not as much as many seem to think. In March 1863 Carroll noted in his diary that he had begun a poem in which he meant to embody something about Alice. This was not an unusual sort of thing for a poetic Victorian gentleman to do. He also remembered her later in his life as 'an entirely fascinating seven year old maiden',[16] but perhaps by the time she had grown up, Mrs Hargreaves was not as appealing as she had been in her childhood. In December 1885, Carroll told a Mary Manners that his heroine had been 'named after a real Alice, but [was] none the less a dream-child'. And in a letter to Alice's mother on the retirement of her husband on 12 November 1891, he was again careful to say that 'many of the pleasantest memories of those early years ... are bound up with the *names* [my italics] of yourself and your children.'[17]

Even for the paradoxical Lewis Carroll, this seems a bit odd. Nonetheless, Carroll tended to speak the truth, even if he spoke it in ways which were not clear to other people. Here, as on several other matters, his 'serious' poetry has something to tell us. As always, no author's poems and stories should be assumed to be autobiographical, however tempting it may be to assume that they are. The only things that poetry and fiction can reliably reveal are the themes and ideas that were on the author's mind when they were written.

In Chapter 4, some of Carroll's poems, including 'Stolen Waters', are shown to reveal that certain themes were on his mind at around the time he wrote *Alice in Wonderland*. He was struggling with great personal distress at the time, and the themes he repeatedly used included poisoned love, obsession, and the idea of female children offering relief from the sense of sin. There is also a correspondence of several themes between the *Wonderland* story and 'Stolen Waters'. 'Stolen Waters', with its message that a sinless little girl offers salvation to the male sexual sinner, was written in early 1862, shortly before Carroll told 'Alice's Adventure's under Ground'.

In late 1862, Carroll wrote another poem 'Beatrice', which also includes this unusual theme of redemption from despair through a child's purity. It is not, perhaps, his best poem, but in it he describes a five-year-old child, Beatrice, who is full of the joys of life. She reminds him of another child he knew, and he says to her:

> Beatrice! Still, as I gaze on thee,
> Visions of two sweet maids arise,
> Whose life was of yesterday.

In this poem, the two past-time Beatrices share a life, so they are in fact the same person. The first version of Beatrice, like the child in 'Stolen Waters', is dying:

> ... pale and stern, with the lips of a dumb despair,
> with the innocent eyes that yearn –
> Yearn for the young sweet hours of life ...

The second Beatrice is an angelic vision. She is glorious and bright, '... a sainted, ethereal maid, whose blue eyes are deep fountains of light ...'. And this angel of the dead Beatrice cheers 'the poet that broodeth apart,/filling with gladness his desolate heart ...'. Just as in 'Stolen Waters' only a few months before, a dying little girl offers hope to the desperate young man. Here, in 'Stolen Waters' the child with long, fair hair becomes a joyous angel, free from her lifetime's suffering, and she shows the narrator that his path to happiness is to:

> Be as a child –
> So shalt thou sing for very joy of breath.
> So shalt thou wait thy dying
> In holy transport lying –
> So pass rejoicing through the gate of Death
> In garment undefiled.

The correspondence of these themes suggests that the idea of a pure child with long, fair hair redeeming sin was emotionally important in Carroll's mind at the time he was writing *Alice in Wonderland*. As mentioned in Chapter 4, Carroll at this time was tormented by particular feelings of sin, and a lovely fair-haired child is what he especially wanted Tenniel to show. The fair-haired 'Alice' of his story was to be his companion through his world-away-from-the-world. She remained with him. He referred years later in another poem to the 'childish sprite/earthborn and yet an angel bright' who stayed with him always.[18] This pure and sinless child would be – and has, indeed, proved to be – forever young, forever companionable, and forever free of the bonds of conventionally moral society.

Was this dead, golden-haired child a real person? An Alice Beatrice, or a Beatrice Alice, perhaps; or merely 'Beatrice', the famous epitome of pure love, leading Dante from purgatory to Paradise? For sure she was not the real, dark-haired Alice Liddell. Carroll knew that Alice Liddell would, God willing, grow up. *She* could not remain his muse forever.

Alice Liddell did indeed grow up, and she joined conventional society. She never made the aristocratic marriage of which her mother had dreamed, but married a man called Reginald Hargreaves, inheritor of a large fortune. She became a noted society hostess, and what her granddaughter referred to as a 'formidable woman who dominated the family'.[19] Late in life, in the memoir which her son wrote with her, Alice commented unkindly on Carroll's stiff-backed posture, and described his sisters as 'stout', although they do not seem to have been stout at all.[20] She certainly was, to put it politely, tough-minded. Among other things, she forbade her three sons to marry, and she disliked the daughter-in-law she acquired when one of her sons eventually defied her and married in middle age. In adult life, Carroll and Alice Hargreaves were not good friends. His dream child, on the other hand, did not change.

Carroll made a comfortable, though not a particularly affluent living from his *Alice* books. He did not choose to discuss the books face-to-face with anyone. However, in 1887, when he was 55, he contributed an article to *The Theatre* magazine. A stage presentation of *Alice* had opened in London, and Carroll decided to say what he thought about the books and their characters.

His piece is affectedly sentimental, and written in the flowery language he always used for high-flown thoughts. It is intended for an adult audience, and it reflects the man he had become in his later years, increasingly eccentric and increasingly concerned with his new imaginary dream-child, the sugar-sweet Sylvie. Nevertheless, it shows what *Alice* meant to him by then, around quarter of a century after he wrote the first book. It shows the mark that it had left on his mind. Once again, he emphasized that 'Alice' was not Alice Liddell:

> Stand forth, then, from the shadowy past, 'Alice' the child of my dreams. … what wert thou, dream Alice, in thy foster father's eyes? How shall I picture thee? Loving, first, loving and gentle: loving as a dog (forgive the prosaic simile, but I know no earthly love so pure and perfect) and gentle as a fawn; then courteous – courteous to all, high or low, grand or grotesque, King or Caterpillar. … then trustful, ready to accept the wildest impossibilities with that utter trust that only dreamers know, and lastly, curious – wildly curious, and with the eager enjoyment of Life that comes only in the happy hours of childhood, when all is new and fair, and when Sin and Sorrow are but names – empty words signifying nothing.[21]

Once again, Carroll went out of his way to say he was describing an unreal child, the 'child of my dreams'. He also made the specific point that Sin and Sorrow had nothing to do with her. A man struggling with his own sin could love his dream-'Alice' with nothing to fear.

Interestingly, Carroll did not think much of his *Alice* books in later life. He told his friend Gertrude Thomson that he could not really imagine what people saw in them, and he said that he had devoted far more thought to *Sylvie and Bruno* than he ever did to the *Alice* books.[22] He was a constructive man, not one to dwell on negatives, and it is not impossible that he associated the writing of the books with sinful times and sad feelings of his own.

But of course, his *Alice* – his dream Alice – was to make another famous appearance in his life after he had written *Alice in Wonderland*. After his father's death, grief-stricken from what he later described as the worst blow of his life, he returned to his imaginary Alice and created and recollected more adventures for her through a looking-glass, adventures which he could 'tell' the vanished little Liddells in his head.

Once more, in his imagination, his cheerful child friends might gather and enjoy his company as the river swept and sparkled by. Once more in his Wonderland, in his role of beloved storyteller, he was popular and happy. True, the children for whom he mentally told the stories that comprise *Through the Looking-Glass* no longer existed in real life. They were not dead – but the sunny days of their youth had gone forever and they lived now only in the dim eyes of a dreamer. He himself was that dreamer, and his 'Alice' was part of his consoling dream. The slightly chilling poem he appended to *Through the Looking-Glass* says most of this openly, and it is, of course, an acrostic on the name of Alice Pleasance Liddell.

A boat beneath a sunny sky,
Lingering onward dreamily
In an evening of July –

Children three that nestle near,
Eager eye and willing ear,
Pleased a simple tale to hear –

Long has paled that sunny sky:

Echoes fade and memories die:
Autumn frosts have slain July.

Still she haunts me, phantomwise,
Alice moving under skies
Never seen by waking eyes.

Children yet, the tale to hear,
Eager eye and willing ear,
Lovingly shall nestle near.

In a Wonderland they lie,
Dreaming as the days go by,
Dreaming as the summers die:

Ever drifting down the stream –
Lingering in the golden gleam –
Life, what is it but a dream?

Is it surprising that so many readers have instinctively detected dark shadows in both the *Alice* books? Just as the terror of depersonalization hangs over *Wonderland*, so the shadow of Death lies blackly athwart *Looking-Glass*.

In 1885, Carroll decided to issue a facsimile of the original story, and asked Alice Liddell, then aged 33, if he could borrow the manuscript. She did not exactly break down his door in her eagerness to help. She wrote to her father about it, and her letter is now lost, but his reply, in March 1885, suggests what her views were.

Dearest Alice, I think you cannot refuse Mr. Dodgson, although he has sold 120,000 copies. If you like to ask for the plates when he has done with them I do not suppose he will object. Probably he will re-process the pages by the new photographic process, so the reproductions will be very exact.

Ever your loving Father, HGL[23]

Mrs Liddell, Alice's mother, made Alice destroy all the letters Carroll had sent to her, according to Alice's son. This may have been mere motherly tidying-up, but in the biography of her husband which Mrs Liddell commissioned after his death, a whole chapter is devoted to the Dean's family, but there is not a single mention of *Alice in Wonderland*, nor of Lewis Carroll. Alice herself was also reluctant to tell her story, and was only persuaded to do so by her son, shortly before her death. However, in 1928, when she was in her late seventies, Alice sold Carroll's original manuscript for a then record price of £15,400, so her earlier snobbishness about Carroll's commercial success had obviously faded. In 2001, Alice's entire Carroll collection of letters, memorabilia and photographs was sold by her descendants for a sum of just under £2 million. Whoever his 'Alice' really was, Carroll's *Alice in Wonderland* did Alice Liddell and her family proud.

Carroll's picture of Xie Kitchin as a Dane, taken in 1873, was one of his particular favourites. A relative of his sister-in-law, named Alice Emily Donkin, later used this photograph as the basis for her painting 'Waiting to Skate' which Carroll then hung in his rooms. Xie was the daughter of Revd George Kitchin, Dean of Winchester.

7

'That awful mystery'

Religion and the Supernatural

'And he, who allows himself the habit of thus uttering
holy words, with no thought of their meaning, is but too
likely to find that, for him, God has become a myth, and
heaven a poetic fancy – that for him, the light of life is
gone, and that he is at heart an atheist, lost in "a darkness
that may be felt".'

Preface, Sylvie and Bruno Concluded

People who knew Carroll usually described his religious
belief as straightforward and childlike. Some said it was
the foundation of his existence, and in many ways this was
true. Without the devout underpinning of his faith, and his
constant awareness of God, he would have been an unimagi-
nably different person from the man that he was.

So his religion sustained, guided and supported him; and
yet there is ample evidence that it also confined and concerned
him, and made him twist and turn like a trapped eel in his
efforts to reconcile his sincere beliefs with the logical approach
to life that was so important to him. In fact, the more closely
his religious beliefs are examined, the harder they are to grasp.
Carroll once suggested that other people might find them
'strange and wild',[1] and in some ways, they were. As with so

many other aspects of his life and work, the apparent simplicity was deeply deceptive.

Carroll was a minister of the Church of England, and everyone knew it. He rose faithfully each morning to attend chapel, and he sometimes went to several services on Sundays, just as he had done in his childhood. He owned hundreds of books on a huge variety of religious topics, and he spent a good deal of his time reading, meditating upon and debating moral and theological ideas. It is less well known that he had been very reluctant to become a clergyman, and that although he was a reverend, he was only a deacon and never became a fully ordained priest. This failure to take priest's orders was one of the most important issues of his whole life.

His family had not expected there to be any problem, it seems. His father had probably hoped that all his sons would follow in his own footsteps and become clergymen. Even better if one or two could be clergymen scholars, working and studying at Christ Church as he himself had done, until the time came for them to marry and earn their livings in a parish.

Edwin and Skeffington Dodgson duly became clergymen, although neither showed any inclination to be scholars. Wilfred, the third son, was exceedingly bright, but he had no wish to be either a clergyman or a scholar – his tastes ran towards country life, and he became an estate manager, ending up considerably wealthier than his brothers.

Carroll had no interest in a business career and was willing and able to take on the scholarly lifestyle. His father's friend, the famous churchman Dr Pusey was impressed by Carroll, and agreed to nominate him in due course for a Studentship (similar to a Fellowship) at Christ Church. Pusey made it plain that he was not doing this out of nepotism but because he genuinely thought Carroll was worthy of the post. His high opinion of Carroll might sadly have rubbed salt into the wounds when Carroll later found himself unable to progress to priest's orders.

As explained in Chapter 2, Carroll needed to accept various conditions laid upon him under the medieval rules that were still in operation. These included the obligation to remain celibate during his Studentship, and to take priest's orders within four years of becoming an MA – that is, deacon's orders by 1861 and priest's orders shortly after that. His subject of mathematics had nothing to do with religion, but Christ Church had a semi-ecclesiastical history, and the requirement to be ordained was, to some extent, an anachronistic relic of this.

So it was all settled, and at first Carroll did exactly what was expected. In an early letter which his father wrote to him about organizing his finances, he assumed Carroll would be a scholar and a celibate priest, and then, after a few years in Christ Church, would accept one of the Christ Church livings, marry and have a family.

In the earliest surviving diaries, Carroll referred sometimes to his clerical training and his possible future as a clergyman. Yet, although he was a dutiful son, there were hints that all was not well in his mind. His anxiety first surfaced in an argument he recorded with his brother Wilfred in 1857, when Wilfred was an undergraduate at Christ Church. Wilfred's somewhat unconventional view was that people ought to decide for themselves which college rules they wanted to follow. Carroll believed that, in order to respect discipline, people should obey rules even if they did not want to do so. He was completely unable to bring Wilfred round to his own point of view, and his failure to convince even his little brother of what seemed to him like a self-evident matter left him racked with doubts. 'If I find it so hard to prove a plain duty to one individual, and that one unpractised in argument, how can I ever be ready to face the countless sophisms and ingenious arguments against religion which a clergyman must meet with!' he agonised.[2]

Further diary entries show that he found it hard to keep up with the divinity reading he had to do in preparation for ordination. By the eve of New Year 1858, he was planning to settle the subject of being ordained priest 'finally and definitely' in his mind – a clear indication that he was still *not* settled about it. A page has been removed from his diaries at this point, suggesting that his family wanted to prevent posterity from learning the full extent of his religious difficulties.

Much of Carroll's intellectual problem with religion lay in the difficulty of reconciling the belief-based approach of traditional religion with the demands of rational argument. With his particular and precise turn of mind, he would always find it difficult to assert anything that he himself did not entirely understand or believe, let alone persuade others that it must be true. His studies in preparation for ordination at Cuddesdon Theological College obviously did not help him resolve his difficulties. As most of his diaries for the period are missing, there are large gaps in the information, but it is known that he delayed taking deacon's orders until the very last possible moment. In fact, he only took the plunge just before Christmas 1861, less than two months before the final deadline. If he had delayed any further, he would almost certainly have lost his Studentship.

Not only are there no diaries, but no contemporary letters survive to give any insights into the matter. However, a letter he wrote 25 years later to his godson Willie Wilcox gives a glimpse of his state of mind. His language is measured, but he tells Willie that shortly before the time when he was to take deacon's orders, he realized he had 'no inclination' to work as a vicar with a parish. Indeed, his work as a mathematical lecturer was well established, he added, and so he had wondered if it might perhaps be his duty *not* to take Holy Orders of any kind.[3]

This was, of course, a non-sequitur. His own father had been an educator, and many schoolteachers at the time were clergymen. Typically, in his letter, Carroll left Willie to fill in the gaps for himself, and did not actually say that he believed educational work was unsuitable for a clergyman himself. If Willie chose not to question the assumption – and it seems that he did not – Carroll would not expand further.

After discussing the matter with his bishop, Carroll continued to Willie, he had conceded that there was no conflict between teaching and the priesthood after all. Yet still he had not left the matter alone. He had gone to his holy friend, the preacher H P Liddon, for more advice. This time he had wanted to know whether he could take deacon's orders without taking priest's orders afterwards. Perhaps he could take deacon's orders as a 'sort of experiment', he had suggested to Liddon, to see how the occupations of a clergyman suited him. Liddon had reas-suringly replied that that was fine, adding that a deacon was in a totally different position from a priest, and 'much more free to regard himself as practically a layman'.[4] So Carroll had gone ahead as a deacon, but even after this, he did not give up on debating the matter of how much further he should go.

Less than a year after being ordained a deacon, he approached Alice's father, Dean Liddell, to ask whether he was really obliged to continue onwards to priest's orders. This time, he offered yet another reason to justify his reluctance. He tried to interpret the Christ Church rules to make the case that he need not become a priest because he had been a lay student of the college and not a clerical student. This was just not so, and the Dean, not surprisingly, disagreed. At the very least, he said, Carroll was bound to take priest's orders as soon as possible. In fact, he should have done it already, and since he had not, he had probably already lost his Studentship. Liddell now talked of laying the whole matter before the college electors.

This was a serious matter which would take the issue onto a different and more dangerous plane. What the Dean was proposing could have cost Carroll his job. It could have meant the loss of his home and the ruination of his prospects. He must have been terrified. All he wrote in his diary, laconic as ever, was 'I differed from this view'[5]

The Dean finally decided not to take the matter further. Nobody knows quite why, but Liddell was a reformer, impatient of old ways, and the issue was certainly archaic. He had plenty of plans for Christ Church, and he would be facing opposition about these, so may not have wanted to cause a fuss over something which Carroll sincerely felt that he could not face. He was a kindly man in his own way, and perhaps Carroll's obvious distress also struck him as sincere.

Although the Dean's decision took the college's ordination pressure off him once and for all, Carroll continued to fret over the matter. His increasingly desperate efforts to escape his sworn obligations, and his misery (discussed in Chapter 4) about his own unspecified 'sins' raise the real possibility that his difficulties over Biblical truths were not the only reason for his reluctance to become a priest. There is no doubt that he was very troubled by the conflict between the impossibility of accommodating his two intense needs: to believe in God and to think logically. He knew that as a clergyman he would be in line for many searching questions about religious truths, and it does not seem that he felt competent to deal with these in depth.

Somewhere along the line, also – probably during the 1858–1862 period for which his diaries are missing – he seems to have done something which made him hate himself for what he perceived as evil behaviour. Whatever this matter was, it was now also tormenting and oppressing him.

At the end of 1863 he wrote miserably of 'how much of neglect, carelessness, and sin have I to remember! I had hoped, during this year, to have made a beginning in parochial work, to have thrown off habits of evil, to have advanced in my work at Ch. Ch. – how little, next to nothing, has been done of all this!'[6] In 1866, hearing from a friend about his work as a clergyman among workmen, he was again plunged into depression, as he concluded that he himself was unfit for such work. 'Oh Lord, make me Thine indeed. Make me a clean heart, oh God, and renew a right spirit within me,' he wrote.[7] Things appeared to get worse. By 1867 he was writing that 'To have entered into Holy Orders seems almost a desecration, with my undisciplined and worldly affections.'[8]

Collingwood admitted in his biography that Carroll's mind was 'much exercised' about becoming a priest, and he conscientiously listed the arguments which his uncle had given the family both for and against the idea. In favour of the priesthood, said Collingwood, Carroll had thought that being ordained would increase his influence and his power to do good among the undergraduates. On the other hand, he added, Carroll thought that his speech impediment would stop him carrying out his clerical duties, and he had not wanted to live with the 'almost puritanical strictness' which was then considered essential for a clergyman.

The Bishop of Oxford had forbidden men in Holy Orders from attending theatres or operas, although he later said that applied only to parochial clergy, not deacons. In fact, Carroll could have avoided that stricture by refusing to take a parish. But in any case, it is scarcely possible that going to the theatre was more important to Carroll than doing his duty by God. He was capable of vigorous wriggling in order to escape from things he did not want to do, but he never showed any sign of shirking difficult tasks once he had accepted that they were his duty. From a young age, as his argument with Wilfred had shown, he had thought one should conform with rules *on principle*, as a form of discipline.

As for the speech impediment, it was true that it made preaching fearsome to him sometimes. He loathed the idea of having to read from the Bible in front of an audience and making people laugh when they should be feeling reverent. Yet there is plenty of evidence from those who knew him, and from his own letters, that he did force himself to preach even though the idea distressed and intimidated him.

None of these many reasons seem quite enough to justify taking the huge step of risking his job, his home and his prospects. Nor were they enough to justify the dismay that his refusal to become a priest would be likely to cause in his family circle.

Collingwood also added that Carroll's preacher friend H P Liddon believed that a deacon should not have to do parish work *if he felt himself unfit for it*. Carroll had also used the concept of 'unfitness' about his own clerical work.[9] Further, on 24 July 1862 he wrote in his diary: 'I have also been asked by Hackman and by Chamberlain to preach for them: till I can rule myself better, preaching is but a solemn mockery – "thou that teachest another, teachest thou not thyself?" God grant this may be the last such entry I may have to make! that so I may not, when I have preached to others, be myself a castaway.' Carroll, who knew enormous passages of the Bible off by heart, was quoting from Romans 2 and Corinthians, Chapter 9, in reference to himself:

> Thou therefore, that teachest another, teachest not thyself: thou, that preachest that men should not steal, stealest. Thou, that sayest men should not commit adultery, committest adultery: thou, that abhorrest idols, committest sacrilege: Thou, that makest thy boast of the law, by transgression of the law dishonourest God. For the name of God through you is blasphemed ...

and

> But I keep under my body, and bring it into subjection: lest that by any means, when I have preached to others, I myself should be a castaway.

His entry makes it clear that he felt his own preaching was a mockery and blasphemy, because he had failed to 'rule himself' physically and done something that transgressed the Commandments of God. He was not fit to preach because of the gravity of what he saw as his own moral failings.

By destroying or mislaying the relevant diaries, one or more members of the Dodgson family made sure that posterity will never know exactly what the sin was that caused Carroll so much distress, but it is clear that the issue was for him a really important one. Some commentators have stated that Carroll was merely hypersensitive about sin, or that he felt bad about oversleeping sometimes, or not working hard enough at his mathematics. The lengths to which he went show that the issue was more important than this, and to pretend otherwise is to trivialize his difficulty.

Throughout all his miseries, there was never any sign that his faith was wavering. His personal problems were compounded by the fact that, like others of his generation, he was also having to navigate through the maze of contemporary religious discussion and decide on his own position on the new thinking. He lived at a time of great religious energy – of church-building, of debate, of evangelizing. Both before and after the appearance of Darwin's *Origin of Species* in 1859, a fundamental reassessment of the basis of Christian belief was occurring. So lively was the subject of religion that young people would gather in their droves to hear famous preachers when they arrived at local churches.

Oxford's own religious upheavals of the 1830s and 1840s had arrived with the traditionalist High Church Oxford Movement, which aimed to take the Church back to its Catholic roots. Carroll's father had attended Christ Church at this time, and was High Church and orthodox, although he drew the line at Roman Catholicism. Mr Dodgson Senior looked only to the past for religious authority, and accepted only orthodox sacraments and words as holy. His beliefs sometimes got him embroiled in religious controversy with those who had less authoritarian views.

Carroll owed his position at the college to Dr Pusey, not only a friend of his father, but a leading light of the Oxford Movement and a hard-line religious conservative, in the modern sense. Pusey was quiet and austere, with long, curling side-whiskers; the Pope is reported once to have said of him that he saw him as the bell which called people to church (by this he meant the Catholic Church), yet stayed outside it himself. Several of Carroll's colleagues and friends were also very High Church, and the Christ Church at which the young Carroll arrived was still old-fashioned and strongly ecclesiastical in tone.

However, the Oxford Movement had lost its fire by Carroll's time, and Pusey was getting old. A new liberalism had begun replacing the backward-looking ideas, and Carroll took a deep interest in this new wave. All his life, he was more than willing to give new ideas a hearing, however challenging they might be. As early as April 1856, Carroll attended a lecture by the Italian preacher Alessandro Gavazzi, who, as an anti-Papist, was at the opposite end of the religious spectrum from Pusey. Gavazzi was booed and hissed throughout by his undergraduate listeners. Carroll did not approve of the booing, and thought Gavazzi spoke well, but he felt his arguments were nonsense.[10]

He was also at Christ Church, and in his late twenties, when Darwin published his *Origin of Species* and of course it was the huge idea of evolution which would be the greatest challenge of the period. By the middle of the 19th century, it was becoming increasingly difficult for an educated person to deny the scientific and historical evidence accumulating against the literal truth of the Bible. Even the most devout had begun to suspect that the Biblical description of the Creation might not be literally, scientifically true.

Darwin had crystallised this subject in the public mind. He had been the one to develop a bold and intellectually coherent theory, though some of his contemporaries developed less structured, less scientific theories on evolutionary themes, both before and after the publication of *Origin of Species*. The Bible itself was still taken as the Word of God, of course, but now people began to reflect upon the fact that the Bible had been translated – not necessarily very accurately – from archaic foreign language sources. Some of its content, furthermore, reflected a world whose attitudes were very different from those of 19th-century England.

Carroll's library contains several books which develop the theme of evolution, although, rather surprisingly, there is no copy of *Origin of Species* in the auction catalogue of his effects. It is all but inconceivable that he would not have read the book, and it is known that he paid a considerable sum to attend the seminal debate on evolution between Thomas Huxley and Bishop Wilberforce at the newly built Oxford Museum of Natural History in 1860. Unfortunately, his diaries are missing and so we will never know what he thought about the debate itself. However, it can be assumed that he felt fairly positively towards Darwin, since in later life he wrote him a friendly letter offering him an extraordinary photograph he had taken as a possible illustration for Darwin's book *The Expression of the Emotions in Man and Animals* (1872).

As well as reading widely on the subject of evolution, Carroll also became friendly with F D Maurice, the founder of Christian Socialism. He was almost certainly introduced to Maurice's ideas by his good friend the writer George MacDonald, who was also one of Maurice's friends and disciples. Maurice had been close to and influenced by the poet Samuel Taylor Coleridge, and Coleridge's *Aids to Reflection* (1825) was an important book to Carroll, who read it more than once. In the book, Coleridge addresses the difficulties faced by those for whom traditional forms of worship no longer seemed relevant, and considered a more inward approach to religion. Maurice was a firm, yet humane man whose views were, of course, significantly at odds with those of Pusey – and, of course, with Carroll's father. Despite its name, Christian Socialism was essentially a religious movement. It focused on the idea that God's Kingdom already existed on earth and, if allowed to surface, would (among other benefits) put an end to divisions between rich and poor.

Maurice stood firmly against the concept of eternal punishment in Hell, and taught that God would not condemn any man to live forever without His love – a view which he backed with quotations from Holy scriptures. His ideas were revolutionary, and for these and other reasons he had been dismissed for heterodoxy from his posts (including the Chair of Divinity) at King's College London.

The concept of God's goodness transcending written dogma suited Carroll's temperament. What is more, his favourite poet Tennyson also admired Maurice, and Carroll and his sisters had already put together an index to Tennyson's 'In Memoriam', a long and closely wrought poem which viewed human systems of religion and philosophy as mere specks within God's eternal existence. The view of religion that Tennyson expressed in this poem was essentially that religious and philosophical systems helped man to organize his thoughts, but did not provide true knowledge of God. For Man, true knowledge could be experienced only through faith. This 'Power in the Darkness whom we guess', as he put it, was a call against atheism, replacing rational doubt with inward emotional certainty. It was a message which resonated with Carroll and many others of his generation.

It was all part of the movement away from slavish adherence to the literal truth of the Bible, and it had a huge effect on Carroll. It was during the 1860s that the 'dual personality' which some commentators insist that he had starts to make its presence felt. Those who knew him insisted that he did not have a dual personality, but in fact his behaviour did begin to change and he started to become inconsistent in certain ways, as if a wish to defy convention vied with an equally desperate desire to live a conventionally religious life. He was conscious of his own sin, he found it hard to accept his faith without understanding it, and he had to deal with the developing revolutions in religious thought of which Oxford was an epicentre. He was under a lot of pressure from several directions, and at first it was not clear which way he would go.

The fantasy Wonderland Carroll created, underground and out of sight, simply sidestepped the whole matter; it was notable for having no elements of sin or virtue. Perhaps Wonderland's freedom from all hint of religion, and the relief it must have afforded Carroll to write it, is part of the reason why Alice's adventures are so oddly compelling.

Alice's lack of moralism was certainly very unusual among Victorian children's stories, many of which even had a tag at the end proclaiming the moral message, just in case anyone had possibly managed to miss it. Carroll parodied these books in *Alice in Wonderland*, as in the passage where Alice is enduring the conversation of the Duchess, who inconsequentially declares that:

> ... the moral of that is – 'Oh, 'tis love, 'tis love, that makes the world go round!'
>
> 'Somebody said,' Alice whispered, 'that it's done by everybody minding their own business!'

Furthermore, in the 1860s, Carroll wrote to 15-year-old Lilia MacDonald that he had sent her a book of which 'the inside is not meant to be read. The book has got a moral – so I need hardly say it is *not* by Lewis Carroll.'[11]

It can thus be seen to what extent his alter ego of 'Lewis Carroll' was, at this time, prepared to show doubts about belief in his books, even though religion was not specifically mentioned. The conversation between Alice and the Queens in *Looking-Glass* jeers at the inherent ridiculousness of trying to make yourself believe something when you simply can't. Alice says:

> 'One can't believe impossible things.'
>
> 'I daresay you haven't had much practice,' said the Queen. 'When I was your age, I always did it for half an hour a day. Why, sometimes I've believed as many as six impossible things before breakfast.'

The depth of Carroll's inner confusion is shown by the sharp contrast between the perceptive, free-speaking, independent-minded rationality of 'Alice' and the over-religious emotional anxiety which clouded so much of his other behaviour. Alas, no amount of literary scepticism about conventional morality could stop him from yearning to be good, or craving redemption from whatever he felt his sin was.

Shortly after writing *Alice in Wonderland* but before *Through the Looking-Glass* Carroll put together an idea for a sentimental and unrealistic play called 'Morning Clouds', which stands in fascinating juxtaposition to both *Alice* books. The play was never completed, but its sketchy plot revolves around a mother, and also, as is so often the case with Carroll, a motherly sister and their son/brother. This boy has been stolen and used by various evil men. The section which most caught Carroll's heart was the final scene, which was central to his vision of the play. He explained to the impresario and playwright Tom Taylor how, in this final scene, the erring boy was returned to the loving arms of his mother and sister. Against all expectations, he was going to take his rightful place in the family once more. The play ends with a highly conventional vision of idealized happiness around the family fireside.

Interestingly, there are no women, good or bad, in the play, except for the widowed mother and the sister. Carroll said that he wished specifically for no love interest, and wrote that 'I should much like to see a piece without any lovers at all: it would be a feat in dramatic writing, and a bone for the critics.'[12]

One wonders what his own family's reaction was to his religious difficulties, but not a single public word of their views survive, even though his determination not to embrace the priesthood must have caused a good deal of discussion in his home. Whatever the cause of his confusion, it was obvious after 1861 that he could no longer progress on the conventional route.

He probably never did beat out a new religious path to his own satisfaction, but he tried bravely to graft elements of progressive, even somewhat revolutionary religious ideas onto a much simpler, straightforward approach to religion which he made his own. His essential approach, as his colleagues commented, was in some ways almost childlike. He accepted the idea that Man was continually sinning, and so constantly in need of God's forgiveness. He saw moral improvement as a constant struggle to do good and be good. He both adored and feared God.

But he was probably only partially successful in his efforts to reconcile his conflicts. As he passed into middle age and then later life, his torment at his own grievous sin became less acute, but the horror of sin most certainly did not disappear from his mind. The older he grew, and the nearer his death came, the more he seems to have worried about it. The preface to *Sylvie and Bruno*, first published in 1889, shows that towards the end of his life, Carroll developed a constant fear of dying suddenly and meeting his Maker while in a state of sin. A long passage in the preface to the book explains how no man can defer his own death for a single moment, and may at any time hear the call: 'We dare not live in any scene in which we dare not die.'

The simple and pure-minded company of children was a

consolation for him as he continued to dwell on problems of good and evil. He wondered who should be considered sinful and who blameless in various different circumstances. An as yet unpublished manuscript entitled 'Theatre Dress',[13] which he wrote in 1888, shows that he had not entirely resolved his ideas about sexuality, as he mused upon who was to blame for the fact that women dancers in theatres wore provocative costumes.

Typically, he did not blame the young and beautiful women – and it clearly never crossed his mind that they themselves might enjoy wearing flimsy, provocative costumes. His rage and anger were nearly always directed at bullying old women or at grubby-minded males, for he rarely hated young and beautiful women for any reason. So the guilty ones in the theatre world were, in his view, the men. There were the male managers who made the girls dress this way to pull in customers, and the lecherous male customers who demanded such things. In a telling aside, the 56-year-old Carroll conceded how extraordinarily hard it was for *young* men seeing these women to refrain from doing what they would bitterly regret later.

By the end of his life Carroll had moved entirely away from the non-moral refuge of 'Alice'. Instead, he had adopted a ludicrous and egregious moralism, apparently to assuage his anxieties about being caught in any form of sin. He tried to control every aspect of his mental life and, famously, the preface of *Curiosa Mathematica Part II: Pillow Problems* (1893), a book of mathematical recreations, recommends mathematics as a way of blotting out 'sceptical thoughts, which seem for the moment to uproot the firmest faith' in the middle of the night.

At around the same time, he wrote a clever and interesting double acrostic for the young actress Isa Bowman. Both the first letter of each line and the first letters of each verse spell her name. The restrictions involved in writing acrostics often pushed him to write particularly well, and many of his acrostics contain interesting ideas. That may be because he was concentrating on perfecting the technical form rather than on trying to push a message, thereby giving his usually-controlled unconscious thoughts an opportunity to see the light of day.

His little poem has nothing whatever to do with Isa (or Sylvie, or Bruno), but instead has a chilling, glooming quality which spotlights the loneliness of the man writing in the dark shadow of a God who might not be a loving God – or might not be there at all.

> Is all our Life, then but a dream
> Seen faintly in the golden gleam
> Athwart Time's dark resistless stream?

> Bowed to the earth with bitter woe
> Or laughing at some raree-show
> We flutter idly to and fro.

> Man's little day in haste we spend,
> And, from its merry noontide, send
> No glance to meet the silent end.

As his life went on, Carroll also devoted increasing time to trying to codify rules by which he and others could identify and hate Sin yet still remain humane and loving human beings. An unpublished letter of 1894 to his cousin Herbert Wilcox set out some of his carefully developed views on more general manifestations of Sin. He argued that someone who is offered bad advice or a bad example in his formative years may show catastrophically wrong behaviour as a result of it, yet could not necessarily be considered sinful for it. He quoted one of his favourite philosophers, Herbert Spencer, in citing a 'bad environment' which might diminish or even remove this person's guilt in the sight of God. However, as he wrote to Wilcox, to set this distinction between Right and Wrong against the conventional religious view that God was almighty, led to a contradiction. A *genuinely* almighty God would, in theory, be capable of turning Wrong into Right. Since the distinction between Right and Wrong was unmovable, Carroll would, in those circumstances, deny that God was 'almighty'.

More detail of some of the beliefs Carroll arrived at late in life are set out in written discussions he had in 1889 with the grown-up child-friend Mary Brown. He told Mary that he believed that he was responsible to a personal Being for everything he did in his life, and he referred to that personal Being, he said, as 'God'. He believed God to be perfectly good.

The first and most important tenet of his belief, he explained, was that there was an absolute, self-existent, external distinction between Right and Wrong. He defined Right as 'what we ought to do' and Wrong as 'what we ought not to do', without reference to rewards or punishments.[14] He also denied the absolute power of God to Mary Brown when he was considering the question of eternal punishment. He really was unable to countenance the idea of a God who was able to condemn people to endless suffering.

He and Mary Brown discussed the question of whether God would punish two people equally if they committed the same sin as each other, even though the temptation may have been, owing to difference of circumstances, irresistible for one, and easily resisted by the other. Carroll decided that God would take account of all circumstances in judging any action, and would only punish *wilful* sin and not punish anyone who wanted to repent. 'And if any one urges "then, to be consistent, you ought to grant the possibility that the Devil himself might repent and be forgiven," I reply "and I do grant it!"' he wrote. He concluded with a resonant piece of advice, clearly hard won. He said that when two things contradicted, one should decide which belief to hold to personally. 'I think you will find peace and comfort in such belief,' he concluded.[15]

In addition, while prepared to allow that God may not be all-powerful, he also considered the possibility that God was not all-loving either. In 1893, in a circular which he distributed to booksellers, Carroll stated that he wished to buy a copy of Hamilton's *Animal Futurity*, which discussed whether animals had souls that could survive death. The conventional view is that they do not and cannot. However, Hamilton's book made the point that if animals are not compensated for the suffering they undergo in this life, then the idea of a just and loving God is compromised. Carroll's search for this book shows that he was prepared to consider this possibility in order to satisfy his own mind.

By the time he was elderly, Carroll had begun to feel that he should be taking his religious views out to a wider public. As he had never been ordained priest, he did not conduct services, but, just as he had done for F D Maurice, he sometimes assisted priests at services, and would preach when invited to do so.

He did not, of course, enjoy any occasions where he was obliged to speak to the congregation, and often found the prospect completely terrifying, but he eventually concluded that it was his duty to preach when asked, and so he did. In his diary for 31 October 1862, he described the humiliating experience of reading through a service perfectly well until he came to the first verse of the hymn before the sermon. There, he said, the two words 'strife, strengthened' coming together were too much for him, and he had to leave the verse unfinished. This and other incidents haunted him through his later years. It was desperately important to him that all aspects of his religious expression should remain pure and unsullied but, unfortunately, his speech hesitation did make people laugh at him, and, by extension, at the Word of God.

His friend Margaret Mayhew gave a vivid description of his difficulty. Recalling her first sight of him speaking in public, she completely failed to remember what he had been talking about, but did recall that he 'opened his mouth wide enough for his tongue to be seen wagging up and down, and in addition to this, carried away by the theme of his discourse, he became quite emotional, making me afraid that he would break down in tears.' She was unable to stifle her giggles, despite feeling terribly ashamed of herself.[16]

As a means of dealing with his humiliating speech hesitation, Carroll developed a method whereby he never wrote his sermons down, but jotted down headings only, and then prepared them mentally beforehand. Having laid the headings out in his mind, he would then progress through them logically. He spoke with great earnestness, usually slowly, and was described as sometimes almost forgetting his audience as he spoke.

Reading this and other descriptions of his preaching, one gets the impression that he was not an inspiring preacher, just as he had not been an inspiring lecturer. He sometimes felt so anxious before a sermon that he would feel he could not go through with it at all. It was a relief all round that he was rarely asked to preach.

As well as grimly struggling through church services in this way, he tried increasingly stridently to make others behave in what he considered to be a reverent manner. This is one of the aspects of his religious life which has been best remembered, probably because most of those who left recollections of him only knew him in later life. It happened, like the rest of his transformation, rather gradually. As he left his thirties, this light-hearted, tolerant and mischievous man gradually and deliberately boxed himself inside a grotesque prison of moral self-regulation. The younger writer who would not allow 'Lewis Carroll' to offer his friends anything with a moral gradually became the older man whose concern for 'morality' became one of his defining characteristics.

Some of the more extreme elements of his behaviour may

have been an eccentric attempt to copy his father, who died when Carroll was 36. Whether Carroll felt he was now taking on his father's religious mantle as head of the family, or whether it was a hardening of his response to whatever sin he felt he had committed in his twenties, it is hard to say. His father was notable for his upstanding morality and absolute refusal to jest upon any religious subjects.

Yet, although it was not in Carroll's gentle and sympathetic nature to be a zealot, in another of the contradictions which make him so puzzling his personal image in fact eventually became so extraordinarily moralistic that at times it almost resembled a caricature. Perhaps, unconsciously, it *was* a caricature. Carroll was an incorrigible parodist, even though he took his own moralizing deadly seriously. He presented his reverence, devoutness and propriety in a way which often aroused some amusement, yet got the message over with such bold strokes that even the most stupid and unobservant onlooker could recognize and remember it. Then, having been presented so unmistakably with what they were supposed to see, people obligingly saw it.

His friend Mrs Shute mentioned that he would avert his eyes and 'turn his back as much as possible' while helping her over stiles, so that he could not possibly catch a glimpse of her legs and feet. The mental picture this evokes is comical, and even she, as a respectable Victorian lady, thought it rather strange. Yet, however ridiculous, this elaborate charade successfully conveyed to her his intended message that he was, in her words, 'the pink of propriety'.[17]

Some of his colleagues are reported to have been genuinely intimidated by his primness and, considering that they were nearly all Victorian clergymen, he must have behaved primly indeed. He kept a close eye on would-be funny stories in the Christ Church Common Room and could be guaranteed to ruin any anecdote that touched upon his religious sensibilities.

He also spent considerable thought on laboriously working

out every detail of the personal moral guidelines with which he regulated his own behaviour. The details of many of these personal guidelines were, needless to say, a mystery to most people, and sometimes raised a smile. His irrepressible illustrator Harry Furniss was probably not too startled to receive a note from Carroll curtly informing him that he had returned four tickets to Furniss's forthcoming cabinet entertainment because it promised 'clever imitations of Dr. Talmage's sermons', and Carroll was sure these were bound to be profane.[18]

Carroll was also outraged at the sight of men dressed as women in theatricals, even though cross-dressers had pleasantly entertained him in his younger days. He also annoyed, upset and irritated his actor friends by lecturing them on the morality of the plays in which they appeared. Even the characters which his actor friends *pretended* to be did not escape his anxious moralizing. Ellen Terry remembered how she was made to feel thoroughly bad by his criticism of one scene in which her character had to remove some clothes. Isa Bowman recalled in her memoir that he was never quite as nice to her when she was playing bad characters, as when he saw her playing 'nice' girls.

Yet this was the man who was dogged with gossip about women in every recorded decade of his life. His friendship with Isa alone attracted so much that he had to lodge her with neighbours. As for Terry, she seems to have had a running joke with him about the only-too-grown-up 'little girls' he brought to her performances, and her letters to him contain several humorous references to these.

Carroll seemed unable to realize that he himself was striving to achieve freedom from the oppressive morality which he had driven himself to adopt. He did not perceive any contradictions in his own behaviour. The fact that his desperate grasping at freedom sometimes scandalized others merely irritated him and made him complain about 'Mrs Grundy'. The moral minefield through which he picked his way in later life was very real to him, but the bigger picture, if there ever had been one, seems to have entirely disappeared from his view. So one day he was turning his back on young ladies at stiles in case he caught a glimpse of their precious ankles. The next he was taking photographs of other equally respectable young ladies wearing gymnastic dress which showed off their ankles and a lot more besides. He was willing to deny that God was almighty, yet raged at anyone who demonstrated the slightest hint of disrespect for Almighty God. He was a man living in a permanent state of mental stress about religion, yet his faith was genuine and his religion was absolutely central to his picture of himself.

Carroll would no doubt have been outraged at the idea that religion and superstition had much in common, but his library and also his diary show that he had an interest in everything and anything pertaining to magic and the supernatural. Perhaps here was an area in which his festering spiritual anxiety did not torture him. In magic and fairy tale, he could think what he liked about non-material life without the spectre of God's disapproval and the pain of his own sins looming over him.

He was a founder member of the Society for Psychical Research, and his nephew Stuart Collingwood wrote that he took a great interest in occult phenomena. He was not alone. The huge upheavals in religion during the Victorian period led many people, of all social classes, down these particular by-ways. It is not for nothing that the Victorian period is the great age of the ghost story and the scary gothic fantasy. Although Darwin had, as Samuel Butler later put it, effectively 'banished Mind from the Universe', many books appeared detailing various ways that Darwinism did *not* preclude eternal life. So, with the advent of Darwinism, old beliefs in spirits and witches were dusted down and converted for the modern age as people clamoured to find some real evidence that there was another world beyond the tangible one.

Mediums became popular, with their strange powers and

manifestations of sounds and sights, their levitation, automatic writing, telepathy and clairvoyance. Carroll's personal library included a large variety of intriguing publications (some rather sensational) on medium confessions, demonical possession, miracles, ghosts of the living, the supernatural in nature, and the history of the black arts.

It will, perhaps, be no surprise to learn that his diary did not go into these matters, but it did at times refer to some of the more weighty publications he was thinking about. From this, and other sources, we know that he owned a number of important books on the supernatural, ranging from Henry Drummond's carefully considered *Natural Law of the Spirit World*, which endeavours to link spiritual and physical existence scientifically, to *Lights and Shadows of Spiritualism* by the celebrated medium D D Home and Cotton Mather's *Wonders of the Invisible World, Being an Account of the Trials of Several Witches Lately Executed in New-England*. Some of his books on magic and witchcraft were also rare and valuable, such as *Saducismus Triumphatus, Full and Plain Evidence concerning Witches and Apparitions* by the 17th-century preacher Joseph Glanvil, and Daniel Defoe's *A System of Magick or A History of the Black Art*.

It is tantalising to think of Carroll sitting reading these or similar works on a dark and stormy night by the light of a guttering candle, as he probably really did, and yet not know what he thought. Still, we do know at least that he liked to read his sinister supernatural books at night, if the *Eastbourne Gazette* of 19 January 1898 is to be believed. This paper contains an anonymous recollection of Carroll by a man who had been an undergraduate at Christ Church. Although Carroll was often criticized for being uninterested in undergraduates, this was not true, for he was very willing to help those who wanted to learn. The author of the letter to the *Eastbourne Gazette* had been invited to Carroll's rooms for a study session, and had been kindly received. While he was there, he noted that, 'the books which lined the walls of his bedroom were nearly all of them volumes relating to psychic phenomena in its many different forms.'

The comment that Carroll's bedroom was 'lined' with these books suggests that there were many of them. In his book on Carroll's library, Jeffrey Stern lists only 32, so either the anonymous undergraduate was wrong, or else many of the books were disposed of before they were catalogued.[19] The undergraduate went on to say that Carroll told him that his especial interest was in the investigation of hypnotic and will power manifestations; in other words, the calling up spirits while in a trance.

Nothing that Carroll may have written about hypnotic and willpower suggestions survives to give an insight into why these aspects of the paranormal particularly interested him. He dropped vague hints that, during his times of deepest spiritual distress, something unusual had happened to him to encourage him, and the tone of these hints suggests that a manifestation or ghostly vision may have occurred. As always, he was not going to let posterity know about it.

It was also Carroll's interest in ghosts that led to his meeting with the artist Thomas Heaphy, who experienced one of the most elaborate and best-known ghostly encounters of the 19th century. In his diary, Carroll notes that he 'called and introduced myself to Heaphy the artist, with no further pretext than my admiration for his pictures ... and the fact that Arthur Wilcox had corresponded with him about the ghost-story he wrote in *All the Year Round*.'[20]

Heaphy was keen on ghosts, but he was a deeply religious man, and his story was commonly believed to be true. If so, it was indeed most amazing; if not, it was an excellent story. It involved several inexplicable meetings and extraordinary coincidences, taking place over several months. In the course of these, Heaphy unwittingly dined with a lady ghost, who sat down at the table with the family and ate with surprising heart-iness for one so insubstantial.

Carroll viewed the portrait which Heaphy had painted of the ghostly lady, but it is not clear whether he believed that Heaphy really had his experience. However, he noted some further details which Heaphy gave him of the extraordinary meeting, including that the mystery ghost had been cramped and crowded out by the family governess who had also come down to join the dinner table that night.

Despite his keen interest in spirits and hypnotic manifes-tations, there is no record that Carroll attended any séances, although he would undoubtedly have heard all about them and it seems unlikely that a man so curious would have completely refrained from investigating them in person.

Table-rapping séances, introduced into England in the 1850s, were at first regarded as a kind of parlour game and were not taken too seriously. Churchmen were divided about them – although Bishop Wilberforce, predictably, came out against them. Séances were by no means always immoral (although some séances were said to be 'introducing' sessions between men and women), but they were known for their socially relaxed atmosphere and certain normal restrictions on conven-tional middle-class behaviour did not apply. This was part of their attraction: people of opposite sexes who barely knew each other could sit in the dark together, sing together and hold hands. The Dodgsons' rigorous beliefs probably did not include trivializing any contact there might be with spirits of the dead, and they probably did not approve of the hand-holding either.

Carroll left no comments about his thoughts on séances, although the final scene from *Looking-Glass* with its levitating tables and flying food has distinct echoes of the Victorian séance experience. But a little incident in Paris also raises the slight and intriguing possibility that Carroll may have encountered the famous medium Mrs Guppy shortly before her marriage, when she was still known as Miss Nichol.

In 1867, he went on a trip to Russia with the renowned preacher H P Liddon. On the way back, in September, the two men stopped for a few days in Paris. Carroll soon checked out of the Hotel Louvre where he was staying with Liddon and went instead to stay in L'Hotel des Deux-Mondes (Hotel of the Two Worlds). The reason for his move, he noted in his journal, was that the hotel where he was staying with Liddon was 'too large' for comfort.[21]

This was an extremely strange reason for moving out. No doubt the Louvre hotel *was* too large, but throughout the rest of the trip Carroll had endured many discomforts cheerfully and hardily. He had shown no desire for alternative accommodation, however grisly the sleeping arrangements may have been – and they had sometimes been very uncomfortable indeed. He and Liddon seem to have established a reasonable *modus vivendi* together during their journey, and remained friends after the trip.

But he was writing the journal of his Russian trip up in two special volumes, giving far more full an account than for his regular diary, and illustrating it too. He almost certainly intended to pass it around family and friends after he returned home so that they could read what he had done on his travels. The Louvre's uncomfortable size undoubtedly provided a truthful reason for moving out, even if it was not the complete reason. It might mask another reason, which he would not then have to explain.

Carroll had been told about the Deux-Mondes by an American lady with whom he had socialized in Moscow. The hotel was a respectable place, but it was of particular interest to spiritualists, who had enthusiastically adopted the idea of there being 'two worlds', and used the phrase in a number of connections. And, as it happens, Miss Nichol, (who would became Mrs Guppy later that year) spent most of the late 1860s on the continent, living in Italy and touring other cities, and L'Hotel des Deux-Mondes was the place in which she conducted her séances when she visited Paris at that time.[22]

She was, as one might expect, a fraud; but her séances were most entertaining, and made a particular feature of flowers and food. She was known to shower the assembled spectators with flowers, apples, grapes, candied pineapple, live ducks and even chunks of ice as part of her interesting communications with the dead. It sounds intriguing, and if the ever-inquisitive Carroll had wished to research a séance, Paris would certainly have been the place to do it, well away from his ordinary life.

Yet even if he did experience the manifestations of Mrs Guppy or one of her colleagues, and even if (as suggested later) he used some of this material in *Looking-Glass*, it hardly seems likely that attending séances would have convinced him to believe in them. When it came to spirits and ghosts, Carroll demonstrated a sturdy rationalism which kept his inexhaustible curiosity in check. In a letter to his friend James Langton Clarke, written some years after the trip abroad, he declared that he did not think psychic phenomena could be *entirely* put down to trickery, although he did not think that disembodied spirits were much to do with it.[23]

He was corresponding with Clarke about the 'two rings' experiment devised by Johann Zöllner, a professor of physics at the University of Leipzig who was convinced that spirits lived in the Fourth Dimension. Carroll had touched upon the Fourth Dimension himself in a mathematical paper of 1859. He had also read a Society for Psychical Research pamphlet on thought-reading, and given it serious consideration. He had concluded that the evidence available suggested there was some kind of natural and yet unidentified force, allied to electricity, by which brains could act upon each other. So although he believed that the spiritual medium upon whom Zöllner had conducted the experiment was a fraud, he suggested that everything seemed to point to the existence of a yet-unknown natural force, 'allied to electricity and nerve-force, by which brain can act on brain'.

It was a sensible conclusion, and one which may yet turn out to be true. Carroll told Langton Clarke that he thought this 'force' would be eventually classed among known natural forces, and its laws set out. 'The scientific sceptics, who always shut their eyes till the last moment to any evidence that seems to point beyond materialism, will have to accept it as a proved fact,' he continued.[24]

Caroll never laid claim to any psychic abilities himself, although he believed that he had had at least one telepathic experience in 1891, which he duly recorded in his diary.

> Before giving out the second hymn, the curate read out some notices. Meanwhile I took my hymn-book, and said to myself (I have no idea why) 'it will be Hymn 416,' and I turned to it. It was not one I recognized as having ever heard: and, on looking at it, I saw 'it is very prosaic: it is a very unlikely one.' And it was really startling, the next minute, to hear the curate announce, 'Hymn 416!'[25]

In general, Carroll's attitude towards spiritualism, rather like his attitude towards religion, was a mixture of an intense interest and wish to believe, and an inherent scepticism and rationalism where non-material matters were concerned. His view of himself was immovably grounded in his identity as a Christian, and his parents' devoted religious training and the continuing piety of his own large, close family, were strong lifelong influences upon him. Yet it would not have been like him to brush aside the difficulties and doubts which increasingly became part of Victorian intellectual life.

As his revealing aside to Mary Brown has shown, he eventually took the decision to settle on what he intended to believe, and stick to it. His resulting simple and luminous piety was noted by several of his friends, but the hundreds of theological books in his library show that this apparently childlike sincerity was hard won – and not quite as clear and bright as it seemed. The mathematician in him yearned for indisputable certainties, the uneasy clergyman sought closeness with a loving, personal God, and the clear, rational and independent thinker needed to confront whatever the cold truth might really be. He never stopped trying to reconcile these views. He might have been a less interesting man if he had succeeded in doing so, but also, perhaps, a rather happier one.

are ferrets! Where <u>can</u> I have dropped them,
I wonder?" Alice guessed in a moment that
it was looking for the nosegay and the pair
of white kid gloves, and she began hunting
for them, but they were now nowhere to be
seen — everything seemed to have changed
since her swim in the pool, and her walk
along the river-bank with its fringe of
rushes and forget-me-nots, and the glass
table and the little door had vanished.

Soon the rabbit
noticed Alice, as
she stood looking
curiously about
her, and at once
said in a quick
angry tone, "why,
Mary Ann! what
<u>are</u> you doing out
here? Go home this
moment, and look
on my dressing-table for my gloves and nosegay,
and fetch them here, as quick as you can
run, do you hear?" and Alice was so much
frightened that she ran off at once, without

The three Alices: Carroll's own hand drawn version (p 211) Tenniel's version and Carroll's photograph of the little Alice Liddell, aged 8, sitting by a potted fern, two years before he told her the story of 'Alice's Adventures in Wonderland'.

8

'And would you be a Poet?'

Literature and Storytelling

Then proudly smiled that old man
To see the eager lad
Rush madly for his pen and ink
And for his blotting-pad –
But, when he thought of *PUBLISHING*,
His face grew stern and sad ...
'Poeta Fit, Non Nascitur' (A Poet is Made, not Born*)*

There is a famous story about Queen Victoria and Lewis
Carroll. It tells how the queen is so touched by her children's
devotion to *Alice in Wonderland* that she issues a royal command
that she should be the first person to receive a copy of Mr Carroll's
next book. After a couple of years, a beautifully wrapped package
arrives addressed to the queen. When Her Majesty opens it, she
finds inside an inscribed personal copy of Carroll's next work –
*An Elementary Treatise on Determinants with their application to
Simultaneous Linear Equations and Algebraic Geometry*.

It is a good story, but, like so much that is written about
Carroll, it is not true. It fits the conventional picture of a boring
don producing two amazing children's books, and then running
out of steam; but nothing could be further from the reality.
Carroll was creative all his life. However, like many creative

people, he needed certain conditions in order to do his best work. He did not need to separate himself from the world, like many writers. Far from it – what he needed was an audience.

'He was a born story teller, and if he had not been affected with a slight stutter in the presence of grown ups, would have made a wonderful actor. His sense of the theatre was extraordinary,' recalled the actor-manager Bert Coote, who as a little boy had been friendly with the grown-up Carroll.[1]

Carroll told his family stories, he made poems up for them and he gave recitations; for like many stammerers, he had few problems when singing or reciting lines that he knew well. As a child, he created vast games for his brothers and sisters in the garden, and spent hours entertaining them, as his mother mentioned in a letter to her sister:

> … Charlie really has got the Hooping cough [sic], after having been so proof against the complaint during the whole of his last summer holiday, constantly nursing and playing with the little ones who had it. … his appetite and spirits never fail at the Railroad games, which the darlings all delight in. He tries and proves his strength in the most *persevering* way, Edwin [aged 3] *always* being glad to accept any number of tickets …[2]

The youthful Carroll drew cartoons for his brothers and sisters, he mystified them with conjuring tricks, he involved them in writing stories and poems with him. He took careful note of what worked with them, and what did not.

His first ever published work had been called, with some prescience, 'The Unknown One'. No doubt his family admired it when they read it in the Richmond School magazine in which it appeared, but no copy of it has ever been found. After this, Carroll produced several family magazines, of which one of the biggest and best is *The Rectory Magazine*, dating from when he was 18. This was created in what is obviously an old exercise book from Rugby School, for the endpaper, dated 1846, contains notes in various hands saying such things as 'Dodgson excused calling over' and 'C.L. Dodgson, Sick Room'. No doubt he joyfully ripped out whatever had been in it beforehand to begin instead the handwritten 'Compendium of the best tales. Poems, essays, pictures etc. that the united talents of the Rectory inhabitants can produce … 1850', to which he jokingly added 'Fifth Edition, carefully revised and improved'.

Seven brothers and sisters, as well as his Aunt Lucy contributed to *The Rectory Magazine*. The youngest was Louisa, then aged 10, who produced a very creditable 'Ode to Wild Beasts'. Carroll put the whole thing together, complete with amusing and lively illustrations. It contains parodies of the kind of songs and stories that the children would have read, and Carroll also included 'Answers to Correspondents', in which it clearly tickled his fancy to imagine the questions to which he was supplying the answers:

> D.S. Your question is unintelligible. What do you mean by 'withsome'?
> M. We do not know the way in which Indian Rubber balls are made.
> E.L.K. Whatever you please, my little dear! You pays your money and you takes your choice!

As well as needing regular 'fixes' of fun, drama and performance, there was another reason why Carroll liked having an audience. With 10 brothers and sisters, he would have had little personal time with his parents, and would have had to find a way of gaining individual attention and love. Entertaining the children in the family got him noticed and put him in the centre of things, and, according to Collingwood, his brothers and sisters always thought a lot of him.

It would follow that he would assume that entertaining other children would make them love his company too – and this is exactly what happened. After Carroll left home, he still found children, particularly well-mannered ones, an easy and satisfying audience. His family background had equipped him for dealing with them, and they found him so interesting that they really wanted his company. Throughout his bachelor existence in the monastic surroundings of Christ Church, no professional actor could have adored their bouquets more than Carroll basked in his child-friends' attention and devotion. So many of his letters and diaries show how much he put into entertaining them. With them, he could be his creative, human self: direct, funny, spontaneous, and gently teasing; and his letters show how he liked to create ridiculous alternative possibilities to amuse them.

'My dear Gertrude,' he wrote to one favourite, Gertrude Chataway,

> Explain to me how I am to enjoy Sandown without you? How can I walk on the beach alone? How can I sit all alone on those wooden steps? So you see, I shan't be able to do without you; you will have to come ... you will have to engage me a bed somewhere in Swanage and if you can't find one I shall expect YOU to spend the night on the beach and give up your room to me. Guests, of course, must be thought of before children and I am sure that on these warm nights the beach will be quite good enough for YOU. If you did feel a little chilly, of course, you could go into a bathing machine, which everybody knows is very comfortable to sleep in. You know they make the floor of soft wood for that very purpose. ...[3]

As well as his flights of fancy, his listeners also appreciated the way in which Carroll wove aspects of their own lives into his narratives. This characteristic of his can be spotted even in the story of *Alice in Wonderland*. He not only named some of the characters in the book after those who were present at the telling of the original story, but he also drew upon other aspects of the little Liddells' lives, turning them inside out and upside down in the process.

Alice's French book at the time was *La Bagatelle*.[4] It contained a sequence of lessons titled 'The Rabbit', 'The Fall' and 'The little girl who is always crying', while a later lesson is about 'the tea table – take some bread and a little butter'. These lessons must have been dreary for Alice to recite, but it would have been very different when they had been imported into Wonderland and utterly transformed.

The *Alice* poems also mischievously poked fun at songs and poems which the little Liddells themselves recited and sang. Children of the period were forced to learn by heart many 'improving' verses such as Robert Southey's drearily moralistic 'The Old Man's Comforts and How He Gained Them':

> ... 'You are old, father William,' the young man cried,
> 'And pleasures, with youth pass away.
> And yet you lament not the days that are gone;
> Now, tell me the reason I pray.'

> 'In the days of my youth,' Father William replied,
> 'I remember'd that youth could not last;
> I thought of the future, whatever I did,
> That I never might grieve for the past.'

Who could possibly fail to prefer Carroll's version?

> ... 'You are old,' said the youth, 'as I mentioned before,
> And have grown most uncommonly fat;
> Yet you turned a back-somersault in at the door –
> Pray what is the reason for that?'

'In my youth,' said the sage, as he shook his grey locks,
'I kept all my limbs very supple
By the use of this ointment–one shilling the box–
Allow me to sell you a couple?'

Like all good children's storytellers, Carroll had a special gift for re-packaging his own ideas, and even his personal feelings, in ways that children could empathize with, relate to and accept. He never forgot that the children he talked to were also real people with their own emotions. They were less sophisticated than adults, but were more honest and expressive. Carroll knew just what they were capable of understanding, and he did not talk down to them.

He thoroughly disliked outsiders poking their nose into the informal, friendly little world he created with children, and he also resented the interference of anyone he thought might jeer at him or be bored by him and his fancies. He had a real hatred of being expected to perform in front of an unsympathetic audience – mischievous boys and conventional adults in partic-ular. His friend Isa Bowman described how one day when she was young he took her to a Panorama of Niagara Falls which was being exhibited in London, and began to weave her a story about a wax dog on display. When he looked up and discovered that several strangers had gathered round to hear the tale, he was so upset that he began stammering at once, and abandoned the story.[5]

Sometimes, though, an adult (usually a woman) was as charmed by his stories as the children were, and might become a friend. Such was a lady called Mrs J N Bennie, who met him at an hotel in the 1870s. She described how she had spotted the 'grave' stranger at dinner, but had no idea who he was. The next day, as she relates,

Nurse took our little twin daughters in front of the sea. I

went out a short time afterwards and found them with my friend of the table, who was seated between them with his knees covered with minute toys. They were listening to him open-mouthed, and seeing their great delight, I motioned to him to go on. A most charming story he told them, about sea urchins and ammonites. When it was over, I said 'You must be the author of *Alice in Wonderland.*' He laughed and replied, 'My dear madam, my name is Dodgson, and *Alice's Adventures* was written by Lewis Carroll.' I replied: 'Then you must have borrowed the name, for only he could have told the story as you have done.'[6]

Carroll continued to deny it, but Mrs Bennie persisted. Eventually, he confessed, and he, Mrs Bennie and her daughters became lifelong friends.

Mrs Bennie was unusual in that she was able to step across the barriers of convention and communicate with Carroll the man. Something about her must have appealed to him enough to persuade him to let her sit and listen to him, for an audience of adult strangers or acquaintances did not suit Carroll's story-telling gift at all. He needed to relax and forget himself in order to create freely, and the conventions of middle-class English society rarely encouraged relaxation. He was always in some ways an outsider in society, as a letter he wrote as a young man illustrates only too well. In it he described to his friend Mrs MacDonald how he was introduced to the wife of a well-known artist, and made a mess of it: '… I stepped forwards to shake hands with her, my hat being still on my head! My left hand was full of coat and umbrella, so my only alternative was to offer her my hand or my hat, to shake: I chose the former as the least absurd of the two, but must, I fear, have made her an enemy for life!'[7]

Pity the man who makes enemies by wearing his hat at the wrong time! Carroll never ceased to find conventional society a bore, and often a stressful bore. Throughout his life he was impatient of the unspoken rules that hedged all social interactions. He often stayed still and silent in formal company, performing only when he was with family, with good friends – or with children.

He does not seem to have had the slightest problem in appealing to children. The actress Irene Vanbrugh recalled how his entertaining stories during rehearsals so enthralled the child actors that on occasions Carroll was sent away by the harassed manager, desperate to get his actors back to work.[8] And not only did Carroll enjoy the experience of performing, he also loved watching others perform. Perhaps the glare of the limelight and the high emotion of the drama offered him a kind of freedom, an escape into an alternative reality where the normal rules of life did not apply.

It is not known what Carroll's father thought about his son's views on the theatre and theatre-going, but he was probably not very enthusiastic, for theatres and theatrical life were frowned upon in many respectable households during his lifetime. Carroll's sisters did not visit playhouses, and his father, as a Church of England parochial clergyman, was forbidden even to set foot within a theatre's doors.

Until the second half of the 19th century there was, it must be admitted, some justification for the Church's disdain. As so often in Victorian times, sexual morality was the issue. Then, as now, glamour was an important part of the drama's popular appeal, and contemporary playhouses were gaudy places tricked up with cheap gilt and flaring lights. They were particularly known for popular songs, dances, and 'ballets' featuring bevies of pretty dancing-girls twirling around in flimsy dresses and showing off their legs. Men flocked to see these young beauties and it is no surprise that theatres were also well known as places where the company of dancers (or that of other girls) could be purchased after the show.

In addition, many theatrical performances were anything but intellectually elevating. Although Shakespeare was reasonably popular, most theatres tended to show short runs of hastily produced plays backed with sensational or humorous supporting acts. In 1867, a typical evening out for Carroll at the New Royalty Theatre featured 'Meg's Diversion', 'Sarah's Young Man' and 'The Latest Edition of Black Eyed Susan'. Carroll enjoyed these very much, and claimed in his diary that the latter was 'a good burlesque, in which a song (and dance for five) "Pretty Susan, don't say No" was encored four times!'[9]

He happily attended many other low-brow plays and pantomimes like *The Statue Bride*, *Goodnight Signor Pantalon*, *A Bottle of Smoke*, *The Boots at the Swan* and *Fee Fo Fum*. The fantasy and fun of these, not to mention *Hanky Panky the Enchanter* and *The Maid and the Magpie*, were probably not too warmly received back at the rectory, but no amount of disapproval appeared to put Carroll off. He seemed to *need* the theatre. His nephew said after his death that the clerical ban on attending theatres had been one reason Carroll had refused to take the priesthood. It is unlikely to have been the whole reason, but it is a measure of the extent of his lifelong passion for the stage that it could be given as a reason at all. In the 36 years of theatre-going which are documented in his surviving diaries, Carroll saw several hundred plays, concerts and operas, and undoubtedly attended many more that nobody now knows about, since several of the diaries are missing.

The theatre's magic, glitter, and ability to create other worlds and other lives were not its only attractions for him. There were the performers themselves, the people who inhabited this enchanted world. In the catalogue of his possessions made after he died is an album of more than 160 photographs of actors and actresses. Each photo is inscribed with the sitters' names in Carroll's own hand, and there was also a register listing each one separately – a real fan's collection.

The perceived immorality of his favourite recreation caused Carroll considerable stress, particularly as he became older, and the way he coped with this may have contributed to his growing reputation for eccentricity. After his father's death, Carroll stayed away from theatres for two years, perhaps as a sign of mourning, for he had inadvertently attended two performances on the day the old man had unexpectedly died. His biographer Stuart Collingwood says that those two years sent Carroll into a depression from which he feared he might never recover, and perhaps staying away from the theatre deepened his unhappiness during this time.

There were no moral conflicts, though, where amateur theatricals were concerned. Large Victorian families often made their own entertainment by staging amateur dramatics, charades and recitations, and Carroll joined enthusiastically in these. One of his favourite party turns was a short play which he had originally seen on a visit to the theatre It was J M Morton's farce *Away with Melancholy*, a tale of cynical betrothal and love between two disreputable men and two greedy women.

The play contains some comical 'business' with idiotic servants, plus several popular songs of the time. Carroll used different voices and characteristics for each part during his solo performances, and sang the songs as well, and the whole thing probably lasted about half an hour. He also noted in his diary that he used the voice of one of *Away with Melancholy*'s main characters, Mr Trimmer, when giving a magic lantern show to around a hundred children in Croft-on-Tees for the children's Christmas treat of 1856. This was an ambitious marathon which lasted nearly three hours. As well as the food, bran-pie and sweets, he presented 47 lantern slides and 13 songs (of which he performed six and the children sang the rest) and he employed seven different voices altogether.

It was not only when performing his parlour pieces that he used multitudes of voices. Some of his child-friends remembered being entranced at how his use of different voices brought the characters of his own stories to life. He also drew lightning sketches to illustrate what was going on visually in the stories as he spoke. It is tempting to wonder what he might have made of film animation, for he would have been well suited to its combination of finicky production techniques and lively, expressive caricatures.

Like so much else about him, his storytelling sessions were difficult to describe accurately. His friend, the artist Gertrude Thomson, another of the few grown-ups that Carroll allowed to listen to him, was frustrated at how impossible it was to convey the magic of his tales. 'It was like pages out of the Alices ... I used to try and recall and record it. It was impossible – as impossible as to catch the gleam of color on sunlit water ...' she wrote.[10]

Ruth Waterhouse, who met Carroll when he was elderly at a children's party, recalls that the party soon became *his* party. He talked and told them stories 'delightfully, and I remember how exasperating it was to be asked whether I would like another piece of cake when I was trying so hard to hear what he was saying at the other end of the table'.[11]

The crucial point, throughout his listeners' accounts, is that Carroll was *telling*, not writing these tales. These fascinating stories disappeared forever because they were never recorded. His letters to children who wanted them were charming and full of fun, and if another of his favourites had asked him to write a whole book for her, perhaps he might have created something else as good as *Alice in Wonderland*. But there is no record that a single one of his child-friends after Alice Liddell ever thought to ask.

Of course, Carroll wished to be taken seriously as a professional man, and success as a children's writer was certainly not an unmixed social asset in the rarefied academic environment of 19th-century Christ Church. Today, Christ Church has joined the modern age. It runs *Alice* tours for its thousands of annual visitors, and earns a good deal of money from tourism. As well as the Harry Potter's 'Hogwarts' Refectory', its porters boast about something called a 'Jabberwocky Tree' – although it is a little hard for the sceptical eye to discern what is quite so specially magical about this gnarled and leafy relic.

It was all very different in the 19th century. Carroll had a public position to keep up and, as a clergyman, he was expected to have serious ideas. Christ Church had produced many great and important men, and it is safe to say that few of them would have concerned themselves with mere children's stories. Carroll's whimsies could, quite literally, have been seen as little things for little minds. At worst, the stories were also the reason why embarrassing groups of gawping trippers kept on turning up at the college specially to catch a glimpse of him, and why the porters had to deal with so many stupid enquiries addressed to 'Mr Lewis Carroll'.

In fact, most of Carroll's large written output was *not* for children, and it was extremely patchy in quality. Much of it deals with mathematics or logic, or with topical issues that interested him and his colleagues at the time. Apart from *Alice*, his main claims to literary fame lie in some excellent comic poems and his long story-poem 'The Hunting of the Snark'. It seems that he made no serious effort to develop his talent for children's writing or comic poetry, being apparently uninterested in analysing it and quite content to say it that it 'came of itself' for no reason that he knew.

On the other hand, he very much liked to create and communicate, and he took a huge interest in every detail of the way his books were presented to the world. Also, in later life at least, he had no hesitation in speaking out in print as 'Lewis Carroll' about public issues that concerned him.

In short, as usual, he wanted things both ways. The solemn don who wasn't 'Lewis Carroll' was only too happy to be a hugely famous author when it suited him, but the performer and storyteller with his comical songs, cartoons and poems was forever being bundled into a cupboard by the dry and silent Reverend Mr Dodgson, who did not choose to entertain his serious-minded contemporaries.

In these circumstances, it is not surprising that the quality of his literary output was so patchy. In particular, the *Sylvie and Bruno* books, written late in his life, were a real disappointment to many who had expected another book in the style of *Alice in Wonderland*. Really two halves of the same story, these books were published separately, in 1889 and 1893 respectively, under the titles *Sylvie and Bruno* and *Sylvie and Bruno Concluded*. Almost entirely lacking in structure, they nevertheless have their own peculiar charm, and contain many gems of strangeness, wit and wonder. They have been hailed as the first deconstructed novels ever written, and have their fans, notably in France, where their peculiar ideas have been said to provide topics for café philosophers.

Their main attraction for the student of Carroll is the unparalleled insight that they offer into his mind as it was in later life, as in them he set out his carefully nurtured thoughts for the benefit of his readership. Alas, shut up inside his head all alone, the thoughts seem to have gradually grown into strange shapes, like sprouting onions kept in a dark cupboard for too long. Both books are written from the point of view of an elderly male narrator, who is never given a name. He is generally assumed to speak for Carroll, as he expresses views which Carroll is known to have held at the time. He moves between a dream world and a real world, meeting strange creatures and characters en route.

The fragmentary plot hinges on a novelette-type romance between two young adult characters, Arthur and Lady Muriel. These, though, are not the real main characters. Those are two child fairies who can be perceived by the narrator while he is in a dream-state. The male fairy is called Bruno, and the female, and the heroine is called Sylvie. Much of the tale is stream-of-consciousness, as Carroll's work often was when he had no particular audience in mind, and nowhere does his literary instinct fail more profoundly than in connection with Sylvie.

As has been described elsewhere, Carroll was deeply attached to idealized sister-mother figures, and little Sylvie was exactly this. She was protective, loving, gentle, good-looking and radiantly, sinlessly pure. Sadly for the reader who does not share Carroll's taste, Sylvie is also mystifyingly unappealing. She moralizes incessantly, and the very sexlessness of her beauty and her unrelenting virtue make her seem cloyingly sentimental. Further, she is a prig, always preventing her argumentative little brother Bruno (who resembles a young Carroll, with curly hair, unclear speech and a playful nature) from doing anything even mildly sinful.

This means, though, that Bruno does not have to cope with evil all alone. In Carroll's personal paradise, it is the adoring sister-mother who vigilantly prevents the horror of sin creeping upon the boy unawares. She unconditionally loves him, kisses and embraces him, and shows him by example what he must do to be a good person. Sylvie will never be cruel or insincere, nor will she reject or hurt her little Bruno, the beloved centre of her life. There is something very poignant about it all.

Strangely – and thought-provokingly – the interesting, beautiful and intelligent Lady Muriel changes into little fairy Sylvie and back throughout the story, and the male narrator has a great interest in her. He feels distress and even bitterness that he is not supposed to have love affairs, but is seen by her only as a harmless old man. However, she is amusing and kind to him, and she is one of the most likeable and realistic characters in the book. Perhaps those who wish to untangle how Carroll saw the opposite sex should study this two-sided Sylvie-Muriel creature. Or perhaps she is three-sided, for she also occasionally surfaces as My Lady, a gross, obese bully with more power than she deserves.

In any event, Carroll's powerful emotional needs and fantasies had a very bad effect on his writing style in this book, and it is hardly surprising that so many people deduced from it that he had lost his storytelling gift as he grew older. Here, for instance, is Sylvie at her most saccharine:

> [Sylvie] sang timidly, and very low indeed, scarcely audibly, but the sweetness of her voice was simply indescribable. I have never heard any earthly music like it. On me the first effect of her voice was a sudden sharp pang that seemed to pierce through one's very heart. I had felt such a pang only once before in my life, and it had been from seeing what at the moment realized one's idea of perfect beauty ... then came a sudden rush of burning tears to the eyes, as though one could weep one's soul away for pure delight. And lastly there fell on me a sense of awe that was almost terror – some such feeling as Moses must have had when he heard the words 'Put off thy shoes from off thy feet for the place whereon thou standest is holy ground.'

Some might feel that this extract provokes entirely the wrong kind of tears. It hardly seems possible that the same writer could also create the following simple and elegant passage from *Through the Looking-Glass*, which is also about singing and tears:

> 'You are sad,' the Knight said in an anxious tone 'Let me sing you a song to comfort you.'
>
> 'Is it very long?' Alice asked, for she had heard a good deal of poetry that day.
>
> 'It's long' said the Knight. 'But it's very, very beautiful. Everybody that hears me sing it – either it brings the tears into their eyes, or else –'

'Or else what?' said Alice, for the Knight had made a sudden pause.

'Or else it doesn't, you know. The name of the song is called "Haddock's Eyes".'

'Oh, that's the name of the song, is it?' Alice said, trying to feel interested.

'No – you don't understand' the Knight said, looking a little vexed, 'that's what the name is called. The name really is, "The Aged, Aged Man."'

'Then I ought to have said "That's what the song is called"?' Alice corrected herself.

'No, you oughtn't: that's quite another thing! The song is called "Ways and Means": but that's only what it is called, you know!'

'Well, what is the song then?' said Alice, who was by this time completely bewildered.

'I was coming to that,' the Knight said.

Never good at setting priorities, and increasingly interested in pinning life down logically, by the 1880s Carroll was entirely unable to give *Sylvie and Bruno* a decent plot. He filled it with a hotch-potch of ideas on all kinds of topics, forcing his readers to wade through pages of moral and theological discussions intermixed with sentiment and whimsy. Worse, the clergyman in him increasingly felt that he had a duty to insert virtuous opinions, for the older he became, the more he regretted that he had not used *Alice* as a means of morally improving children's minds. He seems to have had so little empathy or sympathy with his younger self that it either did not occur to him, or else he did not want to know, that Alice's very lack of moralizing – the deliberate opposition to moralizing, indeed – had been part of her great appeal.

It is a relief to turn back to his earlier work, particularly to *Alice* which is a showcase for some of his best comic poetry.

For instance, the Knight's song, when he finally gets around to singing it, is a masterpiece of nonsense and a wickedly irreverent satire upon Wordsworth's 'Resolution and Independence', in which the narrator meets a poor but inspiring old man who scrapes a humble living. As Wordsworth wrote:

> … He told, that to these waters he had come
> To gather leeches, being old and poor;
> Employment hazardous and wearisome!
> And he had many hardships to endure:
> From pond to pond he roamed, from moor to moor;
> Housing, with God's good help, by choice or chance;
> And in this way he gained an honest maintenance.
>
> The old Man still stood talking by my side;
> But now his voice to me was like a stream …

Carroll's old man also earns his living on the moor in difficult and eccentric ways, but his voice 'trickled through' the narrator's head 'like water through a sieve', and he was certainly not above soliciting for a tip:

> 'I sometimes dig for buttered rolls,
> Or set limed twigs for crabs:
> I sometimes search the grassy knolls
> For wheels of Hansom-cabs.
> And that's the way' (he gave a wink)
> 'By which I get my wealth –
> And very gladly will I drink
> Your Honour's noble health.'

Generations of people have enjoyed Carroll's comic poems, and they are still so fresh and funny that it does not matter that they are mostly pure nonsense, for in their ideas and images they are also pure poetry. Their rhythms, their choice of words, their flashes of luminous strangeness still connect with us despite the huge cultural differences that separate Carroll's time from ours.

Most of Carroll's good comic poetry was written when he was young, but even in *Sylvie and Bruno* the edgy, witty, off-the-wall Carroll sometimes pushes past the worthy Dodgson to give us unsettling moments, such as the oddly disturbing 'Little Birds' poem with its cast of crocodiles and tigresses, and its crimes hidden in carpet-bags.

> ... Little Birds are tasting
> Gratitude and gold,
> Pale with sudden cold:
> Pale, I say, and wrinkled –
> When the bells have tinkled,
> And the Tale is told.

Even more extraordinary is the surrealistic 'Mad Gardener's Song', in which an unnamed narrator believes he sees one thing, only to find that it is something entirely different; something perhaps that could never be seen at all.

> He thought he saw a Rattlesnake
> That questioned him in Greek:
> He looked again, and found it was
> The Middle of Next Week.
> 'The one thing I regret,' he said,
> 'Is that it cannot speak.'

The 'Mad Gardener's Song' is the only poem from *Sylvie and Bruno* which is widely quoted in anthologies today, and it is perhaps significant that the verses were first told to Enid Stevens, one of Carroll's favourite child-friends. She was a very bright, perceptive child, and she described how they would go for walks and he would make up the verses to amuse her, then rush home and note down any that he particularly liked.[12] Once again, Carroll was producing good work for an intelligent, appreciative audience, and happily using his creative gifts to produce laughter in a friend.

Although Carroll's particular talent was for comic poetry, he was technically very skilful and he loved experimenting with form, with sometimes extraordinary results. A poem he wrote for the birthday of his friend Robert Bosanquet has half a hyphenated word at the end of each first line; surely never seen in any poem before. When read aloud, the hyphenated line introduces a pronounced pause, like a sneeze, in each verse, to rhyme with 'Bosanquet' and this is highly relevant to the subject of the poem, which is about catching a cold. It begins:

> The year when boilers froze, and ket-
> -tles crystallized the fender
> The natal day of Bosanquet
> Dawned on us in its splendour
>
> For those who wear wool hosen, cat-
> -ching cold's a thing unheard of,
> But this great maxim Bosanquet
> Would not believe a word of. ...[13]

The undescribed horrors which sometimes appear in his comic poetry – the Jabberwock, the Boojum, the Snark and the Bandersnatch – are also memorable, for one of the things that makes Carroll's poetry most compelling is the unexpected touch of darkness within it. Like that other great storyteller Walt Disney, Carroll instinctively understood how people are moved and thrilled by a flicker of fear. A touch of fear came naturally to him, for his own acute self-contradictions, his terror of sin and his questions about his own identity helped to give an eerie tinge to the cute little girls and the talking flowers, the argumentative animals and the clever wordplay. In Carroll's best work there are always elements of strangeness and craziness, of frustration, anguish and loss.

As discussed in Chapter 6, both *Alice* books were written at times of great mental stress, which suggests that as well as having sympathetic listeners in mind, he needed an emotional impetus to help him to create his best work. Making nonsense seems to have helped him to deal with his own feelings, so that in entertaining and amusing those he loved, he was also able to please, calm and control himself. 'The Hunting of the Snark' was the last major work which showed this particular genius all the way through.

It is a long poem which was begun in 1874 and published in 1876. It is not specifically intended for children, and Carroll wrote it in his sisters' house in Guildford while he was helping to nurse his adult godson Charlie, of whom he was very fond. Charlie's lungs were being destroyed by tuberculosis, then more usually known as consumption. Carroll made up some of the poem during long, solitary walks which he took on the downland outside Guildford. He maintained that he had no idea what it all meant, but his unfortunate godson died by fits and starts and the poem is sub-titled 'An Agony in Eight Fits'.

The story is about a boat trip into uncharted seas in search of a sinister but wholly unimaginable creature, and it has a cruelly inevitable vanishing at the end. The crew who embark into the Bellman's crazy boat with its blank sea charts include a Barrister, a Banker, a Beaver, a Butcher, and a doomed Baker. The Baker is an over-dressed, over-heated character who has been warned against the fearsome Snark by a dying uncle. He has forgotten his own name, so is known by a variety of cries such as 'Fry me!', 'Candle-ends' or 'Toasted-cheese', and he has a heart like 'a bowl brimming over with quivering curds'.

The scholar Fernando Soto has pointed out that contemporary

medical books compare certain signs of consumption to curds and melting cheese,[14] and it is indeed the feverish Baker who finally succumbs to the Snark. He has one final fit, with waving hands and wagging head, before coming face to face with the grim and unknowable Snark, and disappearing entirely.

> They hunted till darkness came on, but they found
> Not a button, or feather, or mark,
> By which they could tell that they stood on the ground
> Where the Baker had met with the Snark.

> In the midst of the word he was trying to say,
> In the midst of his laughter and glee,
> He had softly and suddenly vanished away –
> For the Snark WAS a Boojum, you see.

Although Carroll was constantly being asked what the poem meant, he consistently said that he did not know. Eventually he said he thought he agreed with a lady who had interpreted it as an allegory of the pursuit of happiness.[15] It is an illuminating comment, for despite the darkness and fear which runs through the poem – the horrifying end of the Banker who turns black in the face, the terrified Beaver who purchases a 'second-hand dagger-proof coat' and the utter disappearance of the Baker – the overall effect is somehow comical and entertaining.

Some of Carroll's lesser-known poems are full of private jokes, and so have never achieved such a wide circulation, although they are also witty, thought-provoking and even haunting. He created some good ballads for the entertainment of his family household, apparently inspired by Scottish traditional ballads and Aytoun's popular *Bon Gaultier* parodies, among others. One, 'The Two Brothers' (1853), a spoof old-world song, could easily have made a music hall turn. It was none-too-subtly based on the tragic Borders ballad 'There Were Twa Brothers At the

Scule'. For Carroll, however, there was no tragedy, and the first line was 'There were two brothers at Twyford School'. It refers to Carroll's two younger brothers Wilfred and Skeffington, who both attended the school at Twyford and liked to fish from the bridge ('brigg') over the River Tees near their home.

It is too long to quote in full, but in its entirety it creates a punning and dryly witty picture of the fate that befell the two quarrelsome schoolboys:

> … He has fitted together two joints of his rod
> And to them he has added another
> And then a great hook he took from his book
> And ran it right into his brother.
>
> Oh much is the noise that is made among boys
> When playfully pelting a pig
> But a far greater pother was made by his brother
> When flung from the top of the brigg …
>
> … Said he 'Thus shall he wallop about
> And the fish take him quite at their ease.
> For me to annoy, it was ever his joy,
> Now, I'll teach him the meaning of 'Tees'! …

Carroll's poem ends genially with the brothers being called in for tea, in cheerful contrast with the real ballad, which concludes with an ominous dirk dripping with 'the blude of my a'e brother'.

'The Three Voices', first published in 1856, also seems to relate to some family incident or joke. It has been described as a parody of Tennyson's 'The Two Voices', but actually it is nothing like Tennyson's poem. It describes a naive young man walking on the beach, as Carroll and his family often did at the nearby coast, and meeting with an aggressive and deeply boring umbrella-wielding lady who seems to have been lying in wait. Although Carroll himself described it as "'slight', the poem has been the subject of intense analysis for mysterious hidden meanings in recent years. No solutions have been proposed, but one verse suggests that Carroll was mischievously referring to a real and deeply unwelcome habitual visitor to the family home, since:

> He saw in dreams a drawing-room,
> Where thirteen wretches sat in gloom,
> Waiting – he thought he knew for whom ...

So perhaps the 13 members of Carroll's immediate family knew only too well who the irritating and intimidating lady with the umbrella might be. The poem remains entertaining and readable despite its mysteries.

As he grew older and more famous, Carroll's light-hearted creative genius was, then as now, at risk of exposure to the withering attention of unimaginative adults. He took steps to deal with it as best he could. Not only did he consistently refuse to own up as 'Lewis Carroll' in most social situations, but when he did entertain groups of children – for he never liked to disappoint children – he worked up certain tried-and-tested stories as 'parlour turns'. He saved his original poems and stories to tell informally, and usually privately, to children he liked, and who liked him. He simply refused to co-operate with any of the grown-ups if he did not feel like it.

However, he continued to display a great deal of creativity in his amusing letters to his friends of all ages and both sexes, and there was a light-hearted unconventionality even in his communications with outsiders. A letter he wrote to his dentist six years before his death must have been more imaginative than any of the other business correspondence the good man received that year, and it shows that Carroll's comic fancies were still part and parcel of his approach to life:

Dear Mr. Whatford. The appearance of a small gum boil, opposite that double tooth which you thought you had quite killed, has, I think, convicted it of being the cause of the pain I have had. And the aching of the front teeth seems to be due merely to a brotherly sympathy between tooth and tooth, which, however creditable it may be to the teeth themselves, is decidedly inconvenient to me! I enclose the well earned 5 guineas. Very truly yours, C.L. Dodgson.[16]

Little Lorina 'Ina' and Alice Liddell pose in Chinese garb for Carroll's camera. Carroll liked creating imaginative pictures and had a collection of fancy dress costumes and 'props' which he sometimes used in photography sessions.

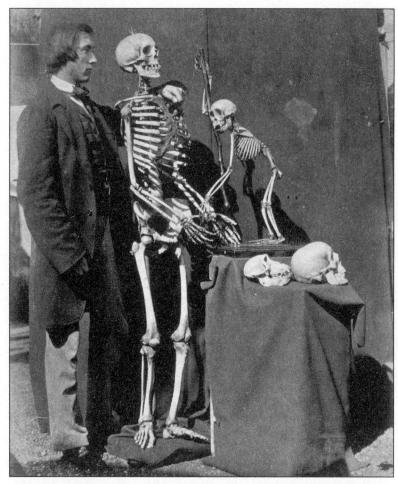

*Carroll's 1857 image of his friend Reginald Southey with his arm
affectionately round a human skeleton, which in its turn is clasping
the hand of a small monkey skeleton*

9

'… the camera of rosewood'

Photography

Finally, he fixed each picture
With a saturate solution
Which was made of hyposulphite
Which, again, was made of soda.
(Very difficult the name is
For a metre like the present
But periphrasis has done it.)

from 'Hiawatha's Photographing'

Carroll was fascinated by the visual world. He liked to accompany the stories that he told children with wild and impish sketches of his own, full of humour and life. He was under no illusions about his academic drawing ability, though, and nor, it seems, was anyone else. He lived in an age when draughtsmanship was highly valued, and even comic *Punch* cartoonists drew in what would seem today an academic style. Nobody was much impressed by amateur caricatures, however lively and entertaining they might be. No less a critic than John Ruskin scanned Carroll's portfolio, and made it witheringly plain that he did not think much of it. Carroll, said Ruskin, did not have enough talent to make it worth his while spending much of his time sketching.[1]

Yet despite his lack of technical drawing skill, Carroll had a highly developed artistic sensibility. He loved attending galleries and exhibitions, and he bought original artworks, sometimes at considerable expense. He also looked closely and carefully at the world with an artist's eye, as is shown in a letter he wrote to his sister Mary in 1861:

> … Brown glossy hair would (in the light) have a line of white where the eye caught the reflected light, and gold on the two sides of that while (in the shade) it would all be dead brown … shadows are coloured but the colours don't depend on the thing that throws them, nor does it depend on the colour of objects which another part of the shadow falls on …[2]

Had he lived even 20 years earlier, he would probably have languished on the sidelines of the visual arts, admiring other people's work but not contributing much himself. But by the 1850s, middle-class amateurs were starting to get involved in photography. By the time Carroll reached his early twenties, he too was earning enough money to take up the hobby, and it was rather an exciting one.

Photography, the 'pencil of nature', had thrown a bombshell into the Victorian art world. 'From today, painting is dead,' Delaroche the painter had said, on first clapping eyes upon a daguerreotype. That was not quite true, but photography certainly did liberate a whole generation of artists – artists who could not draw. A man (or, not infrequently, a woman) who had previously struggled to catch a likeness with pencil and paper now had the chance to create convincing art. At last it was possible to capture in just a few short minutes the authentic lineaments of a human face and figure. There was something very personal about the whole process too. As the subjects looked out at the viewer from the picture, so would they originally have stared at the photographer's face, surrendering their images to him for ever.

Carroll's early humorous story, 'A Photographer's Day Out', published in 1860, is one of several comic works he wrote on the subject of photography, and it describes the lure of capturing another person's image. In this cynical little tale, the narrator spends the day in a fever of desperate anxiety, for he wants to take and own a photograph of Amelia, a lady he secretly admires. Nothing goes well. He describes how he photographs the family: pompous cross-eyed Papa, simpering Mamma, who was 'very fond of theatricals in her youth', and the three youngest girls,

> as they would have appeared, if by any possibility a black dose could have been administered to each of them at the same moment, and the three tied together by the hair before the expression produced by the medicine has subsided from any of their faces. Of course, I kept this view of the subject to myself, and merely said that 'it reminded me of a picture of the three Graces' ...

To his glee, the lovely Amelia consents to sit for him. First, though, she says, she would like him to photograph a particular cottage for her. He ecstatically agrees, and rushes off to take the requested picture; 'muttering "Amelia, 'tis for thee!" removed the lid of the lens; in 1 minute and 40 seconds I replaced it: "it is over!" I cried in uncontrollable excitement, "Amelia, thou art mine!"' Just as he is about to get his hands on Amelia, of course, everything goes sadly wrong. Here, as so often, Carroll's references to grown-up love resonate with feelings of ignominy, betrayal or heartbreak. In this case, the photographer ends up beaten black and blue, then discovers that the faithless Amelia was engaged to an army captain all along. He does not obtain his yearned-for photograph.

The idea of capturing likenesses was attractive, but the actual business of making photographs was cumbersome, chancy and expensive. Still, it suited many aspects of Carroll's nature. Although his fussiness did not become excessive until he was much older, he had a painstaking approach and a love of sheer complication even as a young man. Both these traits were amply satisfied by the use of the wet collodion process. This was the first really popular photographic technique, and its exposures, at just a few seconds, were shorter than most other processes of the time. It also had the great advantage that many paper copies could be made of the same picture, because the plate gave a negative rather than a positive image, which allowed prints to be made easily.

To make a wet collodion negative, bromide, chloride or iodide salts were first dissolved in a solution of pyroxylin in ether and alcohol. This made the collodion. An immaculately polished glass plate was coated with this sticky, freshly mixed solution, and it was left for a few moments. It was then taken into a darkened place and dipped into a silver nitrate solution which would convert the salts into silver bromide, chloride or iodide respectively. It was then ready for use.

Meanwhile, the subject would have been waiting, ready posed. A few final adjustments on the part of the photographer, and the lens cap would be removed from the lens for a few seconds. This would expose the plate inside the big wooden camera while it was still wet. Although exposures with wet collodion were not enormously long, the subject often leaned against a post or chair back in order to avoid the slight movements that might lead to blurring.

The photographer would then remove the plate from the camera, and hurry into the darkroom, and develop it in a solution of iron sulphate, acetic acid and alcohol in water. In Carroll's day, the darkroom had either to be rigged up on the premises or brought along on every photographic trip, for there would be less than 20 minutes available to coat, process and develop the wet plate.

Each part of the procedure had to be done deftly and correctly: the chemicals must be evenly spread on the plate, no dust or smudges must contaminate any surfaces, and the chemicals had to be at the right temperature. Contact prints were made, since enlargers had not yet been developed; if a large picture were required, then a large plate had to be used. It was a primitive system, but the results could be very good, and the best wet collodion photographs have excellent detail and gradations of tone.

The equipment was large and heavy, and transporting the glass plates, clanking bottles of chemicals, blankets, gauzes, tripod, dishes and so on involved much careful packing and the use of a barrow or even a cab. To add to the challenges, the light had to be bright enough to give contrast to the image, otherwise it would be flat and lose detail. The artificial light available in those days was very dim, so photographs were usually taken outside on a bright day, or at least in a studio with a glass roof. Some of the photographs Carroll apparently took inside were in fact taken outdoors against a backdrop, as some surviving untrimmed prints reveal. The brightness of the scene had to be judged by eye, since there were no exposure meters and photographers had various dodges by which they could assess the exposure. The Swedish photographer Gustav Rejlander actually used his cat, checking to see how much its pupils were dilated in order to assess how long an exposure to give.

One of the reasons Carroll succeeded in photographing children so well is that he was able to entertain them and keep them cheerful during these lengthy procedures. Even so, according to Evelyn Hatch, whom Carroll photographed as a young child, being photographed 'meant much patience, for the photographer was always determined to get his picture "just right".'[3] Carroll sweetened the pill for his young subjects by allowing them to come into the darkroom afterwards to see how the image magically appeared. 'What could be more thrilling than to see the negative gradually take shape, as he gently rocked it to and fro in the acid bath?' remembered Alice Liddell, looking back nearly three quarters of a century in her little memoir of 1932.[4]

Between 1856 and 1880, Carroll made nearly 3,000 negatives, and he is acknowledged as an important amateur photographer of the Victorian age. In their careful layout and varied selection of images, his surviving albums offer mute testimony to his perfectionism, his care and his pride in his work. His pictures were mounted to accord with a set of registration marks he made on each album page in fine pencil, and he considered the shape of each picture very carefully. Few of them were plain and simple rectangles.

He has gone down in posterity as a photographer of little girls, but really just over half of his output shows children, and at first he did not specialize in taking photographs of individual children at all. Many of his early diary entries record his pursuit of distinguished and celebrated 'victims' – the contemporary slang word for photographic subjects – and his camera caught many colleagues, friends and celebrities. Among them were Alfred, Lord Tennyson, George MacDonald, Thomas Huxley, Holman Hunt, John Everett Millais, Michael Faraday and Ellen Terry. He even managed to capture royalty with his camera. In mid-November 1863, he reported the exciting news in his diary that his friend Kitchin had called at about 11.30 to say that he would bring 'The Prince' to be photographed at half-past twelve. This was Crown Prince Frederick of Denmark, who was staying at Christ Church at the time. Carroll hurried over to his studio, and when the prince arrived, he took two negatives, a 6 × 5 inch half-length, and a 10 × 8 inch full-length. The prince chatted pleasantly to him, and the gratified Carroll confided to his diary that he thought him 'a much brighter specimen of royalty than his brother-in-law'.[5]

The camera also offered Carroll the chance to record places that were of interest to him: these included, among others, pictures of scenery in Oxford and Yorkshire, and of his childhood home at Daresbury, Cheshire. The parsonage he photographed is plain and small, and it rather resembles a farmhouse, with animal sheds and fields beyond. It burned down in the 1880s, and so his pictures of it are the only ones that now survive to show its appearance.

He also photographed scientific specimens, including some splendid fish skeletons. One amusing image, taken in 1857, shows his friend Southey with his arm affectionately round a human skeleton, which is in its turn clasping the hand of a small monkey skeleton. It was two years before Darwin was to publish *Origin of Species*, so either Carroll showed scientific foresight or – more likely – was just having a joke.

In those early years, he kept busy photographing his family, making numerous pictures of his ever-patient brothers and sisters, father, aunts and uncles. They were portrayed with a variety of props: chess sets, dogs, or, in one case, a penny-farthing bicycle. Of these family pictures one of the most ambitious shows five of his seven sisters sitting on chairs. Edwin, the smallest and very outnumbered brother, is squashed in their midst, and a sixth sister lurks on the floor almost entirely swamped in the voluminous skirts of the other five.

Photography was often used in its early days to record works of art which otherwise would not have been available as cheap reproductions, and Carroll's albums also contain many photographs of sculptures and paintings. He bought some of the photographs and took some himself, and his diary records his excitement at an invitation from the sculptor Alexander Munro to roam at large in his studio with his camera.

Just as important as photographing artworks, as far as Carroll was concerned, was the chance to create original works of art himself. Like many of his contemporaries, he loved genre painting, in which the picture tells a human story, points a moral, or both. He, too, wanted to create art that illustrated poems, expanded on ideas or suggested stories. Today, many art critics disparage what could be called 'fictional photography' of this kind. When the photographs display the twin Victorian penchants for fancy dress and heavy-handed moralizing, it is hardly surprising that some of them seem ridiculous; but they were not all bad. Many, including Carroll's, are as worthy of consideration as any other contemporary art form.

Carroll's genre photographs are very well designed and grouped. Some resemble scenes from charades or amateur theatricals, of which he was very fond. In 1858 he exhibited *Little Red Riding Hood* at the London Photographic Society. This showed young Agnes Weld, daughter of Tennyson's sister-in-law, with a basket of goodies and an apprehensive expression. It charmed the poet so much that he later accepted Carroll into his home on the strength of it. *The Elopement*, taken in 1862, shows Carroll's future sister-in-law, 11-year-old Alice Jane Donkin, balanced precariously outside an upper window with a rope ladder. In *St George and the Dragon*, the young models – three boys and a girl – are posed wearing extraordinary head-dresses with lances and a rocking horse, in a representation of St George slaying the dragon and rescuing a damsel in a long white dress.

Sometimes Carroll added poetry to his pictures, creating a careful matrix on the page into which each handwritten letter fitted individually. In one of the albums now held in the Princeton Collection, he matched up an image of Agnes Weld with a neatly calligraphed seven-stanza poem, 'O fair the blossom on the bough', which had been specially written for little Agnes by the poet and critic F T Palgrave.

Carroll also sometimes created photographs that exploited an interesting prop that came to hand. The outfits that Carroll's models wore in these story-pictures were chosen for their artistic and emotional effect, and some had actually been purchased from theatres where they had been used for panto-mimes. During a visit to his friend the artist Henry Holiday in 1870, Holiday supplied a suit of chain mail, and Carroll made several elegant pictures of young ladies clad from head to foot in it. Marion Terry struck a particularly noble pose with a caption taken from Sir Walter Scott: 'Come one, come all! This rock shall fly/From its firm base as soon as I!' Other images with poetic captions also show individuals wearing splendid costumes, such as that of Miss Rose Lawrie, cross-legged and boyish in elaborate Chinese men's clothing above a verse by Bret Harte.

Looking at these photographs, it is easy to imagine what fun it must have been to devise them, and how delightful it must have been for the sitters to see themselves transformed into exotic characters so very different from their ordinary selves. It is not hard to see, behind the work of the grown-up photog-rapher, the boy who had conducted his own marionette shows decades before – or even the man who would love to play with toys for the rest of his life. In fact, playfulness, in every sense of the word, characterized most of Carroll's artistic successes.

There are sometimes gentle allusions contained in his photographs which a modern viewer might find difficult to spot. Certain images of Alice Liddell show her sitting next to a distinctly ordinary potted fern. The fern itself may not add much to the picture, but in the Victorian language of flowers, which was very widely used and understood at the time, 'Fern' meant Sincerity and also Fascination, both qualities which the clever, lively little girl possessed in abundance.

The distinguished photographer and photo-historian Helmut Gernsheim was an admirer of much of Carroll's work, even though he was scathing about its allegorical and story-telling aspects, commenting that 'the sentiment of these pictures is a lamentable concession to Victorian taste ...'. Otherwise, he thought Carroll a 'genius', and he was among the earliest critics to say so. 'With [Carroll], the whole arrangement of the figures is expressive' he went on to say, and the accessories he used – a folding ladder or even a toy gun – revealed an individual taste and lightness of touch that was unusually effective: '… the position of the figure, the placing of accessories, the disposition of the empty space around them, the trimming of the print: everything plays a part, everything is arranged in a decorative manner. He was a master of composition … In grouping, too, Lewis Carroll is infinitely superior to his contemporaries.'[6]

Gernsheim felt that Carroll's pictures of children were particularly accomplished, and noted the care with which he made his photographs of family groups seem fresh and interesting. Not for them the hackneyed photo sessions that Carroll himself so mercilessly parodied in his comic poem 'Hiawatha's Photographing'.

> … Last, the youngest son was taken:
> Very rough and thick his hair was,
> Very round and red his face was,
> Very dusty was his jacket,
> Very fidgety his manner.
>
> And his overbearing sisters
> Called him names he disapproved of:
> Called him Johnny, 'Daddy's Darling,'
> Called him Jacky, 'Scrubby School-boy.'
>
> And, so awful was his picture,
> In comparison, the others
> Seemed, to one's bewildered fancy,
> To have partially succeeded …

Carroll was interested in others' photographic work as well as his own. He kept a special album, now in the University of Texas, to hold his collection of pictures taken by other people. Of these, the most striking are those by the famous Swedish photographer Oscar Gustav Rejlander, whom Carroll knew personally.

Rejlander was creative and highly original (as his use of his cat as an exposure meter suggests). Much of his work was narrative in style, sometimes combining many negatives to illustrate his concepts in a most technically skilful way. Carroll owned several Rejlander photographs, among which were *Non Angeli, Sed Angli*, a famous image showing the heads of two cherubs, and *Poor Joe!*, which shows a barefoot, ragged boy crouched on a step in despair.

In 1863, Carroll chose Rejlander to photograph him, and the result is probably the most famous picture of Carroll in existence. In this portrait, Rejlander presents Carroll as a photographer, and the image conveys harmonious collaboration between artist and sitter. Carroll holds a large camera lens with a cloth draped partly over it, and he is gazing pensively away from the viewer. His pose is dynamic and must have been difficult to hold. His body is turned, one leg is raised, but every line – from the curves of his hands to the angle of his white bow tie – is elegant.

Unfortunately, Carroll, in his usual laconic style, recorded the visit to Rejlander's studio without saying anything about his own thoughts and impressions on how Rejlander worked. Still, when he set up his own studio in Badcock's Yard, Oxford, Rejlander was the man to whom he turned for advice. A studio was an expensive outlay, and it has been suggested that Carroll might have considered becoming a professional photographer, or 'Photographic Artist' as they were then often known.

Some support for this theory comes with a list of photographs for sale which Carroll issued in 1860.[7] He even signed some of his photographs 'From the Artist'. His bank account shows that he did receive payment for the pictures, and the Ashmolean

Museum in Oxford owns some enthusiastic 1864 letters from Dante Gabriel Rossetti who was apparently prepared to spend when it came to Carroll's pictures: 'I come boring you about the [photographs]. Everyone concerned has reached such a pitch of excitement about them,' he wrote, before ordering no less than 30 extra prints.

At one point, Carroll also entertained the hope that he might be able to obtain some funding from Christ Church for his hobby. Christ Church had a fund to be 'apportioned somehow to the encouragement of Physical sciences' he wrote hopefully in his diary, and he went on to speculate that his cultivation of photography might entitle him, as a college tutor, to claim some of it.[8] Any such hopes came to nothing, however.

In reality, however attractive the idea of professional photography may have seemed, it would never have been feasible. The life may have offered a more artistic and relaxed existence than the monkish routines of Christ Church, but professional photographers did not have high social status, and, most importantly, Carroll had an excellent job at Christ Church which his father had taken great care to help him obtain. He could not lightly exchange this for the insecure life of an artist, especially since, as the eldest son, he would shoulder heavy financial responsibilities after his father died. He must have known, too, that photography was unlikely to provide him with a solid professional career. As the 1850s turned into the 1860s, even the great Roger Fenton had realized there was no serious money to be made in photography – and the gifted Rejlander died in poverty. So Carroll remained an amateur, albeit a devoted one.

During the early years, Carroll created quite a portfolio of photographs taken outside Oxford. He would pack up his equipment – a fastidious process which could last for a morning or more – and would travel with all his bags and boxes to see friends, family or extended family. He would photograph his hosts and their children during his visits, and stay for meals or overnight, sometimes for several days. This social aspect of his photography was probably a major part of its appeal. The photography enhanced, or provided an excuse for, many a pleasant social occasion, and his diaries show that when he was at home he liked to show his photo albums to his guests, partly as a polite way of soliciting friendly commissions, partly to entertain, and partly to be sociable.

One of the best known of his social photography visits during this early time was to the Isle of Wight, where he had come to know Tennyson and Tennyson's neighbour, the celebrated photographer Julia Margaret Cameron. He arrived on the island in July 1864 with his equipment and some of his photographs. Perhaps he was hoping to repeat the earlier success when his *Red Riding Hood* photograph of Agnes Weld had enchanted the poet.

On arrival in Freshwater, Carroll's photography immediately gave him an entrée into local society, with a local photographer lending him some photographs to look at. There was also, as he told his sister Louisa, 'a gentleman and a lady (real ones, as my peculiar skill in physiognomy told me)' who wished to see his own photographs. That same evening, there was yet more photograph-viewing. This time he and Mrs Cameron showed each other their photographs. Hers were mainly taken out of focus, he told Louisa, and he thought some of them were very picturesque and 'some were merely hideous'. However, Mrs Cameron talked about them as though they were artistic triumphs, he added, and '*she* wished she could have had some of *my* subjects to take out of focus – and *I* expressed an analogous wish with regard to some of *her* subjects.'[9]

Neither Carroll nor Mrs Cameron were to know that soon photography would start to take second place in Carroll's artistic efforts. The success of *Alice in Wonderland* would intervene to soak up his time and (initially, at least) a good deal of the money which he might otherwise have devoted to photography. The book was published in 1865 and by the end of the 1860s it was clear that it was a great success. After this, Carroll understandably directed his commercial aspirations, such as they were, towards the writing of books. He moved away from being a photographic jack-of-all-trades and became more selective about how he spent his photographing time. He began concentrating on the type of photography he enjoyed best – portraits. He liked taking pictures of people, particularly girls.

Earlier chapters have described how, as Carroll moved through his thirties he began to seek out little girls as companions. They seem to have offered the combination that he needed of loving, uncritical warmth and essential apartness, and many of his most striking photographs of them hint at this contradictory mixture of feeling. The children stare frankly out of the pictures, happily aware of being observed by a beloved friend, yet ready to run away and play when the session is over.

After he built a studio in his rooms at Christ Church, parents began to bring their children to him to be photographed, and he started to make a name for himself for his pictures of children. By the early 1870s he had published *Looking-Glass*, and Alice and her two closest sisters were grown up. He had made one final photograph of them in 1870, the nearly-adult Alice staring rather glumly out of a large chair, completely unrecognizable as the responsive child she had once been.

In the second stage of his photographic career, roughly covering the 1870s, one of his favourite subjects was a girl called Xie Kitchin. Xie was the daughter of one of his colleagues, George Kitchin – the one who had brought in the Prince of Denmark for him to photograph. Carroll was very friendly with the whole family, and Xie was a natural model, graceful and unselfconscious. He portrayed her both in costume and in regular dress, the first picture when she was five, and the last when she was 16, shortly before he gave up photographing altogether. One of his favourite pictures of her shows her attired in a gorgeous coat trimmed with Santa Claus fur, a furry pillbox hat and gloves – she had links with Denmark and looked the part to brave a Danish winter. Later, it would be Xie's mother, Alice Maud, to whom Carroll confided the problems which led him eventually to abandon photography.

The 1870s, Carroll's final photographing decade, were to see a change in the public attitude towards photography. Quick, convenient photography would not become a serious proposition until the 1880s, but by now the art had reached the mass market. Hundreds of photographic studios had opened in towns up and down Britain to cater for the public's wish to have its photograph taken. These little studios churned out thousands of beautifully decorated and engraved cards upon which were pasted either cartes-de-visite or the larger 'cabinet' photos. Thousands of men and women, boys and girls put on their best clothes and posed stiffly for their pictures, and stationers' shops stocked ever more elaborate photograph albums to hold this unstoppable flood of images. These commercial family albums boasted everything from gilt-edged silken pages painted with flowers or countryside scenes, to carved wooden covers, brass locks and keys, and even built-in musical boxes. New picture card formats were hastily introduced, with names like the Victoria, the Imperial and the Boudoir, and they just as speedily disappeared.

Throughout this busy time, Carroll ignored new technical developments, continuing to use the wet collodion process which suited him. After he built his studio in Badcock's Yard, near Christ Church, he used that for a while. When he moved into a much larger suite of rooms at college, he abandoned Badcock's and constructed a studio and darkroom within his own home.

He was highly methodical in his record-keeping, and kept a numbered register of all the photographs he ever took. This register contained a brief description of every image, and would have been a useful document for anyone seeking an overview of his work and an impression of its scope. The sheer hard work that went into it is suggested by some of Carroll's diary entries during July and August 1875. In these, he describes spending the whole week in registering and arranging photographs, taking up about 10 hours a day. He arranged, and nearly completed, his alphabetical index of negatives, he wrote up the chronological register of his photographs nearly to date and numbered them all. He arranged in albums nearly all his unmounted prints and his mounted cartes and cabinets, and entered them into his photographic register. He then went on, he said, through all the 4¼ × 3¼ and 6 × 5 negatives by means of the register, erasing some, and finding places for others. The register survived his death perfectly safely. Sadly, at some time afterwards, the careful and comprehensive record disappeared. It is just one of many major documents which are known to have existed after his death but which have subsequently vanished.

The disappearance of any document inevitably raises speculation about its contents. Just as the loss of the diaries and letter register has made it harder for researchers to understand Carroll, so the loss of the photographic register has made it hard for researchers to trace the development of his photographic art. Perhaps most unfortunately, the loss of the register clouds Carroll's reason for giving up photography in 1880, and it adds mystery where perhaps there would have been none.

His abandonment of his hobby was, apparently, very sudden. One day, after years of hard work and apparently continuing enthusiasm, he simply put his camera away and never took it out again. From 1880 onwards, if he wanted to obtain photographs of his friends, he had them professionally taken at studios.

Various reasons have been suggested as to why he might have done this. Summer, with its bright light, was the best time for the increasingly old-fashioned style of photography which he favoured, and, as the photographic historian Douglas

Nickel points out, by 1880 his summers were being spent at Eastbourne, away from his studio.[10] Yet Carroll had been going away on his summer holidays for years, if not to Eastbourne then to somewhere else, and he had not abandoned photography before. Furthermore, he was not at all busy in 1880. He was shortly to resign his mathematical lectureship and would be aware that this would offer *more* time for photography. Indeed, after he quit his job, his diary tells that he became lonely and concerned at his 'reclusiveness'.

There is a persistent rumour that Carroll quit photography because of a scandal involving little girls. This rumour is probably partly based on remarks in an essay of 1969 by Helmut Gernsheim prefacing the revised Dover edition of his book *Lewis Carroll, Photographer*.

In this, he described a conversation he had had with a lady called Ella Bickersteth. She had been one of Carroll's child sitters, and she remembered him with great affection. When she talked to Gernsheim, she would have been extremely old – in her nineties. Gernsheim reports that, despite Carroll's scrupulousness when taking nude photos of children, the aged Miss Bickersteth remembered that a scandal had developed about him in Oxford around 1880. As a result, Carroll decided to abandon his photography altogether.

By the time Gernsheim wrote his essay, a piece by Margaret L Woods had appeared in the press. Ms Woods had met Carroll twice as a teenager but had *not* become a friend. In her piece, she stated confidently that Carroll had 'invited a very little girl to be photographed and took her almost unclothed. Her mother shrieked at the impropriety of this.'[11] Ms Woods' piece was crammed with inaccuracies and conjectures, of which this (as will be seen) is one, but her readers could not be expected to know this.

As previously mentioned, several learned commentators had also put forward psychoanalytical theories which supposedly showed that Carroll was unable to fall in love with women and was fixated on little girls. They had little scientific basis, but it would have been reasonable at that time for Gernsheim to assume that little girls were involved in any 'scandal' there might have been. Significantly, though, Ella Bickersteth did *not* report that the scandal involved little girls, but as so often happened with Carroll, this salient fact was widely overlooked.

So what were the relevant facts?

Carroll directed that after his death certain packets of private material should be destroyed unopened by his executors. He had told Mrs Henderson, the mother of two children that he photographed nude, that he would add the negatives of her nude children to these items. 'I haven't destroyed the other prints. Perhaps you may be wanting more some day,' he said.[12]

He felt that these and other nude photographs might embarrass their (by then much older) subjects and their families if strangers were to see them. The reference numbers of the missing nude photographs in question suggest that they depicted the Hatch girls and Gertrude Chataway. All three stayed close to Carroll until the end of his life and were very fond of him, so the photographs obviously did not cause any problems either for the children or their parents.

Yet so much has been written about Carroll's nude photographs, that it is worth looking at the subject more closely before continuing with what actually happened in 1880. Edward Wakeling, a world expert on Carroll's photography, has estimated that of nearly 3,000 negatives made by Carroll, only around 1 per cent is thought to have shown children nude or partly-clothed.[13] These represent 8 sessions over 13 years with the children of 6 families, and all were done only when the children wanted to do it, and with the parents' full permission.

But even one nude child picture may seem like one too many. Even if there is genuinely no deviant intention, the spectre of child pornography casts a constant shadow over modern life, and modern artists and photographers cannot tinker with our own very strong contemporary taboos without causing anger, suspicion and outrage.

This was far from the case in Carroll's day. Nearly all men yearned to touch and gaze at the heavily protected and well-draped womenfolk, who were usually carefully guarded by their husbands, brothers and fathers. Small girls were considered to be sexless (when they were even considered at all), and photographing children naked was considered compatible with a wish to portray human beauty in its purest and most inoffensive form.

There are no assertions, no reports of gossip and no hints or suggestions that any parent of any young child portrayed nude by Carroll felt threatened by anything he did. Nor did any of the few children themselves, after they grew up, suggest that they had been upset by their encounters with him: the opposite seems to have been the case. Carroll wanted to portray what he saw as God's handiwork. He considered his nude photographs of little girls as celebrations of this, and he spoke openly – and with all kinds of people, including their parents – about all aspects of child nudity, both aesthetic and moral.

For example, he made no secret of his enthusiasm for portraying Annie Henderson nude to her mother, Mrs Henderson, when he wrote it was 'a chance not to be lost, to get a few good attitudes of Annie's lovely form and face, as by next year she *may* (though I much hope won't) fancy herself too old to be a "daughter of Eve".'[14] Neither he, nor Mrs Henderson (nor Annie, after she had grown up) saw a problem in his nude pictures of her.

But Carroll was equally frank about the moral problems sometimes inherent in nudity in another letter, which was written to his artist friend Gertrude Thomson, in which he said he no longer wished her to use two particular child models in her drawings for his book because he was concerned about the way in which they were being brought up.

> I don't think I have yet told you that I wish no more drawings
> to be made, for me, of either Iris or Cynthia, naked. I find
> they are being brought up in a way which I consider injudi-
> cious and dangerous for their purity of mind, and I will do
> nothing which can add to the danger. It is a real sacrifice of
> inclination ... but if we are to follow the voice of conscience,
> we cannot always do what we should like![15]

Morality was a vital issue. The use of nudity had a complicated moral and social significance in Victorian art. It not only
celebrated the artistic beauty of the attractive human body,
but it aimed to arouse moral ideas in its viewers, encouraging
them to reflect on social or political issues. Just as the storytelling aspects of Victorian photography are still treated with
puzzlement or contempt today, so are its moral aspects usually
overlooked. Yet these moral aspects are important if one is to
understand what many photographers and artists of the day
were trying to do.

One of the most famous nude statues of mid-Victorian
times illustrates this point. Hiram Powers' *The Greek Slave* was
well known to Carroll, who recorded in his diary that he had
met a lady whose brother had bought it for £300 and sold it
for £5,000.[16] This American statue depicts a chained naked
woman sold into slavery by the Turks. The fact that she is young,
delightful and beautiful as well as naked aroused a storm of
protest (and, of course, created wonderful publicity for the
statue), but ultimately, the public accepted the statement of her
maker, Hiram Powers, that 'it is not her person but her spirit
that stands exposed'.

Just as *Uncle Tom's Cabin* portrayed the evils of slavery in
readable fictional form, so Powers' sculpture invited the viewer
to acknowledge the moral evil represented by slavery, and he
did this by showing a beautiful woman abused and ruined by
it. And this evil, to his American viewers, was part of everyday

life, since some of these mid-19th-century Americans owned slaves themselves.

Some of Carroll's photographs, such as the famous image of Alice Liddell in her ragged, off-the-shoulder beggar girl dress, would also benefit from being seen in their full moral and narrative light. Often criticized today for its supposedly provocative air, this photograph of the beggar Alice was admired in its day by many people, including Tennyson, and a copy was carefully preserved by Alice's family.

To its contemporary observers – including Alice's hugely respectable parents – it would have seemed ludicrous to perceive it as sexual in any way. The image would have reminded them of one of the beggar children that they saw daily. They would also have known the very relevant fact that the photograph was one of a pair. In the other picture, Alice is shown in exactly the same corner of the garden – this time wearing her best clothes. So Carroll's child is *the same child both rich and poor.* The pair of images made the point that wealth and social position were only on the surface; and that, in a religious context, rich and poor are alike in the eyes of God.

Alice Liddell was a gifted little model, as she succeeded triumphantly in engaging with the viewer and compelling attention in her role. Those who see nothing in the picture but a provocative, scantily clad nymphet, are perhaps imposing their own modern anxieties and preoccupations on the image, and also upon other Victorian art nude images, including those by Carroll.

As far as young children's naked bodies were concerned, countless contemporary greetings cards showed naked children merrily frisking in cherub wings or splashing comically in tin baths. Photographs of naked women would not have been acceptable under any circumstances on family greeting cards, and even semi-draped mythological figures sometimes attracted adverse comment, but it was obvious that for much of the 19th and 20th centuries, the public saw pictures of naked small children as appealing and endearing. This convention continued right into the Edwardian age, and within English families, as the writer is personally aware, pictures of young children happily playing without clothes were taken and shown around to friends without arousing adverse comment until well into the 1980s.

Nonetheless, nudity of any kind at all was a problem in some social circles, and Carroll knew this. It may not literally have been true that some ladies draped the legs of their pianos, as popular legend would have it, but there were moralists around who were always alert for any sign of anything potentially sexual of which they could disapprove. They saw no beauty or grace in the naked body and perceived sin everywhere.

Carroll himself was morally over-sensitive on certain subjects, and so it was certainly not that he disapproved of moralizing *per se*. But to him, and most other people of his period, it was an accepted fact that children's purity and innocence were the opposite of sexuality and sensual temptation. Carroll worked always on the assumption that it was normal to wish to avoid sin, and he believed his dealings with children were far more godly than any of the potentially sensual situations that inevitably threatened even the most 'artistic' encounters between grown-ups of opposite sexes.

In accordance with this view, he believed it to be a grave sin to persuade children to do anything they themselves had the slightest unwillingness to do. As his comment to Miss Thomson showed, he would flatly refuse to use child models if he thought they had any bodily self-consciousness, for fear of unwittingly leading them to evil ways. So, despite mutterings from those who disliked nudity at any price, no scandal was associated with his small child-friends, and there is no evidence that his photographs of young unclothed children were the cause of any problems either for him or his contemporaries.

The same cannot be said, though, of contemporary reaction to his photographs of older girls and grown-up women. Therein lies a greater possibility that a scandal was threatening to blow in 1880.

Carroll took pains to emphasize to his friends that his own 'romantic' (as he put it) feelings had dwindled with age. Numerous comments he made indicate that he no longer considered himself to be a moral threat to ladies or their reputations by the time he reached late middle age. He seemed to feel that he was now capable of offering a chaste kiss to grown women and admiring their bodies more artistically – and less sexually, one presumes – than before.

Throughout the 1870s, the age of his sitters had been rising, and his last ones recorded, in summer 1880, were the sisters Gerida and Gertrude Drage, aged about 16 and 19. They were friends of Julia Arnold, the granddaughter of Dr Arnold of Rugby. Carroll told Julia that he wanted to portray Gerida, the younger, in 'gymnasium dress' and she could also be 'Comte de Brissac' if she liked, dressing in a feathered hat and doublet and hose. He also expressed the hope that her older sister might also be willing to pose in gymnasium dress.[17] Carroll's photographs of them have disappeared, but gymnasium, bathing and acrobatic outfits could hardly be morally condemned since they were worn in public places frequented by families. Indeed, his faithful model Xie Kitchin had around this time personally presented Carroll with a picture of young women in acrobatic attire.

At the same time, Carroll complained to Xie's mother, Mrs Kitchin, about some increasingly virulent gossip concerning a recent incident in his photographic studio. After photographing a 17-year-old girl, Atty Owen, he had kissed her in front of her father under the impression that she was just 14 – and hence a 'child'. It would have been fine for him to kiss a child, but a young lady of marriageable age was another matter altogether. Atty's parents, who were both of a legalistic turn of mind, were outraged. Carroll noted in his diary that he had written to Mrs Owen that 'the incident had been as distressing to her daughter as it was to myself, but promising to kiss her no more.'[18] This unfortunate little joke went down very badly indeed with the Owens. Soon afterwards, Carroll, who felt he had done nothing wrong, asked to photograph Atty again. The Owens were even more furious.

By July 1880, Carroll was writing to Mrs Kitchin:

> I met Mr. S. Owen a few days ago and he looked like a thundercloud. I fear I am permanently in their black books now, not only by having given fresh offence – apparently – by asking to photo Atty (was that such a very offensive thing to do?) but also by the photos I have done of other peoples' children. Ladies tell me 'people' condemn these photographs in strong language, and when I enquire more particularly, I find that 'people' means Mrs. Sidney Owen![19]

Carroll knew well it would have been disastrous for him to gain a name as 'unsuitable company' among respectable families, particularly those with children of marriageable age.

The Oxford Art & Antique Agency issued a catalogue after his death which listed various items of fancy dress Carroll had used in his photography. They sound charming, but as well as the fairy prince suit, the red fez and so on, there is a 'large bathing dress – elbows to knees' and one large-sized nightdress, listed as 'suitable for use rather than fancy dress – 7/6d'.

Carroll had been skating close to the wind in photographing young lady friends in nighties or showing their calves, especially when he was known to be a man who was interested in 'nudity' – even if it was only children's nudity and even if he *was* 'past it'. Respectable though most bathers, gymnasts and sleepers undoubtedly were, there was no denying their outfits were scanty by comparison with the whalebone corsets, padded bustles and petticoats sported by regular Victorian ladies in daily life. However ladylike his friends' children were, and however gentlemanly Carroll was, this gossip threatened to damage his reputation. He kept joking about it all, but there is a slightly frantic note to some of the joking, both to Mrs Kitchin and to Xie, whom Carroll had been photographing since her infancy.

Apart from the brief written reference to meeting Atty's father, it has been hard to find out more. As with other troublesome matters – like, for example, the Mathematical Lectures referred to in Chapter 2 – Carroll stopped or avoided referring to it in his diary. Had Mrs Kitchin not kept his letters, the event itself would likely have disappeared from public knowledge. But even though his letter and photographic registers are gone, there are comments still extant which suggest that his overfamiliarity with the 17-year-old Atty had provoked gossip. Laurence Irving described how an Oxford lady had been egregiously 'parading her outraged sense of propriety' around town about the incident,[20] and the persistence of Mrs Owens' anger suggests that she would have been only too glad to hound Carroll until he stopped taking photographs altogether.

He, of course, was obliged to find a reason to explain to the world why he had abandoned photography. He told friends that he no longer had time for it, and in a letter to a Mrs Hunt in 1881 he complained that it was 'a very tiring amusement'.[21] What he said would have been the truth, for telling outright lies seems to have been against his complicated inner code, yet it probably was not the *entire* truth. Still, if he was to be persecuted for doing the sort of photography that increasingly interested him, then perhaps it actually was better to fill his time with other things, and let the vicious gossip about young women die away.

In any case, there is no sign that nude *children* were part of the problem. We know this, because Carroll continued to sketch children in the nude, and talk openly about it, for many years afterwards, and nobody complained about that at all.

Alice as 'rich girl' and 'beggar girl'.

10

'He offered large discount, he offered a cheque'

Money

'My dear Fanny,

As we are about midway in the half-year for which I regard my periodical remittance as due, and as it is pleasant to prepay one's debts, I enclose cheque for £30.'

Letter from Carroll to his cousin, Mrs. W.E. Wilcox[1]

Most people think that Lewis Carroll must have been very rich. After all, he wrote one of the best-known books of the century, and his pseudonym, at least, has become a household name. Yet his bank account, discovered after a hundred years unseen in an archive in northern England, tells a different story.

Tracing its spidery way across the thick ledger pages of Oxford Old Bank, Carroll's account began in 1856, when he was 24 years old, and it finished in 1900, two years after his death, when his brother and executor Wilfred had finally wound up his affairs. Its value lies mainly in the fact that it is the only major document about him which is both factual and completely unaltered. His family did not discuss Carroll with outsiders, either before or after his death, and if his friends knew details of his private life, they chose not to share them with the world.

But nobody ever went through Carroll's bank account snipping out the names they did not like, or rubbing out transactions they thought ought not to be there. So these rows of figures and names are a treasure trove of private fact against which to measure other information.

The account offers details of people and places that might otherwise have been lost, and it points up matters that have been skimmed over in the past. It hints at aspects of Carroll's life that have never been guessed at before, and complements the sparse information otherwise known about his finances – a matter on which he kept rather quiet. And the image that has so often been presented of Carroll as a socially inadequate loner is belied on just about any page of it.

The account reveals that Carroll made a relatively modest amount of money from his books, and by no means a fortune. The great media and publicity machine which now dominates the lives of modern authors did not exist in his day – and nor did the huge sums of money which that media machine can generate for a successful book. In fact, Carroll hardly cashed in financially on his fame at all, and his lack of interest in doing this suggests that he may have had a fundamental lack of interest in becoming rich. As the bank's ledgers also show, never in a single year of his life did he earn anything approaching the annual income of Alice's father, Dean Liddell, at the time *Alice in Wonderland* was written.

Carroll's diary never gives the impression that he thought *Alice in Wonderland* would be a goldmine. In fact, he even seemed resigned at first to the idea that he might lose money. In a diary entry of 2 August 1865, he mused that he had committed himself to paying about £600 for the first 2,000 copies, and anticipated they would bring in £500 – a loss of £100. In addition, 'the loss on the first 2000 will probably be £100 leaving me £200 out of pocket', he continued. ' But if a second 2000 could be sold it would cost £300, and bring in £500, thus squaring accounts: and any further sale would be a gain: but that I can hardly hope for.'[2]

Of course, the books did far better than he had cautiously hoped, and after they became well known he was able to earn some money from what would these days be called merchandising. However, by modern standards, this merchandising was very modest indeed. He created a nursery version of *Alice in Wonderland* with charming new illustrations, and issued a facsimile of the original book he had written and decorated for little Alice Liddell. He also invented a nifty *Alice* postage-stamp case, and on one occasion he agreed to let an *Alice* biscuit tin be made.

Rather surprisingly, he did not press hard for *Alice in Wonderland* to be transferred to the stage, although he allowed various amateur entertainers to put on scenes from it without asking them for money. He once approached Sir Arthur Sullivan to write some *Alice* music, but it came to nothing because Sullivan, understandably, was not prepared to write songs on spec and Carroll did not have a definite proposal for paying him. He also considered the idea of a pantomime, starring a children's troupe called The Living Miniatures, and he mentioned the matter of an *Alice in Wonderland* adaptation to the strangely-named Mr German Reed, whose drawing-room entertainments were popular in genteel society. That too came to nothing – which was perhaps just as well, since German Reed's entertainments were held to be rather weak, not least by Carroll himself.

It was only when he was in his fifties, nearly twenty years after *Alice in Wonderland* was published, that Carroll finally agreed to let the dramatist Henry Savile Clarke adapt the books for the stage. Even then, his main concern seems to have been that the production should contain nothing of 'coarseness, or anything suggestive of coarseness', rather than how much money he would make from it. It is hard not to wonder whether things would have been different if he had had an agent. But Victorian gentlemen did not have agents.

Carroll's apparent lack of interest in increasing his own wealth does not mean he let people walk all over him, however. He was no fool, and he was not prepared to allow anyone to make him feel like one. He took steps to protect his copyright in the books, and kept an eye on his percentages. Indeed, an extraordinary correspondence he had with his publisher, Macmillan & Co, is often quoted to show how financially astute he was, although in truth it could equally likely have been used to demonstrate his twin loves of fussing and winning arguments.

After he had analysed the *Alice* accounts in 1875, Carroll complained to Macmillan that on every thousand copies sold, their profit was £20 16s 8d, his was £56 5s 0d, and the bookseller's was £70 16s 8d. This seemed to him 'altogether unfair'.[3] After bombarding the company with letters on the subject, he began fixing the sale prices of his books himself to obtain a larger profit. He thereby earned himself the deep enmity of book-sellers, and enhanced his reputation for financial sharpness. The book did earn more money, but it made him unpopular all round. Still, Macmillan & Co took it in their stride. They were used to getting difficult letters from Carroll.

His bank account, of course, reveals the financial framework behind his various publishing ventures. Carroll funded the publi-cation of *Alice in Wonderland* from his income from lecturing at Christ Church, and the account shows that this income was all he had, other than dividends from a few shares. Spending all this money on publishing his little book was a daring thing to do when he had no plans to become – and never did become – a professional children's writer. In fact, some might think that it shows a certain recklessness.

Most of the accounting was done by Macmillan (this topic was touched upon in Chapter 6, see pp 179–80). Since they published his works essentially on commission, but marketed the books themselves, he gave them in exchange a percentage of the profit after costs for advertising and distribution (including discounts to book dealers) had been dealt with. They paid the bills on his behalf from the income generated on sales, sending him his money half-yearly in arrears. So the bank account shows that the first money he saw from *Alice in Wonderland* took a long time to arrive, because the 1865 first edition made a loss, and he had to wait for the reprint to generate some income.

The Macmillan payments were usually for several hundred pounds (they never topped a thousand a year). They came in towards the beginning of the year, but it is not always possible to identify which incoming payments are from them, for Carroll did not seem to have any system for keeping payments clear in his account. He often told the clerks that incoming payments were simply 'Cash', without any suggestion as to whom they came from. The first credit labelled with Macmillan & Co's name came in on 17 February 1868, but an earlier one was probably deposited under 'Cash' in early 1867.

The many payments that Carroll made for printing, binding, engraving and so on appear clearly over the years. Sir John Tenniel's £138 fee for doing the pictures for *Alice's Adventures in Wonderland* appeared in the account in 1865. That can be seen to be about a quarter of Carroll's entire annual income, but when *Through the Looking-Glass* came out a few years later, Tenniel's fee had jumped sharply to £290. There are eight more drawings in the second book than in the first, and Tenniel's fame had increased still further by then; but even so, it was a large increase.

It has been speculated that Tenniel may have been upping his price to try and put Carroll off. If so, he did not know his man. A later illustrator, Harry Furniss, who did the pictures for *Sylvie and Bruno*, always maintained that Tenniel had told him that Carroll was difficult to work with, but although Tenniel did observe rather pointedly that he had never somehow felt an inclination to do any book illustrations again after *Alice*, cordial relations between the two men were maintained. Many years later, Tenniel asked for only £100 to redraw and colour his illustrations for *The Nursery Alice* (1889).

Carroll's bank account begins in 1856, and there are relatively few entries in the early years. This is mostly because fewer people had bank accounts in 1856 than later in the century, and cash was far more widely used then. As time went on, the number of transactions increased.

Usefully, the account does run right through the early period 1858–62, the time for which most of Carroll's diary record is missing, probably destroyed. Hence, it is one of the very few documents that offers information about Carroll's private life during this period. It shows that in December 1859 he took his first plunge into the stock market, with a few investments. In June 1860 he splashed out the high price of 2 guineas (£2 2s) to the British Association for a ticket to the famous lecture at Oxford in which Huxley and Wilberforce argued about Darwin's work. That debate sustained Carroll's interest in evolution – an interest which lasted the rest of his life.

The account also gives some rough idea of Carroll's movements, showing that he spent Christmas at Croft-on-Tees in 1861, because he drew cash in Darlington at the time. Commission stamps on certain cash payments indicate other times when he drew money away from home, with the extra charges this entailed. The most interesting payment during this missing diary period is one which occurred in November 1861, and this raises a mystery to add to the several other mysteries which shroud those blank years. The payment is for £94 4s 0d, getting on for a quarter of Carroll's whole annual income at the time, and it is to someone called Forster. It left the account on 8 November 1861, just weeks before Carroll, with considerable reluctance, took Holy Orders. The way the bank wrote the details shows that Forster lived in the Oxford area, but no Forster appears elsewhere in the account. Nor is it possible to identify any tradesmen or tradeswomen called Forster in Oxford at the time.

No surviving documentation links Carroll with anyone called Forster, except for a letter written on 13 January 1872, over 10 years later, to John Forster (1812–76) the biographer, historian and friend of Dickens. The tone of the letter indicates that the two men had previously met and were on cordial but distant terms; they had a mutual contact in Carroll's favourite uncle Skeffington Lutwidge, who, like Forster, had been a Commissioner for Lunacy. However, that John Forster did not live in Oxford, and as the bank showed no extra charges for an out of town payment, it does not seem to have been him. Nor did Carroll seem to have any connection with the Revd Thomas Forster of another Oxford college, whose account – which is also at Old Bank – shows no sign of incoming money at that date.

The payment may not have been connected with the feelings of distress so evident in Carroll's writings at around this time, yet there is some mystery as to why he would have been paying such a large sum of money to anyone. Furthermore, he was drawing rather large sums of cash relative to his income at the time. However, until or unless further evidence comes to light, the Forster payment stands as a reminder that Carroll did have a private life, however inaccessible it may be to us today.

The account's incoming payments are not quite as easy to interpret as the outgoing ones, but there is some historical interest in the money he received from Christ Church, especially in the early days. At that time, most of his income came from his teaching work. As was often the case then, he was paid half-yearly. He received in total about £450 a year, but the amounts credited were rarely the same from one payment to the next, and occasionally money from Christ Church appeared at odd times of the year.

These payments obliquely reflect how the Christ Church

that he knew was, in so many ways, still stuck in a quasi-
medieval way of life. Although changes were on the horizon,
Carroll's income, like everyone else's, reflected the exact amount
and character of the work that he did personally. He received
certain small fixed payments associated with his tenure at
the college, and to this was added a proportion of the money
which the college received from the properties it owned in the
countryside. In practice, that depended on harvests and other
farming events. So the fruitfulness of particular orchards and
wheat fields in some remote corner of the land actually had
a direct bearing on how much went into Carroll's pocket. He
also received teaching income from his pupils, but the amount
that they paid depended on their incomes, with wealthy men
paying him more than poorer ones. This is why it is difficult
for the modern reader to know exactly what salary he received
– because that salary was not entirely fixed. To add to the
confusion, dons who held college office often paid for college
expenditures out of their personal accounts, suggesting a mutual
trust and interdependence in the organization which must have
seemed archaic even in Victorian times.

One of the other features which comes out very strongly in
the account is the extent to which Carroll was involved with
other members of his family. Some of the first names to appear
in the account – and some of the last – are those of family
members. He probably opened the account in the first place so
that he could supervise the money his father had set aside for
his brothers Wilfred and Skeffington during their studies at
Christ Church. From the start, his father deposited money with
him via Coutts Bank's agency. In the 1850s, no national cheque
clearing system existed, but there were several companies, like
Coutts, which transferred money between subscribing banks.
It was Carroll's job to allocate and supervise this money, and
render an account at the end of term to his father. So, in his
early twenties, it is clear that Carroll still existed firmly within

the context of his large family and was expected to take care of his siblings.

After his father died in 1868, he, as the oldest son, became official head of the family, and his account quickly reflected his new responsibilities. Shortly after his father's death, it recorded various costs relating to removing everyone from the rectory at Croft-on-Tees, where the family had lived for 25 years, and settling them into the new house in Guildford, Surrey. From then onwards, he made many payments to his sisters, for he was a trustee of the fund that his father had set up to support his daughters after his death. The sums which he began to pay to his sisters probably included not only the money from the fund, but also money from his own pocket, either as gifts to his sisters or as a contribution towards the costs of accommodating himself and his friends when they came to stay.

The name of his only married sister, Mary Collingwood, also begins to appear fairly soon after her marriage in April 1869. Not a great deal is known about Mary's marriage, but her husband was often unwell. Carroll helped Mary educate her sons, and the large number of transactions in her name suggests that perhaps she had also arranged for him to handle any private money that she had; for until the early 1880s, married women were not allowed to control their own money.

Carroll also paid a regular £30 a year, and sometimes more, to the widow of his cousin William Wilcox, of whom he was very fond. The Wilcox clan figure very prominently in the account one way and another, and are involved in some of the largest financial transactions Carroll ever made. The most disastrous of these was in the 1880s, when Carroll invested huge sums in steamships, partly to help out one of his cousins, Herbert Wilcox, who was involved in the business. Sadly, Herbert was ruined, and the steamships were anything but a good investment, and yet this does not seem to have destroyed their relationship. Carroll did his best to recoup his losses, though with only moderate success, and despite years of aggravation and financial anxiety, he was still exchanging friendly letters with Herbert many years later.

In short, Carroll's family could rely on his support and care, and his money, if not exactly at their disposal, was obviously available to help and support them if necessary. His niece, Violet, remembered how unstintingly he helped her as a young woman when she came to study in Oxford, not only with money but with everything else: '… words almost fail me. Every day until we found our own feet and made friends he came to fetch us, showed us round Oxford, gave us tea in his rooms, introduced us to people, saw to it that we had everything we wanted and in short was the perfect uncle.'[4]

Carroll was protective and caring, he was undeniably in charge, he was deeply involved with family members, and he played his role efficiently and well. With such a large family to deal with, there were bound to be personal problems, disagreements and awkward moments, however. Fascinating hints of family tensions are hidden behind some of the entries, such as the payments which Carroll made to his siblings who got married.

Only three of the 11 ventured into matrimony: the second son, Skeffington, the third son, Wilfred, and the fourth daughter, Mary. The account shows that Carroll gave Wilfred £400 when he married in 1871. It was a generous gift that was obviously intended to help Wilfred in setting up a home and eventually supporting a brood of children. His artistic sister, Mary, had a painting for her wedding gift: not as generous a present as Wilfred's, but then Mary was supposed to be supported by her husband. Skeffington, ever the individualist, had not involved the family in his choice of bride. He had not even told Carroll he was planning to marry. And when he did marry, he did not tell him he had done so. Surely there is a touch of huffiness in Carroll's diary for 21 September 1880 as he recorded, 'Read a letter from Skeffington to Fanny, about his marriage (on Sep. 14) to a Miss Cooper, at Bridlington. He had kept it all a secret, and I am thankful to have no responsibility.' Skeffington did not receive a penny.

The account also strikingly displays some of Carroll's fundamental self-contradictions. A kind of fussy obsessiveness ran through his nature and made an impression on those who knew him; but, as was so often the case in his later life, the appearance was a caricature, and the reality was far more subtle.

Isa Bowman's description of the 'fussy' aspect of Carroll is typical of the kind of thing people said of him in later life. She knew him in the 1880s and 1890s, and she described how he would exactly calculate the amount of money that must be spent. He would then, '... in different partitions of the two purses that he carried, arrange the various sums that would be necessary for cabs, porters, newspapers, refreshments and the other expenses of a journey ...'.[5] It is only too easy to imagine the satisfaction with which the ageing Carroll produced these exact sums from his various pockets, conjuror style, at the appropriate moments.

Behind the scenes at Old Bank, though, it was a different story. When he did not have an elaborate plan involving railway journeys or something equally interesting to fuss about, and when nobody else was there to be impressed, Carroll often could not be bothered to notice how much was in his account from month to month, let alone consider what was happening with the odd 10, 20 – or 50, or 100 – pounds.

He began running into overdraft almost from the start. By the eighth transaction, his account was in the red, and he slid in and out of overdraft for ever after. At these times, a glance at the account gives the impression of a careless, emotional and headstrong man with little anxiety about debt and no interest in planning for the future. In fact, it is no exaggeration to say that at certain periods of his life, Carroll's account could be picked out of the many others in the ledger simply by the amount of red ink it displayed. His carelessness must have been as noticeable to the bank clerks as his fussiness was to his friends. Perhaps, standing at their desks in the back room of the bank, they occasionally commented upon Revd Mr Dodgson's habits, as the red ink bottle came out for him once more.

Carroll successfully hid this manifestation of his acute inner inconsistency from outsiders, and in the same way he was able to reconcile some of the forces which pulled him in opposing directions where his money was concerned. Although *Alice* did not make him a fortune, the annual revenues, which quickly reached several hundred pounds a year, became a lifebelt in an ocean which could become turbulent when Carroll's recklessness brought him near to losing control.

The most serious financial problem Carroll had occurred in the early 1880s, when he was in his early fifties. By then, he had decided he was earning enough from writing to be able to quit his unloved lecturing job. Once free of the lecturing, however, he seemed to start feeling a little lonely and cut off from life. Even an uncongenial job leaves a gap when it has gone, as many retirees quickly discover. Carroll had stopped taking photographs in 1880, and the loss of this hobby must have hit him hard. He needed something else to do. In an unusual burst of confidence, he confessed to his diary that his life was 'tending to become too much that of a selfish recluse'.[6] He accordingly took the extraordinary decision to accept the curatorship of the Common Room at Christ Church.

Many worthy people have held this post, which has also been compared with running a tea-shop. It involves the administration of the college dons' social club, and requires some routine hard work, but flair and originality are less in demand. Carroll, who could not help being original, was not an obvious candidate for the job, but he threw himself into the work with desperate energy, allowing no detail of the Common Room's needs to pass unnoticed. He made many improvements, thereby hugely increasing his workload in a job which would not otherwise have been onerous. He modernized the lighting, stocked the wine cellars with excellent wines, introduced afternoon tea and even established a complaints book. He was a good curator, and yet reading the carbon copies of his Common Room correspondence is a somehow uncomfortable, even saddening experience.

The copybook's pages are not large, Carroll's handwriting was looped, flourishing and of reasonable size, and the contents of the letters are excruciatingly pernickety. The overall effect is disturbing, even slightly crazy. It is a glimpse of a man devoting far too much time and emotion to desperately trivial things. Carroll's diary comments that he took the job with 'no light heart' and taking on a heavy responsibility for the sake of the social contact suggests that he, too, felt a certain concern at his own inner state of mind.

The unemotional contemporaneous figures in the bank account reveal how dramatically his frantic nitpicking in the Common Room contrasted with the lack of control in his personal financial affairs which developed in the early 1880s and was to continue for some years. Between 25 September 1883 and 22 January 1885, as he obsessed over pennies in the Common Room, money drained from Carroll's personal account at a noticeable rate. His overdraft rose to over £666 in January 1884, a sum which would (if only it had been a credit) bought a sizeable house at the time. Even his entire annual income from Macmillan was not enough to pay it off. An annotation on the ledger suggests that the bank had correspondence with him about it, and of course he had to pay interest.

None of Carroll's surviving diaries or correspondence even hint at this financial crisis, let alone suggest what caused it, or what he thought about it. Only these figures, penned by bored clerks and preserved by a company with no interest in Carroll's image, provide the truth. They suggest that something was going on. A little further investigation shows what it was.

In Carroll's day, banks always noted the name of recipient or payee beside each transaction. Many of the names in Carroll's account appear nowhere else in the diaries and letters, and refer to people or businesses whose details have not come down to posterity. Other entries suggest that individuals who previously merited only a footnote were more important than they at first seemed. One of these people in Carroll's life was a Mr Thomas Jamieson Dymes. Mr Dymes was an Oxford man (though not a Christ Church one) who had become a boarding house master at Eastbourne College. He is usually mentioned only briefly in biographies, if at all, as a recipient of Carroll's generosity. Yet Mr Dymes seems to be the reason why Carroll got himself into such a secret mess in the 1880s.

According to the letters and diaries, Carroll met Dymes and his wife in 1877, when Carroll called at Eastbourne College on behalf of a friend who thought she might send her son to the school. Over the following years, he spent a good deal of time with Mr and Mrs Dymes and their many children. In 1883, Dymes got himself into financial difficulties, and Carroll resolved to help him. It is known that he sent a printed circular to 180 friends, asking if they could offer employment to Dymes or his family. He also made contact with the historian Frederic Harrison, who had helped Dymes in the past.

Harrison and friends collected money to help Dymes and gave it to Carroll, and Carroll busied himself in paying off creditors, landlords, lawyers. He also contributed nearly £420 of his own money. A letter he wrote to Harrison on 4 October 1883 shows that he considered that at least £200 of the total amount of £419 7s 0d could be written off as a gift, although he was calling it a loan.[7] Yet there was no way that Carroll could afford to pay this money to Dymes. The overdraft he built up lasted for months, and then years, and there was no obvious prospect of his clearing it.

So what was the truth about Carroll's involvement with

Dymes? Was there any reason why Carroll should be paying large sums of money to someone he apparently only knew socially? Dymes' surviving letters do not present an attractive picture. He comes over as a rather incompetent man who felt he had been badly treated by life, and blamed others rather than himself. Nothing from his wife appears in the archives of the London School of Economics, which owns all the relevant letters, but it is reasonable to guess that Dymes' family probably suffered a good deal during their tribulations. Mrs Dymes was an invalid, and Dymes (as he was entitled to do by law until 1882) had spent her only money – an inheritance. Hard-done-by women often touched Carroll's heart, and the fact that Dymes had many daughters probably weighed with him, too. With seven sisters of his own, he knew the responsibility that unprotected females could be – and the risks to which they were exposed when no man was looking after them properly.

Carroll liked the Dymes girls well enough, particularly Ruth and Margie, two of the older ones, whom he tried to help with jobs. But although his letters to them are cheerful, friendly and teasing, he was not particularly devoted to them, as a casual 1882 comment in his diary about a social occasion shows: 'Margie and Ruth Dymes were also a failure, though in a less degree: they do talk, but are dull: the family have not mind enough to interest one.'[8] There is little indication that he saw the Dymes girls as anything other than pleasant companions. Nothing much has come down to posterity about Mrs Dymes, but there is no suggestion that Carroll had especially strong feelings about her, either.

What does come across is that the Dymes family offered Carroll constant contact with their family life. Just as Harry and the other little Liddells had become his substitute siblings when he was young and lonely in Christ Church, so the Dymes family offered domestic companionship when he was restless and lonely in his fifties. His own family no longer contained children for him to entertain and had no scope for the chats he enjoyed having with mothers about their family lives. His generation of Dodgsons did not go in much for marriage and children. Five of his spinster sisters were now spending their time doing good works in Guildford, and a sixth lived in flourishing eccentricity with many cats in Brighton. The seventh, the only married one, lived in genteel poverty with an ill husband and two growing sons far away in north-east England. The two married brothers eventually had twelve children between them, but they too lived far away, and they, of course, were the kings of their own castles.

The Dymes' joys and sorrows offered interest to a bachelor who otherwise had only himself to think of. His diary shows how he dropped by often to see them, and how he became involved in their family affairs. The children spent time with him and accompanied him on outings to Eastbourne, London, Oxford and Surrey, and he helped them sort out various practical matters which bothered them.

So, as Mr Dymes sat at his desk morosely writing long, sad letters to people whom he hoped might help him, Carroll spent time with Dymes' family, making himself more important to them than would otherwise have been possible. Although in truth he was hardly in control of himself, to them he must have seemed a model of competence and a rock of solidity compared with the hapless Mr Dymes.

Could this have justified the outlay of all that money? Perhaps. As an unknown writer, Carroll had been prepared to gamble money he could not afford on publishing a children's book. So he was probably capable of blowing hundreds of pounds of his personal money on making a woman and her helpless daughters feel more happy and secure, especially if it meant turning himself into a well-loved figure within their family circle.

As the years went on, Carroll apparently continued to get on well with Mrs Dymes and the children, but he went right off Dymes, if he had ever been on him in the first place. Eventually matters came to some kind of a head. In 1891 Carroll wrote in his diary, 'The Rev. G. R. Green called to talk about Mr. Dymes, from whom he is thinking of trying to recover some of his debt. I rather encouraged the idea. Mr. Dymes will never pay any of his debts unless forced to do so.'[9] This sour comment covered a falling-out, for after that the Dymes family fades entirely from his diary and are never mentioned again.

As he looked back during the 1890s, did Carroll regret the Dymes involvement which had cost him so much money, and given him so little long-term reward? And did the loss of personal contact with the Dymes family upset him more than losing the money? We cannot know, but it always seems that, for him, money was important as a means to an end, rather than as an end in itself. He had, by that time, recovered his finances, anyway.

Carroll's personal lifestyle was comfortable but modest. As a Christ Church resident, he paid a small sum to the college to cover his daily needs, and when he had friends to stay, he paid the college a little extra. He was not reclusive, and spent about the same on Common Room socializing as other people, as a glance at other mens' Common Room bills in the old ledgers confirms.

Several payments to booksellers appear, for Carroll was a really ardent bibliophile, and may have had a small sideline in book dealing. He certainly acted as a bookseller's contact point for his friends who were seeking particular books for sale. In a privately printed circular to booksellers of 1893, he asked the booksellers to stop sending him their catalogues so frequently. He had, he said, around 80 catalogues on his shelves which had been sent in the last few weeks![10]

The account also shows several payments to artists. In 1869 Carroll paid Thomas Heaphy £14 4s 0d for copying a painting of a fainting child, and, in 1863, Arthur Hughes received £26 5s 0d for the painting *Lady of the Lilacs*. Carroll particularly loved this latter painting, which hung on his wall until his death. There were also frequent payments to the photographic printers Hills & Saunders, and to chemical suppliers such as Telfer's, where payments for chemicals were substantial. There were payments to colourists and, later, to photographic studios, after he had stopped taking photographs himself. And there were gadgets.

Carroll was a lover of gadgets. In later life he became an eager purchaser of peculiar Victorian devices such as the Stylographic pen and Velociman adult tricycle, as well as one of the earliest typewriters. The Stylographic pen had a writing top consisting of a metal tube with a fine wire inside to regulate ink flow, rather similar to a modern drafting pen or rollerball.

The Velociman was a tricycle costing nearly £50. It was an extraordinary contraption, with two large wheels at the front and a small one at the back. It could, it was advertised, travel at six to eight miles per hour. Rather oddly, it was hand-propelled, so must have been intended for invalids.[11] Carroll had perfectly good use of his legs, and it is a slight mystery why he would have purchased such a device. Perhaps he wished to build up his arm muscles, as he later acquired a Whiteley's Exerciser which had that purpose. Unsurprisingly, he could not get on with the Velociman, and the state of the roads in those days cannot have made travelling in it any easier. He spent some time figuring out ways in which it could be improved, and discussing these with the mechanic who supplied it. Finally, he gave it away to his brother Skeffington. What Skeffington made of it is not recorded.

Curious contraptions aside, Carroll's life seems to have been simple enough. Although he helped his family and friends unstintingly, he kept no household and employed no staff of his own. He was abstemious, never travelled much abroad and he was not interested in luxury. Indeed, one side of his complicated nature seems to have disapproved of too much wealth. As he approvingly quoted Goldsmith's *The Deserted Village* in his 1867 parody 'The Deserted Parks':

> This wealth is but a name
> That leaves our useful products just the same
> Not so the loss. The man of wealth and pride
> Takes up a space that many poor supplied.

He took just one foreign holiday in his life, an overland trip to Russia, and his purchase of £100-worth of Circulating Notes (which could be exchanged for foreign currency) shows approximately what it cost him.

The bank account does not offer a great insight into Carroll's social life in general. Not everything he bought appeared in the account: there are no payments for theatre tickets in London, for example. He undoubtedly spent a good deal of money on the theatre, but Macmillan's staff, who were based in London, often bought his tickets for him and deducted the cost from his book revenues.[12] No regular payments to individuals outside his family occur, and no payments suggest that he had a special lady friend, as has sometimes been conjectured. However, other friends appear in flashes with the odd payment here and there.

Payments to 'Vanbrugh' refer to his friend Irene Vanbrugh, the celebrated comedienne, then aged about 20, or one of her theatrical sisters. Several payments to 'Quin' relate to Minna Quin, a distant cousin whom Carroll discovered and helped to support as she began her acting career. The money he gave them may have been to help with tuition, as he took a keen interest in developing the skills of his theatrical friends, whoever they were.

Isa Bowman was another actress who was a close and beloved companion. She always acknowledged how much he had helped her in establishing her professional career. A large payment to 'De Bunsen' of £12 12s od relates to Carroll's diary entry of 24 October 1891 in which he commented that, 'Dear Isa was to go at 11 this morning, to sing to Mddle. Victoria de Bunsen, who is to give her opinion on the capabilities of her voice. I shall then decide about lessons.'

Another friend, Gertrude Thomson, was an artist who socialized alone with him in defiance of Victorian convention, and his letters and diaries suggest they were fairly close. He employed her to create several pictures for him, and his generous payments to her mask the fact that she was not, by all accounts, very good at delivering her drawings on time – or at all.

Others were also beneficiaries of Carroll's generosity. An artist friend, Ethel Hatch, recalled gratefully in her unpublished memoirs[13] how he kindly offered to pay her fees to study with the artist Herkomer, even though she did not take his offer up. The account also shows for the first time how he helped support the writer Henry Kingsley in his dying days. Henry, brother of the more famous Charles Kingsley, had been one of the first adults to spot the commercial potential of *Alice in Wonderland*, and he and Carroll had been friendly for some years. In 1865, when Carroll was publishing the book, he had stayed with Henry in his cottage near Wargrave, and Henry's response to the copy of the book which Carroll presented to him was ebullient and enthusiastic, as his delightful letter of thanks shows.

> I received [it] … in bed in the morning and in spite of threats and persuasions, in bed I stayed, until I had read every word of it … I could not stop reading your book till I had finished it. The fancy of the whole thing is delicious …[14]

He was almost as enthusiastic about *Looking-Glass*. But by 1871, Kingsley, afflicted by debts, had moved back to London. He was not on very good terms with his famous brother. On 10 January 1872, Carroll's diary records laconically, 'Called on H. Kingsley, but he was out.' The diary makes no mention that he had left £100 for him; the cheque was cashed a few days later: Kingsley had obviously needed the money. He died in May 1876, and in November 1876 a repayment of just £37 9s 6d appeared in Carroll's account.

So Carroll gave generously to individuals, but he also gave generously to charity. In fact, his payments to charity are a very marked feature of his overall spending. In early life his gifts were unsystematic, but when he reached the age of 50, he embarked upon one of the frenzies of organization which sometimes consumed him, and he arranged his charity giving from then onwards with ardent precision. From 1882 until his death, he made payments to over 30 charities annually, as well as one-off payments for specific appeals. They differed slightly from year to year, so he obviously considered them all afresh each time.

His choice of charities shows that his main concern was for the ill, unprotected and vulnerable: 'him that hath no helper' as he once put it. As a group, the people whom he helped cover the spectrum of wretchedness that formed the dark side of the generally smug, secretive and sanctimonious Victorian era. He cared, as we have seen earlier, about the countless women and children whose poverty laid them open to illness and abuse. He supported the Homes of Hope for 'fallen and friendless young women' and the Clerkenwell women's prison where 'betrayed' and 'sincerely repentant' fallen women were rehabilitated. For many years he regularly supported The Society for the Rescue of Young Women and Children, which helped women and children who were at risk of prostitution. Until the end of his life, he also regularly supported the Society for the Protection of Women and Children, which fought against sexual exploitation and trafficking of children, and sometimes mounted legal prosecutions against men who abused children.

As already discussed, Carroll is sometimes accused of being a paedophile, or alternatively he is thought to have been too innocent to understand the crime. These regular donations show that he was well aware of the problem, and he loathed it. He did not support these particular organizations for show, nor did he single them out for his special support. He contributed to them quietly as part of a larger system of giving to many good causes over many years.

The Reformatory and Refuge Union was another beneficiary. It operated about 90 homes all over the country to shelter the fallen, destitute and neglected, particularly women and children. Additionally, the quaintly-named Metropolitan Association for Befriending Young Servants looked after ignorant young female servants who were far from home. These girls had nobody to turn to and were often sexually exploited by men in the families for which they worked.

Carroll was always realistic about the human body, and he did not flinch from the ugly side of physical life. There are regular payments to 'Lock Hospital' in the account. The precise Lock Hospital is not specified, but Carroll supported several London hospitals and female refuges in poor areas, and it is likely that this was the one situated in Westbourne Grove, London, which also operated as a refuge for prostitutes. Lock Hospitals were very unpopular, not only among many of those who were confined in them and obliged to accept treatment, but among the moralistic middle classes too. Dr Frederick W Lowndes, who worked in Liverpool Lock Hospital, produced a pamphlet illuminating the moral reasons why they were so reviled. 'Lock Hospitals are principally for the reception and treatment of persons suffering from diseases, the direct result of their own vicious indulgence … this is why they enjoy so little of the liberality so lavishly bestowed upon other hospitals and infirmaries,' he wrote gloomily.[15] It is hardly surprising that Carroll also supported the Society for the Suppression of Vice

– sexual 'vice' being the cause of most of the misery that caused women and children to 'fall' or be cruelly exploited.

His religious faith showed in his many contributions to Christian charities, and his interest in medicine led to several hospitals appearing on the list, for in those pre-National Health days, most hospitals relied on subscriptions to keep going, and those in poor areas were particularly hard pressed. Some of the many other social charities that he approved of included The Workhouse Infirmary Nursing Association, established by Louisa Twining (of the tea family) to improve the standard of nursing in workhouses. He also supported The House of Charity for Distressed Persons, which offered shelter to people of good character who fell on hard times, and the Society for the Relief of Distress, founded in 1860, which helped anyone who needed it, with no distinction of creed or race.'

Carroll never kept pets himself, but he hated to see animals mistreated and he was an early anti-vivisectionist. He supported The Dog's Temporary Home, the forerunner of the Battersea Dogs' Home for unwanted dogs, and he contributed to the Metropolitan Drinking Fountain and Cattle Trough Association, which built drinking fountains for people and water troughs for animals.

Despite all his gifts to charity, Carroll was not gullible. His eccentricity and kind-heartedness always had a steely edge of realism, and he also supported the Society for the Suppression of Mendicity. Subscribers earned the right to direct scroungers and beggars to the society's offices, where their claims would be investigated, and payments only made if they were genuinely found to be necessary.

In all this flurry of charitable giving and gifts for family and friends, one thing particularly stands out. Although he was happy to help and support others, Carroll was strangely uninterested in safeguarding his own future. When he was young, his father had advised him to take out insurance, but although there is an annual 16*s* premium to Norwich Fire (and, in *Looking-Glass* fashion, a strange payment from him to Clerical Medical Assurance after his death), there is no sign that he insured his life.

He probably trusted in God. God looked after him but, as it turned out, his decision had difficult consequences for his dependents. His income mainly came from book sales, and was a respectable but not enormous sum. It had eventually dawned on him to arrange a regular overdraft facility to cover times when he ran out of money, and these arranged overdrafts tided him over till the annual payment arrived, usually in late February or March. When he died on 14 January 1898 the account was overdrawn, by arrangement, by £222 15*s* 8*d*. The annual payment from Macmillan & Co was almost due, but there were bills to be paid immediately and no life insurance.

The money had to be found somewhere. So the family sorted out his most private documents. They chose mementoes for themselves from among his books and personal possessions, and then they auctioned as much of the remainder as possible, as quickly as possible, to get cash in hand.

There was some snobbish criticism of them at the time. One of Carroll's colleagues even wrote a poem decrying the sale. Looking at what the family had to deal with, that now seems unfair. One hopes they did not mind the criticism any more than he would have done. They all knew that their brother had specified that he wanted the cheapest funeral that was, as he said, 'consistent with dignity'. If the bank account is anything to go by, he would have been the first to agree that it was of no importance what happened to his worldly goods and chattels any more.

individualist, a tease and an iconoclast, and the roller-coaster progress of his personal finances and the almost scandalous get-togethers with young women show an irrepressible recklessness at his centre, a recklessness that he strove all his life to control.

Carroll was dramatic, creative and emotional, but none of these qualities were particularly admired in Victorian middle-class society, and he did not choose to express them much in public. Instead, he took pains to adopt the dull and respect-able outward lifestyle that he, his family and the outside world expected and wanted. He seems to have felt more secure when he faded into the drab, black-clad world of the conservative clerical don, hedged in by a thicket of rules and regulations.

His drifting into self-caricature later in life suggests that some parts of that role pinched him, but at least by then he had convinced himself logically that his self-contradictory ideas were consistent with the purity and godliness which mattered so much to him, and he had largely put his mind at rest about himself. Perhaps it was as well that he also possessed a toughness and canniness that was bolstered by his important practical place in his family circle, for, without secure footings and the rigid boundaries he had the sense to impose on himself, one suspects Lewis Carroll could have been something of a loose cannon.

Just as his ultra-moral appearance distracted attention from behaviour that sometimes teetered on the edge of unconven-tionality, so his love of over-elaborated daily planning counter-balanced a certain difficulty in organizing himself sensibly in everyday situations. His Christ Church colleague T B Strong described a characteristic example of the latter which occurred after Carroll agreed to mark some examination papers. Carroll, said Strong, had decided that the fairest way to assess the papers was to read them all at one sitting. However, he did not get around to doing this until the day before the results were due, and Strong discovered him toiling amid a gigantic pile of papers that literally rose higher than his own shoulders. Carroll worked heroically through the night, finishing just before the announcement of the results the following morning. He did not enjoy the experience, yet it did not seem to occur to him that he could have handled it differently. 'Of course,' he told the incredulous Strong, years later, 'I never examined again.'[1]

Carroll's handwriting also gives a hint of his acute self-contradictions. It is precise and clear, and however quickly he has written, it is readable. But it spreads, looping and flourishing, across the page, often hitting the right hand margin before the word is finished, and sporting scrolls and ornaments more appropriate to an artist or actor than an habitually silent mathematics don. In short, the opposing forces in his nature dictated how he lived his life, and ran through him like the letters in a piece of seaside rock.

His family knew what he was like, of course. Early in his adult life he recounted to his sister Mary how he had recklessly led friends to the station by climbing a steep cliff rather than going by road in the normal way. When he was halfway up he realized this was a bad idea, not just for him, but for the friend following him:

> … both my feet had lost hold at once … if the root I was hanging to had broken I must have come down and probably carried him with me … just at the top it was hardest of all; it was only to be done by crawling up through the mud, holding by 2 roots, without whose help it would have been impossible. … [once at the station we] boasted as much as possible of our feat, to prevent ridicule at our appearance …[2]

Carroll used humour like this to entertain, to charm and to cover up his feelings. The normally clean and tidy young man might have felt rather silly turning up covered in mud, but by making his audience laugh with him, he was deftly stopping them from laughing *at* him.

His wit was usually kindly, and he was gentle, sympathetic and compassionate, yet there was a darker side to him, too. He is said by Collingwood to have suffered from depression, and a persistent streak of unfocused horror flickers throughout even his humorous work. Sometimes the grimness is so unobtrusive that it passes almost unnoticed, as the following extract from *Through the Looking Glass* displays:

> 'Seven years and six months!' Humpty Dumpty repeated thoughtfully. 'An uncomfortable sort of age. Now if you'd asked my advice, I'd have said, "Leave off at seven" – but it's too late now.'
>
> 'I never ask advice about growing,' Alice said, indignantly.
>
> 'Too proud?' the other enquired.
>
> Alice felt even more indignant at this suggestion. 'I mean,' she said, 'that one can't help growing older.'
>
> '*One* can't perhaps,' said Humpty Dumpty. 'but *two* can. With proper assistance, you might have left off at seven.'
>
> 'What a beautiful belt you've got on!' Alice suddenly remarked ...'

No wonder Alice suddenly changes the subject here. Was Humpty Dumpty's comment a sinister threat to Alice, a veiled suicidal wish or an indication of Carroll's yearning for the childish lost innocence which preoccupied him? Nobody knows. But the shadows in Carroll's stories put into simple form our diffuse understanding of the insecurity, danger and sadness that underlies all life. Both the books about Alice were written during deeply unhappy periods, which suggests they may somehow deal with Carroll's emotional efforts to conquer misery and pain. Alice alchemically transforms fury, passion and nonsense into calmness, sense and humour, and transforms unanswerable questions into amusing puzzles, double meanings and jokes.

Carroll's love of puzzles and double meanings went alongside a feeling for dreams and marvels and mysteries. His interest in the supernatural is seen in many of his works, although not a great deal of other information about this has survived. There is little documented record of his interest in other-worldly experiences other than his lifelong support of the Society for Psychical Research. The sale catalogue of his effects does not list many books from what sounds to have been a fairly extensive supernatural library, but of course this lack of information does not mean that the books were not originally there. Some super-natural topics blend into philosophy and religion, and books on both these subjects are well represented in the catalogues. Also, his large family had gone through his library before putting it up for sale, and would have removed many books for all kinds of reasons.

Carroll was also particularly interested in what Stuart Collingwood described in 1898 as 'psycho-physiology',[3] which would have dealt with the relationship between body and mind, strange mind states, hypnotism, delusions and hallucinations, curious psychosomatic conditions and early psychology. Unfortunately, his vast collection of medical books was bequeathed to a nephew, and none reached the auctioneer's catalogues, so little is known about them either. Frustratingly little, too, is known about any supernatural experiences he may have had, although he did hint that he had them, and he was sure he had received answers to prayer. He was also superstitious enough to note that Tuesday was his lucky day, although he is not recorded as having explained why.

So the sum total of what is known does not sound very spooky, and yet the closing scenes of *Through the Looking-Glass* are among passages in his work that show a startling sense of horror and the supernatural. The characters are grotesque, from the misshapen, zombie-like servants to the bizarre queens who suddenly fall into a dead sleep, one on each of Alice's shoulders.

Equally chilling are the incidental characters, such as the hunk of meat which Alice prepares to cut, only to find that the meat, although cooked, is not dead after all. Indeed, it knows etiquette, for it raises itself on end and bows to her. As the story lurches towards its climax, the table starts rising too, and the food begins to fly around just as it did in the crazy real-life seances of Mrs Guppy. 'Take care of yourself! Something's going to happen!' screams the White Queen. The candles shoot up to the ceiling, still alight and flaming. The diners change places with the food. A 'hoarse laugh' beside Alice indicates that the piece of cooked meat has somehow left its plate and is now sitting alongside her. It laughs, but it does not speak.

One of the most surprising things about this second 'Alice' book is the way that Carroll has managed to introduce these hideous images in a book for sheltered little children. His preoccupation with death is particularly clear in *Looking-Glass*, probably because he was still emotionally shattered by the death of his father. Yet in the end, in the middle of her terror, Alice shakes the frightening red queen into a sweet little kitten, and all ends well.

Nevertheless, it can be seen that death was a subject that increasingly preoccupied Carroll in later life; the 'silent end' which awaits us all. In public – and perhaps consciously to himself – Carroll used his religion to put a positive gloss on it. How wonderful it was going to be, he mused, when one could awaken at last and realize that the hurdle of dying was now behind! Yet the question of eternal punishment troubled him, and he was terrified at the idea that he himself might accidentally die in the midst of a sinful act and have to justify his own evil-doing to God. He created elaborate intellectual reasons why a loving God would never allow human souls to suffer torture for eternity, and vowed he would rather have a loving God without great power, than an all-powerful God who could hate. But his letter to his friend Mary Brown offered a revealing glimpse of his real feelings when he advised her that the greatest comfort could be achieved by believing whatever seemed right to her.[4]

Religion and morality, plus their ugly sister, moralism, must also have influenced his sexual life. Speculation about that never ceases, but common sense dictates that it is impossible to know all there is to know about another person's sexual life when they have been dead for well over a century. What is certain is that during Carroll's lifetime few opportunities existed for loving, mutual sexual relationships outside marriage. There was no effective contraception, and women were the ones who took most of the terrible risks attached to extra-marital sex. He seems to have had strong feelings about this, and so it is unlikely that he patronized the huge sexual underworld which seethed behind the façade of middle-class Victorian morality and wrecked the lives of so many women and children. His private donations to charity show how consistently he supported charities which helped women and children who were misused by men.

However, he very much liked female company, and was unusual for his times in treating women more or less as equals. This sense of equality could not include anything sexual, for Victorian women did not have the opportunity to behave equally about this matter, and there are suggestions that Carroll may have overstepped the mark sexually at least once with a woman, to his great regret.

He also had many male friends and got on well with men, but they do not seem to have attracted him emotionally and he did not (like so many of those who had been through the public school system) end up gravitating towards sentimental relationships with other men. His time at Rugby school is said to have revolted his sensitive nature, and although Collingwood discreetly does not go into further details, there are many contemporary descriptions of the appalling obscenity of boys' life at public schools, including flogging and the only too aptly named system of fagging, in which small boys were expected unquestioningly to perform tasks for older boys. Carroll seems to have ended up despising overt maleness and masculinity, and perhaps that included his own.

Carroll did not desire men and boys, and he could not have women, so his preoccupation with little girls therefore seemed to his contemporaries to be a total rejection of sexuality. He probably believed it was. We, with a modern perspective, however, can see how ideas of sexuality – even though it was *rejected* sexuality, or non-sexuality – thereby attached to his friendships with girls.

It is not fair to call it paedophiliac, for if he had sensed any inward carnality in his love of children, his highly developed moral sense would have forced him to avoid them, just as he had avoided over-closeness with women during his years of sexual potency. He said that what he got from his child friends was love, which he equated with the pure love of God. It kept him emotionally grounded and did not tempt him to evil.

Of course, marrying might have solved some of his conflicts. It would also have given him more problems, not least the task of finding an occupation sufficiently lucrative to support a wife and family in reasonable style. However, he showed no inclination to marry. The formal structure of mid-Victorian courtship, in which the feelings of individuals were not of great account, had little to do with romantic love and was more a matter of joining families, settling individuals down and rearing children. Carroll, an incorrigible individualist, had enough family life and more than enough family responsibility, and his bachelor life at Christ Church offered the space to make his own decisions in a way that would have been impossible if he had had his own wife and children.

Moreover, a strong vein of fear, distress and cynicism runs through his references to marriage, although these are usually veiled in humour. There was indeed justification for the common contemporary view that women were forever trying to snare a man for his money. Women, after all, had few other chances to get away from home and secure a reasonable life. Carroll's strong romantic and sentimental streak was endearing, but it always made him react strongly to the idea of someone giving themselves to a person who did not value them. He seemed most unsure of whether true, overwhelming marital love ('... second only to your love for Him who Himself *is* "Love",' as he told a friend)[5] could exist for him in the real world.

As he grew older, Carroll was increasingly perceived as a recluse. His diaries belie this, since he records an extensive social life right up until his death. His reclusiveness was experienced mostly by his Christ Church neighbours and the conventional people who formed the backbone of polite Oxford society. He made few efforts to fit in with them, and sometimes one gets the impression that he obtained a decided pleasure from annoying and irritating them. He particularly hated attending get-togethers where he might be lionized as the creator of *Alice*. He had, it seems, ambivalent feelings towards the books, and refused always to answer questions about them. He also refused to elucidate any of the other hidden meanings in his works, although there are undoubtedly many of them. Like so much else, he took these secrets with him to the grave.

Now, in the end, I find that the Carroll who has emerged from my researches is a man that I like, despite his faults. The underlying humour of his precise, kindly, unexpected nature shows in his many letters, which still crackle with life after more than a century. Those letters, thoughtful, quirky, charming and entertaining, now fetch hundreds or even thousands of dollars at auction.

But even if they had not been worth a penny, I still wish my childhood dream had been possible. I really would have liked to receive one addressed to me.

Appendix

Report of Dr Yvonne Hart on Carroll's neurological symptoms, August 2008

[The dates refer to entries either in the *The Letters of Lewis Carroll* and *The Diaries of Lewis Carroll*.]

The descriptions of 'fortifications' followed by headache are most suggestive of migraine. The description of only one eye being involved (first the left, and on another occasion, the right) is unusual, but may occur in 'retinal' migraine. This usually causes either temporary blindness in one eye or a patch of blindness, but may include scintillations. In fact, it is common in medical practice to find people describing visual disturbances involving one eye when they have a disturbance involving the same field of vision in both eyes (as occurs in migraine), but I imagine one may assume that Carroll would have tried closing each eye in turn to establish firmly that only one eye was affected!

Migraine aura not followed by headache (12 June 1888; 2 September 1889) is also very common, and if it was the same as that described in Dr Latham's book on 'bilious headache' (which I confess I have not read), it sounds quite likely that it was migraine.

Epilepsy. 20 January 1886 – I cannot really comment on the episode of 20 January 1886, as there is no description. Certainly after a seizure people may have a headache and not feel their usual self, but it would be unusual for this to last for 10 days. It is possible that the episode on 6 February 1891 was a seizure.

Loss of consciousness for an hour could not be attributed to a faint, unless it was complicated by a significant head injury, and I would be suspicious that it was a seizure (the DVLA[1] would count it as an 'unwitnessed loss of consciousness with seizure markers' if anyone with such a story were to apply for a driving licence today). These days he would be investigated with MRI scan of the brain (showing the structure of the brain) and EEG (looking at the electrical activity of the brain), but even if he had epilepsy, both of these could be normal in between attacks.

With regard to the visual distortions, 'macropsia' and 'micropsia' are recognised in migraine as well as epilepsy. If one were to postulate that they were a manifestation of epilepsy, I would not be put off by the fact that his other manifestations of epilepsy did not appear for decades – it is not particularly uncommon for people to present with their first generalised tonic clonic seizure ('convulsion') and for one then to elicit a history of minor seizures, unrecognised as such by the patient, going on for several years. I agree that although 'eerie' unreal or 'dream states' could be a symptom of epilepsy, they are non-specific and couldn't confirm that diagnosis.

In summary, therefore, I think it very likely that he had migraine. I think it is possible that he also had epilepsy (and there is considerable debate in the medical world as to the extent to which these conditions may be linked), but without further evidence (preferably in the form of an eyewitness description of the episodes of loss of consciousness), I would have considerable doubt about this.

Select Bibliography

Primary sources

Amor, Anne Clark (ed), *Letters to Skeffington Dodgson from his Father* (The Lewis Carroll Society, London: 1990)

Bowman, Isa, *Lewis Carroll as I Knew Him*, with a new introduction by Morton N Cohen, (Dover Publications, New York: 1972)

Cohen, Morton N (ed), with the assistance of Roger Lancelyn Green, *The Letters of Lewis Carroll*, 2 Vols (Macmillan, London: 1979)

Cohen, Morton N (ed), *Lewis Carroll: Interviews and Recollections* (University of Iowa Press, Iowa City: 1989)

Cohen, Morton N (ed), *Lewis Carroll and the Kitchins: Containing twenty-five letters not previously published and nineteen of his photographs* (Lewis Carroll Society of North America: 1980)

Collingwood, Stuart Dodgson, *The Life and Letters of Lewis Carroll* (T Fisher Unwin, London: 1898)

Dodgson C L (Wakeling, Edward (ed)), *Lewis Carroll's Diaries: the Private Journals of Charles Lutwidge Dodgson* (Lewis Carroll Society, Luton: 1993–2007). The complete diary, 1855–98; nine volumes with commentary; volume 10 contains the index and supplementary notes.

Dodgson C L (Lancelyn Green, Roger (ed)) *The Diaries of Lewis Carroll*, Vol I: 1855–67 and Vol II: 1867–98 (Cassell & Co, London: 1953; reprint Greenwood Press, London: 1971)

A and C Hargreaves, 'Alice's Recollections of Carrollian Days As Told to her Son', *Cornhill Magazine*, July 1932

Secondary sources

Clark, Anne, *Lewis Carroll, a Biography* (J M Dent & Sons, London: 1979)

Cohen, Morton N *Lewis Carroll: A Biography* (Macmillan, London: 1995)

Cohen, Morton N and Wakeling, E, *Lewis Carroll and his Illustrators: Collaborations and Correspondence 1865–1898* (Macmillan, London: 2003)

Cohen, Morton N, *Lewis Carroll and the House of Macmillan* (Cambridge University Press, Cambridge: 1987)

Gernsheim, Helmut, *Lewis Carroll: Photographer,* (Dover Publications, London: 1969; revised edition 1970)

Hudson, Derek, *Lewis Carroll* (Constable, London: 1954)

Journals of the Lewis Carroll Society, UK and the Lewis Carroll Society of North America

Leach, Karoline, *In the Shadow of the Dreamchild: a New Understanding of Lewis Carroll* (Peter Owen, London: 1999)

Lennon, Florence Becker, *Lewis Carroll* (Cassell, London: 1947) (Published in the USA as *Victoria Through the Looking Glass: The Life of Lewis Carroll*)

Lovett, Charlie, *Lewis Carroll Among His Books: A Descriptive Catalogue Of The Private Library Of Charles L. Dodgson* (McFarland & Co, Jefferson, NC: 2005)

Nickel, Douglas R, *Dreaming in Pictures, the Photography of Lewis Carroll* (Yale University Press, New Haven and London, 2002)

Phillips, Robert (ed), *Aspects of Alice: Lewis Carroll's Dreamchild as seen through the Critics' Looking Glasses, 1865–1971* (Victor Gollancz, London: 1972)

Reed, Langford, *The Life of Lewis Carroll* (W & G Foyle, London :1932)

Stern, Jeffrey, *Lewis Carroll, Bibliophile* (White Stone Publications, Lewis Carroll Society, London: 1997)

Taylor, Roger and Wakeling, Edward, *Lewis Carroll, Photographer: The Princeton University Library Albums* (Princeton University Press, Princeton, NJ: 2002)

Wilson, Robin, *Lewis Carroll in Numberland: His Fantastical Mathematical Logical Life* (Allen Lane, London: 2008)

Woolf, Jenny, *Lewis Carroll in his Own Account* (Jabberwock Press, London: 2005)

Notes

Abbreviations

Berg: Henry W and Albert A Berg Collection, New York Public Library, New York

Berol: Alfred C Berol Collection, Fales Library, New York University

Bowman: Isa Bowman, *Lewis Carroll As I Knew Him* (Dover, 1972)

Cohen: Morton N Cohen, *Lewis Carroll: A Biography* (Macmillan, 1995)

Collected Letters: Morton N Cohen, *The Letters of Lewis Carroll*, 2 Vols (1979)

Collingwood: Stuart Dodgson Collingwood, *The Life and Letters of Lewis Carroll* (1898)

Diary: Dodgson C L (Wakeling, Edward (ed)), *Lewis Carroll's Diaries: the Private Journals of Charles Lutwidge Dodgson* (1993–2007)

Gernsheim: Helmut Gernsheim, *Lewis Carroll, Photographer* (1949)

Houghton: Houghton Library, Harvard University

Huntington Henry E Huntington Library, California.

Hudson: Derek Hudson, *Lewis Carroll* (1954)

Interviews and Recollections: Morton N Cohen (ed), *Lewis Carroll: Interviews and Recollections* (1989)

Langford Reed: Langford Reed, *Lewis Carroll* (1932)
Lennon: Florence Becker Lennon Papers, Special Collections Department, University of Colorado at Boulder Libraries
Lindseth: Collection of Jon Lindseth
Rosenbach: Philip H and ASW Rosenbach Foundation, Philadelphia
Texas: Harry Ransom Humanities Research Center, University of Texas
Thomson: E Gertrude Thomson, 'Lewis Carroll, A Sketch by An Artist Friend', *The Gentlewoman Magazine*, February 1898, in *Interviews and Recollections*, pp 228–37

Introduction

1. Florence Becker Lennon Collection, University of Colorado at Boulder.

Chapter 1

1. Collingwood, p 11.
2. Letter from Mrs F Dodgson to Lucy Lutwidge, 24 March (no year) in *Diary*, Vol 1, p 24.
3. C L Dodgson to Mrs Richards, 13 March 1882, *Collected Letters*.
4. Facsimile, Hudson, p 27.
5. Collingwood, p 12
6. 31 January 1855, Berol.
7. Private letter to author, 17 October 2008.
8. Sarah Stanfield, 'The Dodgson Sisters', *The Carrollian*, Lewis Carroll Society, Autumn 1998.
9. Catherine Lucy, *Diary* entry quoted in *Interviews and Recollections*', p 214.
10. Private letter to author 17 October 2008.

11. 5 August 1844, Houghton.
12. Collingwood, p 24.
13. Ibid, p 24.
14. J W Ley, 'From Youth Onwards', *Mid Devon Times*, *c* 1895.
15. Collingwood, p 30.
16. Ibid, p 23.
17. *Diary*, 18 March 1857.
18. Collingwood, p 30.
19. Ibid.
20. Ibid, p 29.
21. *Diary*, 20 August 1867.
22. Reproduced in Morton N Cohen and Edward Wakeling (eds), *Lewis Carroll and his Illustrators: Collaborations and Correspondence 1865–1898* (Macmillan, London: 2003)
23. Letter from C L Dodgson to Frances, Elizabeth and Skeffington Dodgson, 5 August [1844], Houghton.
24. Collingwood, p 13.
25. Ibid.
26. Langford Reed, *Lewis Carroll* (W & G Foyle, London: 1932).
27. Privately printed by Parker of Oxford, 1874.
28. Handwritten in *The Rectory Magazine* Dodgson family magazine, *c* 1847.
29. Ibid.
30. 13 January 1870, Berol.
31. Letter from Fanny Dodgson to Lucy Lutwidge, 18 April 1836, (unpublished) Collection of Caroline Luke.
32. Private Dodgson family letter, 1846.
33. 15 August 1877, Berol.
34. 16 June 1895, Guildford High School collection.
35. Anne Clark Amor, *Letters to Skeffington Dodgson from his Father* (Lewis Carroll Society, London: 1990)
36. Ibid, 1 November 1862.
37. 6 Jan 1840, Dodgson Family Collection.

38. Collingwood, p 131.

39. Ibid, p 45.

Chapter 2

1. Collingwood, p 39.

2. *The Rectory Umbrella* (handwritten Dodgson family magazine), 1849.

3. Collingwood, p 85.

4. Ibid, p 29.

5. Margaret Fletcher, *O Call Back Yesterday* (Shakespeare Head Press, Stratford-upon-Avon: 1939) p 29.

6. Letter from C L Dodgson to F P Cobbe, 21 May 1875, Huntington.

7. *Diary*, 26 November 1856.

8. Warren Weaver, 'Lewis Carroll, Mathematician', *Scientific American*, April 1956.

9. H L Thompson, *George Henry Liddell, D.D., Dean of Christ Church, Oxford, A Memoir* (Holt, 1899).

10. This missing volume is mysterious. It apparently only covered three months, while the other volumes covered longer periods. It was still in existence on Carroll's death and it is a puzzle why it was so short and why it disappeared.

11. *The Times*, 19 December 1931, p 6.

12. *Harper's Magazine*, February 1943, pp 319–23.

13. *Jabberwocky*, Vol 5, No 1, Lewis Carroll Society.

14. 18 May 1878, Fitzwilliam Museum, Cambridge collection.

15. C L Dodgson, *Twelve Months in A Curatorship, By One Who Has Tried It* (Privately Printed, 1884).

16. Unpublished manuscript, May 1897, Morris L Parrish Collection, Princeton University Library.

17. Letter from C L Dodgson to S Collingwood, 29 December 1891, Berol.

18. Lewis Carroll, 'Answers to Knot 2, "A Tangled Tale"', *The Monthly Packet* (1880).

19. Lewis Carroll, 'Answers to Knot 10, "A Tangled Tale"', *The Monthly Packet* (1885).

20. C L Dodgson, *Curiosa Mathematica, Part II: Pillow Problems*, (Macmillan 1893) p 2. Problem No 5; the answer is 2/3.

21. This acrostic is quoted in full in Chapter 6, pp 176–77.

22. Texas.

23. *Cornhill Magazine*, March 1898, pp 303–10.

24. Michael Sadler, *Michael Ernest Sadler, A Memoir by his Son* (Constable, London: 1949) p 95.

25. Letter to *The Times*, July 1957.

26. 28 February 1882, Mrs S E Scourfield collection, at present displayed in Oxford University Museum.

Chapter 3

1. *Harper's Magazine*, February 1943, p 319.

2. Thomson, p 235.

3. *Diary*, 25 February 1887.

4. A and C Hargreaves, 'Alice's Recollections of Carrollian Days As Told to her Son', *Cornhill Magazine*, July 1932.

5. John Pudney, *Lewis Carroll and his World* (Thames & Hudson, London: 1976) p 120.

6. Thomson, pp 166–7.

7. Bowman, p 19.

8. William Tuckwell, *Reminiscences of Oxford* (Cassell, London: 1900) pp 160–3.

9. Mark Twain, 'Chapters from my Autobiography', Chapter VI, *North American* Review, 1906.

10. Roger Lancelyn Green, *The Story of Lewis Carroll* (Methuen 1954) and Benson Bobrick, *Knotted Tongues:*

Stuttering in History and the Quest for a Cure (Simon & Schuster, 1995).

11. Edith Blakemore, 1 February 1891, Berol.
12. Letter from C L Dodgson to W E Wilcox, 11 May 1859, Berol.
13. 'More Recollections of Lewis Carroll, *The Listener*, 6 February 1958.
14. Lorina Liddell to Florence Becker Lennon, 4 May 1930, Lennon.
15. James Hunt, *Treatise on the Cure of Stammering* (Longman Brown, 1854)
16. 24 July 1873, New York Public Library collection.
17. 1 September 1873, Facsimile, Collection Dr. Joyce Hines, reprinted in Collected Letters p.194".
18. Ibid.
19. 19 December 1873, Scripps College collection, California.
20. 27 December 1873, Houghton.
21. St. Thomas's Hospital, quoted in visitor information material about the Old Operating Theatre.
22. *Diary*, 19 December 1857.
23. *Diary*, 19 May 1892.
24. Unpublished letter in possession of the Dodgson Family.
25. Dr Selwyn Goodacre, 'The Illnesses of Lewis Carroll. *Jabberwocky*, Vol 1, No 8, Lewis Carroll Society, pp 15–20.
26. *Diary*, 13 September 1867.
27. Hugues Lebailly, 'Charles Dodgson's Infatuation With the Weaker and More Aesthetic Sex Re-Examined', *Dickens Studies Annual*, Vol 32, 2002.
28. *Diary*, 26 May 1884.
29. James Paget, *Clinical Lectures* (Longman, London: 1875), p 285.
30. Dorothy Furniss, 'New Lewis Carroll letters', *Pearson's Magazine*, December 1930.
31. Ibid.

32. *Diary*, 28 August 1875.
33. Dr Hart kindly gave permission to reproduce her report; it is included in full in the Appendix.

Chapter 4

1. Langford Reed, p 92.
2. 21 July 1946, Lennon.
3. Edith Olivier, *Without Knowing Mr Walkley* (Faber, 1938), pp 176–9.
4. Wiliam H Dixon, *Spiritual Wives* (Hurst & Blackett, London: 1868).
5. 13 January 1879 and 5 April 1881, both Rosenbach.
6. http://contrariwise.cc/cldandfemales.html.
7. Jeffrey Stern, *Lewis Carroll, Bibliophile*, (White Stone Publications, Lewis Carroll Society, London: 1997) p 57.
8. 15 August 1888, Linseth.
9. Thomson, pp 229–30.
10. Ibid.
11. Quoted in *Collected Letters*, pp 576–80.
12. 7 January, 1884, Collection of Selwyn Goodacre.
13. 26 August 1886, Rosenbach.
14. 26 November 1893, Berol.
15. Laurence Irving, *The Successors* (Rupert Hart-Davis, London: 1967), p 75.
16. Langford Reed, p 77.
17. Ibid, p 71.
18. 24 November 1899, Harvard.
19. Thomson, p 232.
20. Ibid.
21. Quoted in Bowman, p 118, letter of ?31 July 1892 (Morton Cohen's estimated date).
22. Hudson, p 317.
23. 21 September 1893, Berol.

24. *Diary*, 29 May 1894.
25. 13 September 1893, Collection of Herbert L Carlebach.
26. *Diary*, 17 October 1866.
27. Stuart Collingwood, quoted in *Interviews and Recollections*, p 11.
28. *Diary*, 6 March 1864.
29. Collingwood, p 355.
30. This is part of the reason why Ellen Terry's family did not acknowledge her during the time she was 'living in sin'.
31. A theme examined throughout *In the Shadow of the Dreamchild: a New Understanding of Lewis Carroll* by Karoline Leach (Peter Owen, London: 1999).
32. 21 August 1885, handwritten addition to circular letter, Collection of C Lovett.
33. Collingwood, p 363
34. Harcourt Amory Collection, Harvard.
35. Collingwood, p 362.
36. 27 May 1879, Rosenbach.
37. 28 May 1879, Rosenbach.
38. Hudson, pp 322–6.
39. 16 November 1896, Rosenbach.
40. 21 September 1893, Berol
41. Karoline Leach, *In the Shadow of the Dreamchild – the Myth and Reality of Lewis Carroll* (Peter Owen, 2008) p 156.

Chapter 5

1. Collingwood, p 360.
2. Bowman, pp 59–60.
3. Lewis Carroll, *Sylvie and Bruno* (Macmillan, London: 1889) p 176.
4. Private Dodgson family tape recording.

5. Virginia Woolf, 'Introduction', *Complete Works of Lewis Carroll* (Nonesuch Press, 1939).

6. Virginia Woolf, 'Lewis Carroll', *The Moment and Other Essays* (Harcourt, New York: 1948).

7. Greville MacDonald, *Reminiscences of a Specialist* (George Allen & Unwin, London: 1932) pp 15, 16.

8. Langford Reed, p 95

9. 15 July 1868, unpublished diaries of H P Liddon, copyright Liddon House.

10. Eleanor M. Browne, quoted in *Revisiting Richmond School*, privately printed, undated.

11. *Interviews and Recollections*, pp 191, 192, 194, 134.

12. Ibid, p 175.

13. 23 November 1881, Boston (Massachusetts) Public Library collection.

14. 14 August 1877, New York Public Library collection.

15. 15 August 1877, Berol.

16. 2 October 1877, New York Public Library collection.

17. Letter to *The Times*, 2 January 1932.

18. 16 February 1894, quoted in Gernsheim, p 82.

19. A M E Goldschmidt, '*Alice in Wonderland* Psychoanalysed', in Richard Crossman, Gilbert Highet, and Derek Kahn (eds), *New Oxford Outlook* (Basil Blackwell, Oxford: May 1933) pp 68–72.

20. Paul Schilder, 'Psychoanalytic Remarks on Alice in Wonderland and Lewis Carroll', *The Journal of Nervous and Mental Disease*s, Vol LXXXVII (1938), pp 159–68.

21. M Grotjah, 'About the Symbolization of Alice's Adventures in Wonderland', *American Image*, Vol IV (1947) pp 32–41.

22. *Interviews and Recollections*, pp 109, 139, 126, 133, 105, 201

23. To Bertie Coote, 9 June [?1877], Morris L Parrish Collection, Princeton University Library.

24. John Skinner, 'Lewis Carroll's Adventures in Wonderland, *American Image*, Vol IV (1947) pp 3–31.
25. Florence Becker Lennon, *Victoria Through the Looking Glass* (Simon & Schuster, 1945).
26. 25 November 1962, Lennon.
27. 5 October 1893, Lindseth.

Chapter 6

1. *Diary*, 6 March 1856.
2. Ibid, 5 June 1856.
3. Ibid, 5 February 1857.
4. Unpublished letter, Lorina Liddell to F B Lennon, 4 May 1930, Lennon.
5. *Diary*, 17 May 1857.
6. 20 February 1861, Berol.
7. A and C Hargreaves, 'Alice's Recollections of Carrollian Days As Told to her Son', *Cornhill Magazine*, July 1932.
8. Unpublished letter, Lorina Liddell to F B Lennon, 4 May 1930, Lennon.
9. Unpublished letter, Lorina Liddell to F B Lennon, 22 June 1930, Lennon.
10. Carroll corresponded on logic with Sidgwick, who was later to found the Society for Psychical Research, of which Carroll was a founder member.
11. Anon [John Howe Jenkins], *Cakeless* (privately printed, 1877).
12. Cohen, p 515.
13. Edward Wakeling, 'Two Letters from Lorina to Alice' *Jabberwocky*, Vol 21, No 4, Lewis Carroll Society.
14. *Diary*, 6 April 1865.
15. 10 June 1864, Berg.
16. *Diary*, 1 November 1888.

17. Letter from C L Dodgson to Mrs Liddell, 12 November 1891, present whereabouts unknown.
18. C L Dodgson, Acrostic poem 'Around My Lonely Hearth Tonight', 1878.
19. Vanessa St Clair, 'A Girl Like Alice', *The Guardian*, 5 June 2001.
20. C Hargreaves, 'Alice's Recollections'.
21. C L Dodgson, 'Alice on the Stage', *The Theatre*, 9 April 1887, pp 179–84.
22. Thomson, p 234.
23. 25 March 1885, present whereabouts unknown, previously at Christ Church, Oxford.

Chapter 7

1. Letter from C L Dodgson to Mary Brown, 28 June 1889, Berg.
2. *Diary*, 3 February 1857.
3. Letter from C L Dodgson to W M Wilcox, 10 September 1885, Berol.
4. 10 September 1885, Berol.
5. *Diary*, 21 October 1862.
6. Ibid, 31 December 1863.
7. Ibid, 14 August 1866.
8. Ibid, 14 April 1867.
9. Ibid, 9 July 1866.
10. Ibid, 23 April 1855.
11. 5 January 1867, Beinecke Library collection, Yale University.
12. 25 January 1866, Berg.
13. Harcourt Amory Collection, Harvard.
14. 26 December 1889, Linseth.
15. 28 June 1889, Berg.
16. Hudson, pp 322–6.

17. E L Shute, 'Lewis Carroll as Artist', *Cornhill Magazine*, November 1932, pp 559–62.
18. 12 May 1896, Lilly Library collection, Indiana University.
19. Jeffrey Stern, *Lewis Carroll, Bibliophile*.
20. *Diary*, 23 April 1867.
21. Ibid, 11 September 1867.
22. *Revue Spirite d'Etudes Psychologique*, Paris, March 1869.
23. Letter from C L Dodgson to James Langton Clarke, 4 December 1882, Texas.
24. Ibid.
25. *Diary*, 6 September 1891.

Chapter 8

1. Langford Reed, p 95.
2. Dodgson Family Collection.
3. 21 July 1876, Berol.
4. Published by Robert Baldwin, 1850.
5. Isa Bowman, quoted in Langford Reed, p 75.
6. Langford Reed, 'The Droll and the Don', *The Listener*, 3 February 1932, p 171.
7. 3 August 1863, Beinecke Library collection, Yale University.
8. Irene Vanbrugh, quoted in Langford Reed, p 73.
9. *Diary*, 24 April 1867.
10. Thomson, p 231.
11. Hudson, p 314.
12. E Shawyer, 'More Recollections of Lewis Carroll', *The Listener* 6 February 1958, p 243.
13. Grace Lawless Lee, *The Story of the Bosanquets* (Phillimore, 1966), p 84.
14. F Soto, 'The Consumption of the Snark and the Decline of Nonsense', *The Carrollian*, No 8, Autumn 2001, pp 9–50.

15. Letter from C L Dodgson to the Lowrie Children, 18 August 1884, quoted in 'A Letter from Wonderland', *The Critic*, Vol XXIX, 5 March 1898.
16. 24 September 1892, Berol.

Chapter 9

1. Collingwood, p 102
2. 20 February, 1861, Berol.
3. Gernsheim, p 20.
4. C Hargreaves, "Alice's Recollections".
5. *Diary*, 18 November 1863.
6. Gernsheim, pp 20–1.
7. In the Morris L Parrish collection, Princeton University Library.
8. *Diary*, 5 February 1857.
9. Letter from C L Dodgson to Louisa Fletcher Dodgson, 3 August 1864, Texas.
10. Douglas Nickel, *Dreaming in Pictures: The Photography of Lewis Carroll* (Yale University Press, New Haven and London: 2002), p 21.
11. Margaret L Woods, 'Oxford in the Seventies,' *Fortnightly Review*, No 150, 1941.
12. Letter from C L Dodgson to Mrs Henderson, 30 June 1881, Texas.
13. www.lewiscarroll-site.com/(Talk: Illustrated Paper on Dodgson's photography). Edward Wakeling, 'Lewis Carroll and his Photography: Mystic, awful was the process', a talk given at various venues after the publication of *Lewis Carroll, Photographer* (Princeton, 2003).
14. Letter from C L Dodgson to Mrs Henderson, 17 July 1879, Texas.
15. 6 November 1893, Huntington.

16. *Diary*, 13 January 1881.
17. 7 June 1880, Rosenbach.
18. *Diary*, 5 February 1880.
19. Morton N Cohen (ed), *Lewis Carroll and the Kitchins: Containing twenty-five letters not previously published and nineteen of his photographs* (Lewis Carroll Society of North America: 1980), p 45.
20. Laurence Irving, *The Successors* (Rupert Hart-Davis, London: 1967) p 75.
21. *Diary*, Vol 7, p 280, Note 511.

Chapter 10

1. 29 March 1886, Berol.
2. *Diary*, 2 August 1865.
3. 29 December 1875, extract, Rosenbach.
4. Talk by Violet Dodgson, 21 June 1950. Surrey History Centre collection.
5. Bowman, p 37
6. *Diary*, 8 December 1882.
7. All letters London School of Economics archive.
8. *Diary*, 2 October 1882.
9. *Diary*, 4 August 1891.
10. Jeffrey Stern, *Lewis Carroll, Bibliophile*.
11. Canberra Bicycle Museum catalogue.
12. Morton N Cohen, *Lewis Carroll and the House of Macmillan* (Cambridge University Press, Cambridge: 1987).
13. Private collection.
14. Harcourt Amory Collection, Harvard University, n.d. The letter has also been published in part in *Collected Letters*, p 81, Note 1.
15. Frederick W Lowndes, *Lock Hospitals and Lock Wards in General Hospitals* (Churchill, 1882) p 2.

Chapter 11

1. *The Times*, 27 January 1932.
2. 23 August [1854], Berol.
3. Anonymous, 'Lewis Carroll, An Interview with his Biographer', *Westminster Budget*, 9 December 1898, p 23.
4. 28 June 1889, Berg.
5. Letter from C L Dodgson to Helen Feilden, 7 June 1890, Edward Wakeling collection.

A Personal Conclusion

1. The Driver and Vehicle Licensing Agency, which issues British driving licenses.

Index